MANAGING ARCHAEOLOGY

THEORETICAL ARCHAEOLOGY GROUP (TAG)

MANAGING ARCHAEOLOGY

edited by
Malcolm A. Cooper, Antony Firth,
John Carman, David Wheatley

London and New York

First published 1995
by Routledge
11 New Fetter Lane, London EC4P 4EE

Simultaneously published in the USA and Canada
by Routledge
29 West 35th Street, New York, NY 10001

Typeset in Bembo by Florencetype Ltd, Stoodleigh, Devon
Printed and bound in Great Britian by T J Press Ltd, Padstow, Cornwall

British Library Cataloguing in Publication Data
A catalogue of this book is available from the British Library

Library of Congress Cataloguing in Publication Data
A catalogue record for this book has been requested

ISBN 0-415-10674-5

Contents

Illustrations

CONTRIBUTORS

Gill Andrews has been working as an archaeological consultant since 1984, following a period of six years in field archaeology. She has extensive experience in the design, management and monitoring of archaeological projects and specializes in the provision of advice in these areas and on organizational structures in archaeology. She wrote *Management of Archaeological Projects* (MAP2) for English Heritage.

Marion Blockley is Lecturer and Course Co-ordinator in heritage management at the Ironbridge Institute, University of Birmingham. Her current research interests include the interpretation and presentation of archaeological sites and monuments and the management of World Heritage Sites. She spend fifteen years managing excavations and is currently a member of the Council of the IFA.

Mim Bower is a research student at Cambridge University. Although her research focus is ancient biomolecules and their reflection on the origins of agriculture, she has had an interest in the 'Heritage Industry' for some time. She is currently involved in running a restoration/museum project in Hungary and is finding the birth of a new 'Heritage Industry' most stimulating.

Carole Brooke is Lecturer at Durham University Business School. She has an MA in archaeology/anthropology from Cambridge and a PhD in business studies and information technology from City University Business School. She has nine years' commercial work experience including work in research and development, and recruitment consultancy. Her current research interests include TQM, the management of archaeology, and the human aspects of information technology.

John Carman is a Research Fellow at Clare Hall, Cambridge. After a professional career in commercial administration, he undertook research in archaeological heritage management, receiving his PhD from Cambridge University in 1993. His research interests include the social valuation of archaeological material, its management under legal regimes, the history of archaeology and approaches to writing archaeology.

Malcolm A. Cooper is an Inspector of Ancient Monuments with English Heritage. Prior to this he worked as the Archaeological Officer of Hereford and Worcester County Council where he developed his interest in applying management techniques to archaeology. He is a member of the Institute of Management and has lectured on management for the University of Central England and for the Worcester College of Technology.

Timothy Darvill is Professor of Archaeology and Property Development, Bournemouth University. After taking a degree in archaeology at Southampton University and then completing a PhD on the Neolithic period in Wales and the mid-west of Britain he directed a series of research projects relating to archaeological resource management in England. Current research interests include the British Neolithic, the values placed by society on archaeological materials, and the way that archaeological monuments change through natural and humanly induced processes.

Antony Firth is currently studying the management of archaeology underwater at the University of Southampton. Following his first degree in international relations he became involved in archaeology through diving and then in various aspects of management and campaigning. He has a special interest in past and present management of archaeology, contemporary use of the past and the study of maritime cultural landscapes.

Martin Locock is currently Projects Manager (Assessments) for the Glamorgan-Gwent Archaeological Trust, responsible for managing GGAT Contracts' team of Project Officers. His previous fieldwork included the excavation of the historic garden at Castle Bromwich Hall. His main research interest is in theoretical approaches to the analysis of buildings.

Ellen McAdam is the Post-excavation Manager of the Oxford Archaeological Unit. Her doctorate is in Mesopotamian archaeology, and after nearly ten years in the Near East she returned to British archaeology via a qualification in computer studies. Her research interests include prehistoric figurines, the archaeology of settlements and the application of the techniques of systems analysis to post-excavation processes.

Taryn J.P. Nixon is Head of Operations at the Museum of London Archaeology Service (MoLAS). After training as a prehistorian at University College, London she worked in archaeological survey and cultural resource management in the Far East, and has been working in London archaeology since 1987. In addition to her responsibilities for the project management and fieldwork sections in MoLAS, she is active in drafting archaeological standards and guidance with the IFA.

Francis Pryor is Director of Archaeology for Fenland Archaeological Trust. He has spent his professional life researching the prehistory and early history of the Fenlands in the Peterborough region. His principal excavations include sites at Fengate, Maxey, Etton and, latterly, Flag Fen. His other interests include archaeology and visitors, excavation techniques, experimental archaeology and the integration of regional research.

Bill Startin works for English Heritage and was, until February 1995, head of their Monuments Protection Programme, an initiative reviewing our current understanding of the archaeological resource and its protection. His first degree is in civil engineering but after spending several years excavating he gained a B Phil in Prehistoric archaeology at Oxford and subsequently joined the Inspectorate of Ancient Monuments in 1976. He took up his present post in 1986.

Roger Thomas is an Inspector of Ancient Monuments with English Heritage. He joined English Heritage in 1984 following a degree in archaeology at Southampton and research at Cambridge. His research and professional interests include the British Later Bronze Age, policies for post-excavation work and publication, archaeology and planning policies, environmental assessment procedures and the management of the urban archaeological resource.

Francis Wenban-Smith is an archaeological consultant specializing in Palaeolithic and Mesolithic excavation and lithic analysis, and in all aspects of the evaluation and protection of Palaeolithic and Mesolithic sites. His PhD thesis on the interpretation of Early Palaeolithic behaviour from lithic arte-facts, taken at Southampton University, is approaching completion.

David Wheatley is a Lecturer in Archaeology at the University of Southampton. His main research interest is the application of computer technologies to archaeological problems. His most recent work has included the development of computer simulations for teaching and the investigation of intervisibility between Neolithic burial monuments.

Readers are advised that the views expressed in this volume are those of the individual authors and not necessarily those of their employers.

GENERAL EDITOR'S PREFACE

Why does the world need archaeological theory? The purpose of the Theoretical Archaeology Group series is to answer the question by showing that archaeology contributes little to our understanding if it does not explore the theories that give meaning to the past. The last decade has seen some major developments in world archaeology and the One World Archaeology series provides a thematic showcase for the current scale of enquiry and variety of archaeological interests. The development of a theoretical archaeology series complements these thematic concerns and, by focusing attention on theory in all its many guises, points the way to future long-term developments in the subject.

In 1992 the annual Theoretical Archaeology Group (TAG) conference was held in Southampton. Europe and the world of archaeological theory was our theoretical theme at this EuroTAG conference. We stressed two elements in the structure of the three-day conference. In the first place, 1992 had for long been heralded as the time when the single market would come into existence combined with moves towards greater European unity. While these orderly developments could be planned for and sessions organised around the role of archaeology and the past in the construction of European identity, no one could have predicted the horror of what would occur in former Yugoslavia. Throughout 1992 and beyond, the ideologies of integration and fragmentation, federalism and nationalism vied with each other to use the resources of the past in vastly different ways.

The second element recognised that 1992 was a notable anniversary for theoretical archaeology. Thirty years before Lewis Binford had published his first seminal paper, 'Archaeology as Anthropology', in *American Antiquity*. This short paper was a theoretical beacon in an otherwise heavily factual archaeological world. From such beginnings came the influential processual movement which, in its early years, was referred to as the New Archaeology. Thirty years has clearly knocked the shine off such bright new futures. In the meantime archaeological theory had healthily fragmented while expanding into many areas of investigation previously regarded as off-limits to archaeologists and their mute data. Processualism had been countered by post-processualism to either the enrichment or irritation of by now partisan theoretical practitioners. EuroTAG marked the anniversary with a debate involving the views of Lewis Binford, Chris Tilley, John Barrett and Colin Renfew, supplemented by opinions from the floor. Their brief was to outline the theoretical challenges now set before the subject. The audience heard various programmes of where we might go as well as fears about an uncertain theoretical future. Both optimism and pessimism for another thirty years of theoretical excitement were to be found in almost equal measure. However, the clear impression, exemplified by the number of people (almost 800) who attended EuroTAG, was that the strength of any future theoretical archaeology now lies in its diversity.

How different in numbers attending and diversity of viewpoints from the early days of TAG, an organization whose aims have always been simple: to raise the profile of discussion about theories of the past. The need for such a group was recognised at the first open meeting held in Sheffield in 1979 where the programme notes declared that 'British archaeologists have never possessed a forum for the discussion of theoretical issues. Conferences which address wider themes come and go but all too frequently the discussion of ideas is blanketed by the presentation of fact'. TAG set out to correct this balance and achieved it through an accent on discussion, a willingness to hear new ideas, often from people just beginning their theoretical careers.

EuroTAG presented some of the influences which must now contribute to the growth of theory in archaeology as the discipline assumes a central position in the dialogues of the humanities. As expected there was strong participation from European colleagues in sessions which focused on Iberia and Scandinavia as well as discussions of the regional traditions of theoretical and archaeological research on the continent, an archaeological perspective on the identity of Europe and multicultural societies in European prehistory. Set beside these were sessions devoted to visual information, food, evolutionary theory, architecture and structured deposition. Two archaeological periods expressed their new-found theoretical feet. Historical archaeology argued for an escape from its subordination to history while classical archaeology embraced theory and applied it to its rich data. Finally, the current issues of value and management in archaeology were subjected to a critical examination from a theoretical perspective.

Nowhere was the polyphony of theoretical voices, issues and debates more clearly heard than in the session devoted to world perspectives on European archaeological theory. While EuroTAG was a moment to reflect on the European traditions and uses of theory, a comparative view was needed if such concerns were to avoid the call of parochialism. Here at the heart of EuroTAG was an opportunity to see the debate in action – not as the preserve of individuals, but as a dynamic answer to the question of why does the world need archaeological theory.

FOREWORD

Ask an archaeology unit manager what he or she does for a living and the unequivocal reply will be 'I'm an archaeologist'. Dig a little deeper and you may discover you are talking to someone who manages a team of thirty professional staff with an annual turnover close on a million pounds, who has not stood in an excavation trench (except to satisfy press photographers) for several years. As the editors note in the introduction to this volume, there is a general reluctance amongst archaeologists to accept that management issues are central to their discipline.

In the past management in archaeology has been regarded as somehow intrinsically and ethically dubious – a black art of little or no concern to proper archaeologists. Thus it was with some suspicion that delegates at the 1993 conference of the Institute of Field Archaeologists (IFA) regarded the aptly entitled session 'Sleeping with the Enemy? Managing or making do'. The debate was lively and well attended, a reflection, perhaps, of recent changes in archaeological project funding which have steered us into the realms of systematic project management. Gradually there is a growing acceptance in the profession that good management is fundamental to good archaeology.

The Institute of Field Archaeologists exists to promote professional standards and ethics and to facilitate the exchange of information and ideas about archaeological practice in Britain. The IFA annual conference provides a most effective platform for debate and it is pleasing to see the development of this seminal publication from it. This book presents a variety of issues on the application of management theory to archaeology and its likely role in the future of the profession. *Managing Archaeology* fills a huge void in archaeological literature and will stimulate continued discussion and publication.

David Start
Honorary Chair, Institute of Field Archaeologists
July 1994

Acknowledgements

The editors would like to extend their thanks to everybody who assisted with 'Managing Archaeology' at EuroTAG 92 and 'Sleeping with the Enemy' at ABC 93 in any way, notably Simon Woodiwiss who co-organized and chaired the session at ABC 93 and Tim Schadla-Hall who acted as discussant at EuroTAG 92. We should like to extend our thanks to the organizing committees of the two conferences, notably Clive Gamble, Sara Champion, Simon Keay and Tim Champion and the archaeology students of Southampton for EuroTAG 92, and Stephen Walls, Andrew Fitzpatrick, Chris Gerrard, Cathy Batt and Taryn Nixon for ABC 93. The editors would also like to thank A. Ruiz-Rodriguez and F. Hornos for presenting a paper in the EuroTAG 92 session which is not included in this volume. Our very great thanks go to the contributors to the sessions and to this volume for their hard work and patience. In addition to his role at EuroTAG 92, we must thank Clive Gamble for his efforts as Series Editor.

Thanks must also go to Patricia Carman for providing a way out of our impasse over the order of papers at the TAG session and for reading early drafts of both the Introduction and the Conclusion. The editors also wish to thank the following people for their support in the course of preparing this volume: John Brunsdon, Claire Kenwood, Peter Cooper, Siân Jones, Kathryn Knowles and Julian Thomas.

Malcolm A. Cooper
Antony Firth
John Carman
David Wheatley
July 1994

INTRODUCTION

Archaeological management

JOHN CARMAN, MALCOLM A. COOPER,
ANTONY FIRTH, DAVID WHEATLEY

THE ORIGINS OF THIS BOOK

This book is the result of a collision between three individuals with similar concerns and research interests – all relating to the management of archaeology – but widely differing ideas as to what they were about and how to proceed with them. As discussion proceeded between these three – John Carman of Cambridge University, Malcolm Cooper of English Heritage and Antony Firth of the University of Southampton – it became clear that they all knew of others with similarly divergent views in their field. The immediate consequence was two conference sessions, and out of them this book. We were all three driven by the reluctance of archaeologists to identify management issues as central to the discipline and to debate them as vociferously as other issues. We all saw this reluctance among our colleagues as having serious implications for the discipline, and this volume has been brought together to help stimulate the debate we feel is necessary.

Although we consider every paper published here of international relevance, one characteristic of the volume which will quickly become apparent is its preoccupation with the UK and particularly with England. This has a number of sources. Our principle interest is in *ideas* about management and archaeology, not in the countries where the ideas are being expressed. We believe that the UK provides particular opportunities for discussion of these ideas, especially at the annual conferences of the Theoretical Archaeology Group and the Institute of Field Archaeologists. This is not to deny a link between the context of management and its theoretical development but we have no intention of duplicating Henry

Cleere's two edited volumes (Cleere 1984, 1989). Another volume which sought to offer explanation by recourse to comparative analysis would be interesting, no doubt, but it assumes that nationality is a major variable in the character of management. While this may be so, the diversity of papers in this volume demonstrates that it is not the only, or perhaps even the most significant, variable. Following on from this, it will be apparent that the management of archaeology in the UK is by no means monolithic, and we would hardly expect it to be so elsewhere. Even where an 'establishment' can be identified, differences in interest, understanding and perspective occur. This volume includes authors who might be identified as part of an establishment, and others who clearly feel that they are on the periphery, but we would hesitate to suggest that there is any consistency in the one with respect to the other which reflects a 'real' characteristic of management in the UK.

Archaeology in the UK, and its management, is in a state of considerable flux on many accounts. A number of the chapters make reference to changes associated with the increasing professionalization of the discipline, the division of archaeologists into those concerned with curating the archaeological resource and those concerned with contracting for fieldwork, the growth of competitive tendering, the introduction of new planning guidance, the culture of value-for-money, cuts in core public expenditure, boom and bust in the construction industry, the impact of information technology, apparent paralysis of the legislature on archaeological matters, commercialization of heritage, and so on. The UK has experienced a great deal of social and economic change in the past twenty years, impacting on the conduct of archaeology at many levels. Many other countries have experienced the same sorts of change, in different circumstances, to different degrees and at different times and we would expect readers to identify the situations which approximate, or contrast with, those with which they are familiar in their home territory. A glossary has been included at the end of this volume to assist readers with specific terms current in the management of archaeology in the UK.

To a certain extent some of these chapters reflect their author's attempts to come to terms with these major changes, to reassess their position within the discipline, and to make their own accommodation of earlier beliefs with new externally imposed circumstances. The fact that a volume of this kind can be compiled suggests that such reassessment can be negotiated successfully. As editors we have not sought to remove personal views from the chapters, being of the opinion that while these explanations may not be universalizable, they could certainly resonate internationally.

In summary, we as editors believe that the domestic context of these chapters does not detract from their relevance internationally. If anything, however, rather than making the job of those who would conduct broad-based international comparisons any easier, the true difficulties begin to come to light. There are, it emerges, many more factors to take into account than are apparent in international volumes such as, for example, Cleere (1984, 1989) and O'Keefe and Prott (1984).

The Annual Conference of the Theoretical Archaeology Group, Southampton 1992

TAG is well known as a place where fierce debates rage, and the collective noun for a group of TAG session organizers – although not yet to be found in any dictionary – may well be 'an argument'. Certainly, our experience of putting together first a TAG session and consequently this book would suggest so!

Ours was an argument of ideas and perspectives which first emerged after Malcolm Cooper's paper and John Carman's session at TAG 1991 in Leicester; but to write it off as a simple discussion would be to dismiss the vitality of the issues. Cooper's paper – provocatively entitled 'Management theory *is* archaeological theory!' (Cooper 1991) – prompted interventions by first John Carman and then Antony Firth. Although it was comforting to know that we were not each alone in trying to explain what seemed to be going on, it was equally apparent that the words 'management' and 'archaeology' were virtually all that we had in common. Carman's session – 'Stoned into Silence? "Heritage" and Discourse', comprised chiefly (but not exclusively) of Cambridge-based researchers – compounded our differences by a concern with understanding the cultural significance of archaeological remains rather than the day-to-day practice of archaeology.

It was quickly agreed that the best way of resolving our differences was to run a jointly organized TAG session the following year in Southampton. David Wheatley joined in at an early stage of converting this challenge into something more tangible, offering the title 'Managing Archaeology' as the simplest way out of the conundrum of drawing together still disparate ideas. A measure of these difficulties is that we failed to agree on a themed separation of papers for the session and settled for delivery in alphabetical order, inviting the audience to make up their own minds about what the 'message' of the session was, assuming there was a single idea behind it. What was clear, however, was that if we had such problems, then there was something worth talking about and sharing with the archaeological community.

There were, perhaps, one or two other common strands beyond the use of the two words 'archaeology' and 'management'. We had all encountered resistance to the notion that management, however defined, was a theoretical matter. Resistance ranged from the rejoinder that management was entirely *a*theoretical (and therefore not a fit subject for TAG), to it being classed as the antithesis of theory. We had a common belief that this attitude was mistaken, preferring the notion that if the antithesis of theory was practice, then maybe management (whatever that term meant) was the synthesis. Hence we were concerned with theoretical issues of practical relevance. In this case any perceived distance between academic and field archaeology was not the result of the introduction of management ideas and practices into the latter, but of a lack of understanding of the character of management.

Another common strand was dissatisfaction with the level of discussion of management issues in archaeology. Concepts derived from general management theory had been imported into archaeology with few questions, and quietly accepted as something simple to do. Discussion focused on the subject of heritage management as control of the archaeological resource – a discussion which continues in some contributions here – but rarely on the nature of management itself. Proffered definitions of management were almost entirely descriptive: it is what managers do, it is the purpose of this legislation and that administration. Books about management and archaeology are still rare and tend to follow this pattern; volumes such as Hunter and Ralston (1993) serve an essential role in describing the day-to-day stuff of management but they are less concerned with the philosophy of management and its effect on the resources as a whole. The questions which we wanted to highlight are often apparent in such volumes, implicit and sometimes explicit, but the space available is not devoted to answering them. We believed that a dedicated attempt to offer some answers had to be made, however inconclusive and contradictory the exercise might turn out to be. On this basis the EuroTAG 92 session, 'Managing Archaeology', took place.

Apart from the editors of this book (also the session organizers), contributions included papers by Gill Andrews and Roger Thomas, Mim Bower, Tim Darvill, Arturo Ruiz-Rodriguez and F. Hornos, Francis Wenban-Smith, and (as discussant) Tim Schadla-Hall. Bower and Carman have contributed to this book chapters combining ideas they expressed also at Carman's 1991 TAG session. Andrews and Thomas have merged the papers they gave separately at TAG and the IFA, as has Cooper.

The Annual Conference of the Institute of Field Archaeologists, Bradford 1993

Malcolm Cooper followed up his TAG 1991 paper on archaeology and management with a session organized jointly with Simon Woodwiss at the annual conference of British archaeology's main professional institute. Called 'Sleeping with the Enemy? – Managing or Making Do', the session centred on seeking a general definition of the term 'management' in relation to the archaeological discipline and the nature of its concern to archaeological professionals. The call for papers set the tone for the session:

Archaeology is being forced by external change to alter both the structures which comprise the profession and the functions which its professional practitioners undertake. This in turn affects the nature of archaeological employment and the skills needed to run organizations and projects. The purpose of this symposium is to explore two specific areas of particular relevance to field archaeologists: organizational strategies and project management strategies. In order to stimulate a structured discussion of these areas, papers addressing a series of thematic headings are sought, e.g.: *Organizational strategies*: identifying customers and stakeholders; marketing; implementing change; assessing organizational strengths and weaknesses; *Project management strategies*: what comprises the project design process; how targets are defined and monitored; what management structures are employed for the project teams; how the external environment is controlled.

The impetus for the session came from the recognition – as any visit to a bookshop will reveal – that writing on management is a growth industry and that the term is a very general one, covering a wide variety of subjects as diverse as financial management and the psychology of organizations. Accordingly, at the session speakers were invited to give their views on the nature and relevance of management to the archaeological profession.

Session participants comprised Gill Andrews, Carole Brooke, Marion Blockley, Malcolm Cooper, Tim Darvill, Martin Locock, Taryn Nixon and Francis Pryor, plus a contribution from Ellen McAdam.

Beginning a dialogue

The natures of these two conferences are very different, with TAG much more concerned with theoretical frameworks and the IFA concentrating more on professional and practical issues. We all felt, however, that both perspectives would shed interesting light onto the management debate and that two different approaches would lead to a fuller and more interesting range of discussion than either conference individually would produce. As expected, the results of the two conference sessions were a wide variety of themes and perspectives on archaeology and its management.

This volume comprises sixteen chapters plus this Introduction and a Conclusion, and yet many subjects which can be considered to fall under a general heading of 'archaeology and management' have not been addressed or have only been touched on. From the outset we recognized that it would not have been possible or indeed desirable to produce a definitive volume on archaeology and management. However, we all felt that a series of papers illustrating the very diversity of subjects falling under this heading, and the variety of options and approaches currently in existence, would help the recognition that such themes deserve wider debate and stimulate other archaeologists to join in. At the same time, we intended this collection of papers and the references cited therein to act as a useful starting point for those studying particular applications and experiences of management in archaeology – whether as students, teachers, or practitioners.

BOOK STRUCTURE

The sequence of chapters in the book mirrors two of the main themes which could be detected in the papers and from the discussions at the conference sessions: first, the widespread interest in the theorization of archaeological value; and second, the way in which management theory is or might be applied to archaeology. The papers are thus roughly arranged along a continuum that runs from a greater concern with value to a greater concern with practice, although virtually all contain elements of both theory and practice via chosen case studies. It might be tempting to think of this continuum as one that runs from the abstract to the concrete – as reflected in the book's divisions, from value, through management theory to practical management – but the real-life consequences of whatever is being discussed are always present. The two types of 'abstract' value identified by Carman, for instance, are inevitably associated with particular real-life fates for archaeological material. Similarly, Pryor's 'practical' chapter includes a consideration of abstract concepts such as 'motivation' and 'standards'.

Obviously it would have been possible to group the contributions in a variety of ways other than the one chosen, which in turn would have reflected other themes which run through the contributions. The structure of the book perhaps owes much to our realistic expectation that the consumer may not read the volume cover to cover in one sitting (although we hope that all will be read, in whatever order) and contributions have therefore been placed where we hope most readers will expect to find them.

VALUE: THEORY AND CONSEQUENCES

The concept of valuing the archaeological resource is central to much of the literature concerning the management of archaeology. This is usually approached in terms of the evaluation of individual components of the archaeological resource base for their significance. The term 'significance' is borrowed from the United States where it has a very specific legal meaning (Davis 1989: 97; McGimsey and Davis 1977: 31; King *et al*. 1977: 95–104; Schiffer and Gumerman 1977: 245–6 *et seq*.). In Britain this approach has given rise to the Monuments Protection Programme (Darvill *et al*. 1987; Startin, this volume) and schemes derived from it (Darvill *et al*. 1993). Other approaches to the consideration of value have provided lists of the types of values represented by archaeological material – either as 'givens' (e.g. Lipe 1984); or as historical alternatives (Darvill 1993). The notion of value lies also at the heart of the principle that archaeology and the management of archaeological remains is carried out in the 'public interest' (e.g. McGimsey 1972: 5).

Attention in the area of value is now turning to the consideration of whence the values carried by archaeological materials derive – how value is ascribed to archaeological remains. The chapters in Part I of this volume, 'value', represent some of the new approaches being taken in this direction. The point that they all share is the realization that value does not reside immanently 'inside' archaeological material but is ascribed to it by social processes. The question becomes, then, not 'how valuable is this?' but 'what kinds of social value does it represent and where do these come from?' This common agreement as to aim aside, the contributors are not yet agreed either as to the methodology of understanding valuation nor even an appropriate terminology. While Carman talks of 'value gradients', Firth discusses 'value systems', Darvill both of these together with 'value sets' and Bower avoids use of the term 'value' throughout her chapter in preference to a concern with 'heritage' – something which is 'not a material product but an emotional or perhaps even spiritual one'. Where terms are shared, considerable differences in meaning are evident: Darvill's use of 'value gradient', for instance, is not the same as Carman's. Darvill's three terms are also used by him in a manner suggesting that they are interchangeable, an idea that may not be shared by others using these concepts.

Carman considers value as an essentially dynamic process and composed of two elements: the type of value and (separately) its 'quantity' (however measured). Firth is concerned with conflicting value systems – especially those which are 'archaeological' versus those which are 'non-archaeological'. For Carman the process of valuation is in some sense a 'real' social fact and comes at the end of a social process of selection, whereas for Firth the concept of value is more of an abstraction along with other elements of the management process. Darvill considers values themselves to be 'real' and to derive from a combination of socially prescribed attitudes (especially the expert knowledge of the archaeologist) and private interest, which raises important and interesting questions concerning who has the power to determine which types of expertise and interest are considered relevant – an area he does not, however, enter on this occasion. Bower's 'spiritual' heritage corresponds here to Carman's value gradient.

A continuing concern with the measurement of the 'significance' of archaeological remains is evident in Darvill's and other chapters in the volume. Darvill emphasizes the role of the concept of 'importance' in assessing archaeological remains. *Management of Archaeological Projects* (MAP2) specifically provides for the assessment of the potential of material for analysis as part of the review process of managing archaeological projects (Andrews and Thomas, this volume). Startin looks at the procedure for indentifying material 'of national importance' in relation to legal and other forms of protection. In a similar vein, Wenban-Smith considers the problems of identifying and evaluating Palaeolithic sites. Wheatley takes a wider view, being concerned with the evaluation of landscapes not as 'bounded spatial entities' (discrete sites) but instead as surfaces of 'continuous variation'. Wheatley espouses the views of Carman, Darvill, Firth and Bower that 'archaeology clearly has no inherent value', though there remains an assumption that something can be measured in value terms by appropriate procedures. The precise relationship between ancient material which undoubtedly exists in a physical form and remains which can only be identified as 'archaeological' as a result of a social process will become, one feels, the great area of debate in the immediate future.

Assessment in another sense is also evident in the contributions to this volume. As well as its concern with site potential, MAP2 requires the constant assessment of archaeological work (Andrews and Thomas, this volume). Locock, going one stage further, suggests that the workings of MAP2 should itself be subject to assessment, while Wenban-Smith supports the ongoing evaluation of research programmes.

This link to the practice of archaeology is reflected in the value-laden terminology of McAdam's review of the history of archaeology, where she talks of 'mystics and savants', 'Victorian respectability', 'a Golden Age' and (a negative value) the 'coming of Mammon' – all ideas which force us to confront the other meaning of value – that of a moral standard (cf. Barrett 1993; this is also a sense in which Darvill uses the term). Value as a moral standard is evident in Pryor's concern with the motivation behind archaeological work, Andrews and Thomas claim that MAP2 specifically derives from the 'academic values of archaeology', and Brooke's call for archaeology to 'come to a deeper understanding of itself' requires 'giving values a more explicit role'. Cooper justifies his concern with management issues by reference to the increasing interaction of archaeology with outside forces (and especially the realm of politics) – and the consequent need to explain the value of archaeology as an endeavour to those not involved in the discipline. It is in this connection of the field of valuation with practice that a link is made with the other themes of the book – the management of that practice, the differing levels of importance given to organization or material, the diversity of approaches represented by that practice, and degrees of optimism and pessimism about the future.

MANAGEMENT: THEORY AND PRACTICE

Compared with the variety of topics which find their way onto management bookshelves, the discussion of management in the archaeological literature is extremely limited in scope. The discussions which fall under a 'management' heading are most commonly restricted to those which some archaeologists would term Cultural Resource Management. Where are the texts on organizational change, on the cultures of archaeological organizations, on the problems of developing archaeological research strategies and managing archaeological projects, and the effects of such activities on archaeological theory and practice? Perhaps most importantly, where are the discussions about archaeologists 'as people', addressing their motivations and aspirations?

There is a worrying lack of published discussion which can be grouped together under the heading of archaeological management, and the reason for this is difficult to explain. For some, it may be that management is thought to be solely about concepts such as 'productivity' or 'value for money'. This view – combined with a strongly held belief that such concepts have little or no relevance to the archaeological discipline – may discourage debate. For others it may be diffidence and uncertainty regarding the value of their day-to-day experiences in the profession and its relevance to others. Whatever the reason, we can commonly read the results of large-scale research projects and benefit from the description of the methodologies applied against an explicit philosophical framework. However, the organizations which undertake the work, their structures, the kinds of individuals involved on these projects, the part which such projects play in the strategy of these organizations as a whole, and many other areas of general interest, remain invisible to the reader. Indeed they are frequently relegated instead to non-attributable coffee-break discussions at conferences and elsewhere.

This lack of an explicit concern with debating the application of management ideas and principles in archaeological work is matched, however, by the introduction of professional standards into the discipline (IFA n.d.) and the generation of documents such as *Exploring Our Past* and MAP2 (English Heritage 1991a, 1991b) which effectively constitute policy statements and performance standards for the discipline as a whole. This being the case, there is a danger that management concepts are being learnt by rote and applied in the archaeological profession without a full understanding and appreciation of their derivation, their degree of appropriateness and the reasons for their success or otherwise. Darvill's chapter on training for the management role in archaeology is of particular relevance here.

This lack of published debate also has more far-reaching strategic implications for the discipline by limiting the available examples for study by the younger generation of archaeologists, and reinforcing the idea that management is not a 'proper' subject justifying published discussion within the discipline. Accordingly one of the aims of this book is to forge an explicit link between the discussion of management issues and archaeology as an academic discipline. The book structure reflects this: value is a key concern in the management of archaeological resources, and so we begin with discussions of value; Part II outlines key ideas from management theory and their value to archaeology; the practical implications of their importation into the discipline are taken up in Part III.

In addition to Cooper's, two chapters are concerned to analyse the general nature of archaeological management: McAdam does so from a historical perspective, and Firth from a more synchronic, theoretical standpoint. Current problems in the management of archaeological remains are particularly highlighted by Wenban-Smith and Startin, although Carman, Firth and Pryor also touch on this. But the majority of chapters explore the range of management approaches open to archaeologists and their value: marketing (Blockley); total quality management (Brooke); the impact of information technology on practice (Wheatley); project management (Andrews and Thomas; Nixon); and matrix management (Locock; Nixon). While Darvill considers management training as part of an archaeological education, Pryor provides a useful corrective to a technically managerial approach by concentrating on the specifically archaeological aspects of running a project.

MATERIAL VS ORGANIZATION

Two of the chapters in this collection use the term 'marketing', and the differences between them serve perhaps to heighten awareness of the division in the field of managing archaeology between those whose concern is primarily with the material of archaeology and those whose concern is primarily with the practice of archaeology. Mim Bower's concern is with material – 'archaeological material which is immediately tangible' and the 'emotional or spiritual' product of which can be 'marketed' to create empathy with the past. For Marion Blockley, on the other hand, marketing is 'a corporate philosophy, a set of tools and techniques, and a systematic approach to problem solving in a rapidly changing market' – an approach to archaeological practice.

Those who focus here on material do so in two senses. As a *record* (a term challenged by Barrett [1987]), archaeological material is the focus of research into the past. This is the sense in which material is considered by Carman, Pryor, Firth and Wenban-Smith. As a *resource* it is material to be drawn on and used – and this is the sense applied by Andrews and Thomas, Bower, Nixon, Startin and Wheatley. To some extent, and as pointed out by Darvill on value, these understandings overlap – a focus of research is no less subject to use than anything else, and in the case of Startin and Wenban-Smith this is the kind of use they envisage. If any problem exists here – and any real difference – it is in the burden of meaning carried by the term 'resource'. This is the term most used in the field of archaeological management (Darvill 1987; Schiffer and Gumerman 1977; McGimsey and Davis 1977; Hunter and Ralston 1993) and it carries overtones of 'management' in a highly commercialized sense – rather as Blockley's definition of marketing does. Here we meet Shanks and Tilley's (1987, 23–4) criticism of cultural resource management as a 'pricing of the past' and echoes of the 'Heritage Industry' (Hewison 1987; Bower, this volume). In considering archaeological remains as a 'resource' the possibility exists that its meaning as a 'record' of the past may be forgotten.

A significant proportion of the chapters in the book which focus on organization are concerned with the organization of people. This lies at the heart of project management (and thus of MAP2) (Andrews and

Thomas, this volume), and involves a consideration of the motivating of people – whether as 'total quality management' (Brooke, this volume), 'redesigning the [management] pyramid' (Locock, this volume), 'trying to make it happen' (McAdam, this volume), encouraging change (Nixon, this volume), training (Darvill, this volume) or deciding objectives (Pryor, this volume). Surrounding this concentration on the individual human being is an alternative concern with rather more 'abstract' structures. Here Startin considers the MPP, Wenban-Smith the structures for protecting Palaeolithic remains, Carman the law on Treasure Trove and Firth the legal system surrounding archaeology underwater. Wheatley – in his consideration of the impact of information technology on the management of archaeological material – bridges the space between these two concerns by recognizing the interplay of practice and (pre-existing) structure, an idea that resonates with Giddens's structuration theory (Giddens 1984; and see Firth this volume).

It is here – in the interpenetration of concerns with material on one hand and practice on the other – that the study of managing archaeology will benefit the discipline. It is clear from this volume that no agreement has yet been reached on what constitutes the object of management in archaeology – the practice of the discipline, or the material with which it is concerned. This uncertainty may derive in part from a false assumption – that archaeological management forms part of the discipline of archaeology. A change of perspective may assist here: as one of the editors has argued (Carman 1991; Carman in press), archaeological management may not be part of the discipline of archaeology, but surround and encompass it, serving as a link to other fields and the outside influences that affect archaeology (Cooper, this volume; Firth, this volume). If this is so, then the division between a concern with practice versus that with material falls away and the interpenetration of these fields becomes an essential component of a discourse about the purpose, management and future of archaeology.

DIVERSITY

The grouping and ordering of the chapters outlined above, pragmatic though it is, genuinely reflects some broad common interests among the various authors. However, this superficial coherence should be set against one of the other central aspects of the project which this volume represents: *diversity*. Since the aim of the book is not to make a definitive statement about the management of archaeology, nor to establish a work of reference in which management theories can be fossilized, it is hoped that the book will provoke and stimulate a renewed debate about the future direction of archaeology. The reader should not be surprised, therefore, if there seem to be contradictions and dissent among the contributors: there *are* contradictions and there *is* dissent. Nor should the reader see the volume as the product of an existing coherent body of opinion or theory, because there is no such body. The diversity of the book is not accidental, and is not regarded by the editors as a weakness. That some of the chapters may seem to have little in common to merit their inclusion within the same cover is merely a reflection that these issues have not been brought together until now. The *mélange* should be taken as a statement in its own right: its diversity is therefore emphasized and not concealed.

Cooper sets the tone for diversity in his introduction to management approaches in archaeology by listing the types of archaeological management most commonly encountered: 'managers of archaeological organizations, managers of particular archaeological projects, or managers of particular specialisms and services'; and the wide range of publications encountered in the discipline of archaeology: 'field techniques, analytical methods, theory and theory development, on the management of the archaeological resource, and on the presentation of archaeology to the public' (Cooper, this volume). But this is not his point here. His aim is to survey critically the range of material available in the literature of management studies which is of relevance to archaeology. This diversity is reflected in the other chapters in the second and third parts of the book as discussed in the 'management' section above. Similarly, as discussed in the section on 'value', Carman, Bower, Darvill and Firth take very different positions in understanding value as a phenomenon, and each of them adopts a different position from other authors on the subject. Overall, the aim of this volume is to highlight these differences, to make them explicit, and to encourage debate and discussion.

DISSATISFACTION VS OPTIMISM

Another contrast which can be drawn from these chapters is the contrast between those authors who are pessimistic and those who are optimistic about the management of archaeology. The elements of pessimism in many of the contributions clearly stem from a profound dissatisfaction with current practices and theories of archaeological management. Dissatisfaction, for example, is the central element of Francis Wenban-Smith's chapter. He identifies a management problem – the protection of a particular body of material – and lucidly draws into focus the failings of some current management practices through the use of a simple metaphor. McAdam's historical review of archaeological management starts pessimistically: 'why, despite the dedication of those working in the field, so many projects fail to reach publication and so much unofficial discontentment is expressed' (McAdam, this volume).

There is perhaps an element of resigned pessimism also in the contribution of Firth, whose examination of the role of institutions has led him to suggest that: 'archaeological endeavour, managed through state institutions, will be incapable of challenging the contemporary values of the state, including its conception of nationality or territoriality' but Firth, like the majority of the contributors, is also of a more optimistic bent, observing rightly that the state is not a static phenomenon but open to alteration. Those advocating various management approaches (Cooper, Blockley, Brooke, Andrews and Thomas, Nixon and Locock, all this volume) are in general optimistic and forward-looking. Bower is satisfied for archaeology to be a branch of the 'nostalgia' industry and urges us to exploit this advantage, while Pryor is in general happy with the way archaeologists manage both things and people, if not with some of the results. None, however, is so profoundly optimistic as Wheatley who sees in the adoption of new technology into archaeological management an opportunity to realize some ambitions, and to discard some of the baggage of the past.

If Firth stands between the extremes of optimism and pessimism, then so do Carman and Startin – not so much by fusing the two responses but by avoiding their taint. Carman is essentially concerned to understand how the world works in relation to the legal valuation of archaeological remains: he passes no judgements – but thereby abrogates the right to make recommendations for improvements. Startin, by contrast, is concerned to demonstrate the degree of debate necessary within an existing practice.

CONCLUSIONS

This volume represents a moment in what we hope will become a process. The moment is the current situation, the opening-up of a discussion in archaeology of the contribution of management to the discipline; the process is the continuation of that discussion throughout the archaeological community in the UK and elsewhere.

The chapters which follow this Introduction are ordered as outlined above for the reasons we have set out. After them is a short speculative piece which outlines what we think will be the issues needing clarification and debate in the immediate and foreseeable future. In many ways these represent our own 'pet' concerns, and can be seen as our 'private' debate – the one we started in a corridor at the Leicester TAG – continuing. You, our readers, will have your own concerns, which we hope are reflected somewhere (explicitly or not) in these pages. Our debate continues; we are happy for you to join in.

REFERENCES

Barrett, J. (1987) 'Fields of discourse: reconstituting a social archaeology', *Critique of Anthropology* VII, 3: 5–16.
Barrett, J. (1993) 'Ontology and temporality', paper given at the Annual Conference of the Theoretical Archaeology Group, Durham, December 1993.

Carman, J. (1991) 'Beating the bounds: heritage management as archaeology, archaeology as social science', *Archaeological Review from Cambridge* 10, 2: 175–84.

Carman, J. (in press) 'Wanted: archaeologists not bureaucrats', in H.F. Cleere and P.J. Fowler (eds) *Training Heritage Managers*, London: Routledge.

Cleere, H.F. (ed.) (1984) *Approaches to the Archaeological Heritage*, Cambridge: Cambridge University Press.

Cleere, H.F. (ed.) (1989) *Archaeological Heritage Management in the ModernWorld*, London: Unwin Hyman.

Cooper, M.A. (1991) 'Management theory *is* archaeological theory!', paper given at the Annual Conference of the Theoretical Archaeology Group, Leicester, December 1991.

Darvill, T. (1987) *Ancient Monuments in the Countryside: An Archaeological Management Review*, English Heritage Archaeological Report no. 5, London: Historic Buildings and Monuments Commission for England.

Darvill, T. (1993) 'Valuing Britain's archaeological resource', Professor of Archaeology and Property Management Inaugural Lecture, Bournemouth University, July 1993.

Darvill, T., Saunders, A. and Startin, B. (1987) 'A question of national importance: approaches to the evaluation of of ancient monuments for the Monuments Protection Programme in England', *Antiquity* 61: 393–408.

Darvill, T., Gerrard, C. and Startin, B. (1993) 'Identifying and protecting historic landscapes', *Antiquity* 67: 563–74.

Davis, H.A. (1989) 'Is an archaeological site important to science or to the public, and is there difference?', in D.L. Uzzell (ed.), *Heritage Interpretation*, Vol. 1, *The Natural and Built Environment*, London: Bellhaven Press, 96–9.

English Heritage (1991a) *Exploring our Past: Strategies for the Archaeology of England*, London: Historic Buildings and Monuments Commission for England.

English Heritage (1991b) *Management of Archaeological Projects*, London: Historic Buildings and Monuments Commission for England.

Giddens, A. (1984) *The Constitution of Society: Outline of the Theory of Structuration*, Cambridge: Polity Press.

Hewison, R. (1987) *The Heritage Industry: Britain in a Climate of Decline*, London: Methuen.

Hunter, J. and Ralston, I. (eds) (1993) *Archaeological Heritage Management in the UK: An Introduction,* Stroud: Alan Sutton.

Institute of Field Archaeologists (n.d.) *By-laws of the Institute of Field Archaeologists: Code of Conduct*, Birmingham: IFA.

King, T.F., Hickman, P.P. and Berg, G. (1977) *Anthropology in Historic Conservation: Caring for Culture's Clutter*, New York: Academic Press.

Lipe, W.D. (1984) 'Value and meaning in cultural resources', in H.F. Cleere (ed.) *Approaches to the Archaeological Heritage*, Cambridge: Cambridge University Press, 1–10.

McGimsey, C.R. (1972) *Public Archeology*, New York: Seminar Books.

McGimsey, C.R. and Davis, H.A. (eds) (1977) *The Management of Archaeological Resources: The Airlie House Report*, Washington DC: Society of American Archaeologists.

O'Keefe, P.J. and Prott, L.V. (1984) *Law and the Cultural Heritage,* Vol. 1, *Discovery and Excavation*, Abingdon: Professional Books.

Schiffer, M. B. and Gumerman, G. J. (eds) (1977) *Conservation Archaeology: A Handbook for Cultural Resource Management Studies*, New York: Academic Press.
Shanks, M. and Tilley, C. (1987) *Re-Constructing Archaeology: Theory and Practice*, Cambridge: Cambridge University Press.

PART I

VALUES

CHAPTER ONE

THE IMPORTANCE OF THINGS

Archaeology and the law

JOHN CARMAN

One of the problems with the field variously known as archaeological heritage management (AHM), archaeological resource management (ARM) and cultural resource management (CRM) is that it is seen as a branch of archaeology constituted entirely by practice and therefore essentially non-theoretical. Accordingly, there is a paucity of research in the field (Carman 1991) and its practitioners are relegated to a process of mere training (Carman in press). The field is separated from other branches of archaeology – particularly academic archaeology – to its detriment, and one purpose of my own research is to close this unnecessary and unhelpful rift.

The specific focus of my research is English law and what it does to archaeology when it meets it. The central idea is that the application of the law to archaeological material changes that material into a different phenomenon – no longer an archaeological one but a legal one; Schiffer (1972) might like to extend his list of N- and C-transforms to include an L-transform – a particular kind of C-transform. In particular, I seek to understand the way the law acts upon archaeological material in order to open up the field of AHM to new questions and thus provide a framework for future research. As many commentators have noted (see especially Lipe 1984), questions about the value of archaeological remains lie at the heart of AHM.

LAW AND DECISION-MAKING IN ARCHAEOLOGY

Researchers in Britain and the United States are attempting to apply the analysis of political cultures to decision-making processes (Douglas 1982; Schwarz and Thompson 1990; Thompson *et al.* 1990). A major concern has been understanding the differences between the proponents and opponents of various energy policies and why these differences should be so wide and so fiercely debated. The conclusion is that if energy resource estimates (over which the arguments take place) 'provide justifications for energy policies then energy policies are best understood as arguments for ways of life, as rationalizations for different kinds of desired social arrangements'(Schwarz and Thompson 1990: 91). Instead of selecting your preferred policy on the basis of objective facts concerning energy outputs and spin-off effects 'you start with a socially-induced predilection that leads you to favour the kinds of social arrangements promised by one policy. . . . Having chosen [that policy] you then look around for justifications for it'(Schwarz and Thompson 1990: 91–2).

The conventional sequence of policy selection as we understand it is thus back to front. We do not choose policies on the basis of their likely effects, but instead only look for the likely effects that will justify a policy we have already chosen. Similarly, the entire political process works backwards: '*Political actions chiefly arouse or satisfy people not by granting or withholding their stable substantive demands, but rather by changing the demands*'(Edelman 1971: 7, emphasis in original).

In other words, politicians are not elected to get us what we want, but to ensure that we want what we get – and the passage of legislation is a necessary part of this political value-ascription process. Laws can be seen variously as symbols against threats to the moral consensus (Edelman 1967: 37–8), as a means by which 'groups which present claims upon resources may be rendered quiescent by their success in securing non tangible values' (Edelman 1967: 40), as a signal that 'a group aspiring to a valued status has achieved it' (Edelman 1971: 10), and as the creation of 'space in which to act' (Edelman 1967: 103). Laws are any of these but they are neither 'commands nor predictions of future actions' (Edelman: 1967: 104) since laws may be 'repealed in effect by administrative policy, budget starvation or other means' (Edelman 1967: 37–8). Laws to protect archaeological material fall into this category – they act primarily as symbols of the importance of archaeology.

Few perhaps realize how closely tied together are the development of laws to govern the treatment of archaeological remains and the development of the discipline of archaeology itself as we know it. In 1851 the material of archaeology was divided into three categories: the oral, the written and the monumental (Newton 1851). Newton's paper is an important one in the history of the discipline because its aim was to boost the importance of the study of objects (what the author called 'monuments') over folklore studies of oral history and popular traditions, and the study of written materials. It was during the 1850s – and out of the same organization as Newton – that figures such as A.W. Franks began work to establish a collection of specifically British material in the British Museum. At the same time, out of the same organization, the very same people also tried to persuade the Treasury to use the ancient legal doctrine of Treasure Trove to gain state ownership of certain types of archaeological material. The internal politics of the Archaeological Institute at this time was dominated by an effort to shift emphasis away from the study of folk-lore and historical material to a concentration on objects. This is closely tied to the rise in influence of Baron Talbot de Malahide, who chaired the Institute's 'antiquities' study group and was elected President of the Institute for the first time in 1861. Talbot was an individual who worked very closely with Franks, endeavoured to legislate on Treasure Trove, acted as mentor to John Lubbock and Augustus Pitt Rivers and first called for legislation on field monuments as early as 1859 (*Archaeological Journal*, passim).

Murray (1990) convincingly shows the connection between Lubbock's legislative efforts on behalf of ancient monuments and his archaeological theory, but more than that is involved. One of the striking things about Lubbock's Bill and the 1882 Act that was derived from it is that medieval monuments are specifically excluded from both. The justifications given for this at the time were very thin and contradictory: that medieval remains were already well looked after; that they would cost a lot to maintain; and that there would be 'aesthetic' problems. But Roman monuments, to which these arguments would not apply, were also excluded. This legislation only related to prehistoric remains, and that was all it was intended to relate to (Chippindale 1983). The explanation for this lies in the political context of the time. First, we can see this legislation as a continuation of the drive to promote the object as the proper study of archaeology. There are no direct folklore links with the prehistoric past nor are there any written materials, and the logic of this is almost inexorable: if no oral or written evidence exists to explain the significance of these objects, then we must look for ethnographic parallels – and this is precisely the field in which Lubbock and Pitt Rivers were involved for ten years previously, together with Franks and Talbot as close allies (Chapman 1989; Stocking 1987). Secondly, Lubbock and Pitt Rivers used their prehistoric archaeology and their ethnography to promote a certain political message – essentially, that evolutionary change in human affairs led from above is more 'natural' than revolutionary change. But the late nineteenth century also hosted an alternative politics which looked to a vision of the medieval period as its model, advocating revolutionary change and a more libertarian and egalitarian way of life. This is the real reason for limiting protection to prehistoric remains: to promote the object above the written word inside the archaeological community, and to privilege the ideology of prehistorians over socialist medievalism.

The aim of Talbot and then of Lubbock in the field of legislation was to assert the importance of objects and monuments over other materials, and (in the case of Lubbock) to privilege the study of prehistory within archaeology as a whole. Prior to the late nineteenth century, objects were only a small part of the province of archaeology and the study of pre-history was very unimportant. It was the promotion of law in this field that gave them value and which maintains their value today. The same can be said for every class of material protected by law – in a very real sense they become 'archaeologically important' because they are covered by a body of law, and not the other way around.

This interpretation challenges the current generally held view, which is that archaeological material is valued and therefore requires protection. Twenty years ago, however, writers in this field were fully aware that the passage of laws gave material a value rather than reflecting a value it already had. McGimsey (1972) argued for the need for archaeologists to promote their work in order to gain public support. He recognized that the ultimate justification for laws is that they give the public an interest, not that a pre-existing public interest requires legislative action. Later in the 1970s, McGimsey changed his story and argued in terms of a duty to the public (McGimsey and Davis 1977; McGimsey 1978). What had changed? One key change was the legal situation: in 1969 the US enacted the National Environment Policy Act and in 1974 the Archaeological and Historical Preservation Act (McGimsey 1978: 415–16). By legislating, the US federal authorities gave a value to archaeological remains and it was that newly given value which made it of public concern.

Accordingly, it is the passage of laws covering archaeological remains that gives those remains their value, and the point of passing laws is to promote certain types of material for some ulterior motive (that is, having nothing to do with any 'innate' value of the material itself). What, then, is the process by which this value is given?

THE VALUATION PROCESS

Law gives archaeological material a publicly recognized value. Intuitively, most people will recognize the existence of two distinct realms of action in the modern world – the private and the public. These realms have also been identified by students of social theory (Giddens 1984: 197; Benn and Gauss 1983a, 1983b) and the sociology of knowledge (Berger *et al.* 1973). They are also reflected in the division of people into those with more or less cultural capital (Bourdieu 1984) or social control (Douglas and Isherwood 1979) which allows much greater freedom of movement between the public and private realms. People who are able to move relatively freely between these two realms are those most likely to appreciate the phenomenon we call the 'archaeological heritage' (Merriman 1991).

The division between the public and private domains is not a clear one – rather, it is an area of fuzziness relying on the position of the observer. As a realm of social action, it depends on the position of the actor and the acts of the actor as to whether they take place in the public domain or the private one.

Berger *et al.* (1973: 104) recognize that 'the cleavage between private and public spheres is a basic principle of modernity'. The distinction 'between publicness and privateness is a practical one, part of a conceptual framework that organizes action in a social environment' (Benn and Gauss 1983b: 5). The two spheres are normative categories, applied in relation to social context and there are three dimensions along which measurements of publicness and privateness can be made: access, agency and interest (Benn and Gauss 1983b: 11).

An analysis of liberal conceptions of the public and private realms considered the important institutions of the two domains (Benn and Gauss 1983a: 39). In the private sphere we are essentially concerned with the individual. In the public sphere, it is the group which is the important thing, and especially the state which stands for the entire society. In the public sphere, then, the group acts as a single body, and in the case of the state it acts for everyone. The distinction between the private domain of economic activity and the activities of the state has in particular been recognized by Giddens:

> [A] 'private' sphere of 'civil society' is created by, but is separate from and in tension with, the 'public' sphere of the state. . . . Civil society is the sector within which capital accumulation occurs, fuelled by the mechanisms of price, profit and investment in labour and commodity markets.
>
> (Giddens 1984: 197)

Douglas and Isherwood (1979) have considered the differences between individual and corporate savings and in particular the strong corporate group:

> Because its legal existence is eternal, it can make its demands in the name of unborn generations. . . . No individual acting on his or her own behalf can entertain dreams of such a long-term future. Only the group can develop a full-fledged otherworldly morality, for the group outlives its members.
>
> (Douglas and Isherwood 1979: 37)

Since we devote valuable resources to its preservation and non-consumption, this is the way to view the archaeological heritage – as a form of corporate saving. Looking at it this way, the archaeological heritage can be seen to exist in the public domain, the realm of the group rather than the individual, endowed with an 'otherworldly morality'. The idea of the 'otherworldly' expresses the aura of the public domain quite nicely: it is not of the everyday in which things are used up, discarded, bought, sold, or just ignored. The public domain is a special place – above and beyond the reach of the individual and yet something in which the individual has a legitimate interest and rights.

This raises issues concerning the importance we ascribe to the heritage and how we should apply to the archaeological heritage ideas about the 'social life of things' (Appadurai 1986) and how things gain and lose value

(Carman 1990). Most of such thinking has been about goods in circulation – commodities of various kinds. These have been usefully defined from an anthropological perspective by Appadurai (1986) and Kopytoff (1986). In addition, Thompson (1979) has looked at the mechanism of shifts in the lifetime of an item from a period of declining value to one of increasing value. From the point of view of this paper the concept of commodity – the good in circulation – is not a useful one since the heritage, lodged in the public domain, is not in circulation. The point about a commodity is that 'its exchangeability (past, present or future) for some other thing is its socially relevant feature' (Appadurai 1986: 13). A thing that is not intended for exchange ceases to be a commodity – and that is the situation of items in the heritage.

Michael Thompson's book *Rubbish Theory* (1979) is also concerned with items in circulation. He divides all things into three value categories: *durable* items are things whose value is increasing over time (antiques, works of art, collectables of various kinds); *transient* items are those whose value is decreasing over time (second-hand furniture, everyday things, a motor car unless it is vintage or veteran); and *rubbish* which is things of no value.

Thompson himself is more concerned with the third of his categories – rubbish. These items are not only valueless but also deemed to be culturally invisible. This means that they are held by common agreement not to exist: they have a physical existence, but (unless we are being perverse) we all agree not to see them. Not seen, not discussed. Rubbish exists in a realm below that of discourse. This is very useful, because Thompson's model is a dynamic one that tries to explain how things shift from one value category to another. The rubbish category is particularly important in this, since it is by being reduced to rubbish – culturally invisible, not considered or discussed – that items can be manipulated so as to re-emerge with a new value placed upon them.

Many readers of this book will be happy with the idea that any form of material culture can operate in the social environment at a level below that of discourse (cf. Hodder 1982), a similar idea to Thompson's about things in his rubbish category. The heritage, however, can be said to reside in the durable category. Durable items are deemed to have a permanent existence and constantly increasing value. What happens when they reach a level of value that can no longer be measured is that they are withdrawn from circulation. This is not rubbish – they are not culturally invisible. Instead they become hyper-visible, highly prominent in the cultural landscape.

The distinguishing characteristic of material in the durable category is that its value is constantly rising. Thompson tends to equate value with monetary worth. Accordingly, his only means for dealing with those things that become so valuable they are literally priceless – that is, so highly valued that this cannot be expressed in monetary terms – is to relegate them to removal from circulation. What he does not do is provide any means by which such items can really be identified, nor does he suggest what such removal means. This is of some practical importance for anybody concerned with the heritage.

I want here to make a preliminary attempt to describe what happens when an item of increasing value passes finally into the public domain, when it is given legal status and withdrawn from circulation. There used to be a phenomenon well known to radio engineers called the Heavyside Layer which could be used to allow radio transmission over long distances. The radio beam would be pointed at an angle skyward, and when it encountered the Heavyside Layer the beam would be deflected back to the earthbound receiving station. To use this effect, the beam had to be pointed at an angle that was neither too steep nor too shallow in respect to the surface of the earth. The trick was to hit the Layer at just the right angle to deflect the beam where you wanted it to go, rather like bouncing a snooker ball off the edge of the snooker table.

Something like this happens with 'heritage' items (Figure 1.1). Essentially, if the rate of increase in value is so fast that monetary terms become inappropriate, then the item shoots through the cognitive barrier that has by common consent been erected between the realm of commerce – the private domain – and the public domain. If the rate of increase in value is not fast enough, then the item 'bounces off' this barrier and stays in the realm of commerce. This valuation process is really a matter of perception, and:

> Anything whatsoever that is perceived at all must pass by perceptual controls. In the sifting process, something is admitted, something rejected and something added to make the event cognizable.
>
> (Douglas 1982: 1).

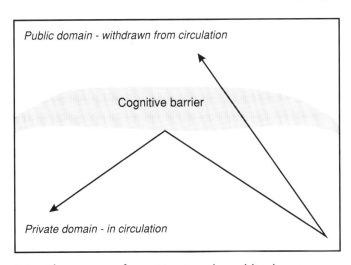

Figure 1.1   The process of transition into the public domain

Lipe (1984: 3) identifies no less than four different types of value which can be contained in the 'cultural resource base' – economic value, aesthetic value, associative/symbolic value and informational value. Lipe is concerned with archaeological material as a totality, and so does not attempt to ascribe particular levels or quantities of value to particular parts of the cultural resource base. It is not, however, too much of a mental leap to realize that any single component of the cultural resource base – any one site, object, structure – may rank differently on each of these four *value gradients* (Thompson 1990: 124–5).

The four different types of value emerge from four different value contexts (Lipe 1984: 3). These values are not somehow contained in the cultural resource base itself – not immanent in objects, structures, sites and so on – but derive from various social contexts in which these things are located – the economic marketplace; traditions of style; structures of knowledge and understanding; academic disciplines; and so on. To take one example – the economic marketplace as exemplified by the auction – we can see how these contexts play their part in ascribing values to things. Two of the functions performed by auctions are the function of (1) resolving ambiguities and uncertainties, and the function of (2) establishing value, identity and ownership (Smith 1989: 162).

> Objects are reborn in auctions. They acquire new values, new owners, and often new definitions. For these new identities to be accepted as legitimate, they must be seen as having a communal sanction. It is this search for legitimacy that underlies the communal character of auctions.
>
> (Smith 1989: 79)

In the case of the auction, the type of uncertainty to be resolved is that of price, and this in turn depends on the category of the object (Smith 1989: 33). So even before entering the realm of uncertainty (the auction room), some kind of decision about the object has already been made. This puts the valuation of the object at the end of the auction process, not at its beginning. This suggests that in any decision process there are at least three phases. First, objects are chosen for a particular form of treatment. Secondly, they are categorized. Only at the end of this process are they given value – just as Lipe suggested, the kind of value ascribed derives from the context in which the thing is placed.

But the auction can only ascribe one kind of value – a commercial money value. In other words, auctions are places where a single context rules and from which only a single kind of value ascription can emerge. But there are three phases to this. First, things are selected for a particular form of treatment, second they are categorized in some way, and only then can they be allocated a place on the appropriate value gradient. These three phases correspond to the three 'perceptual controls' (Douglas 1982: 1):

1 something is admitted – to a particular arena for treatment in a particular way;
2 something is rejected – by categorizing we reject other forms of categorization, other ways of thinking about something;
3 something is supplemented – a kind and a quantity of value.

LAW AND ARCHAEOLOGY IN ENGLAND: THE EXAMPLE OF TREASURE TROVE

The ancient doctrine of Treasure Trove whereby certain items of gold and silver automatically belong to the Crown (and are usually passed on to a museum) (Hill 1936; Palmer 1981) was the first law in England to be taken up by archaeologists. Its manner of operation provides the model for all such law – whether ancient monuments legislation, planning regulation, the protection of wrecks, or the preservation of the natural environment (but see also Firth, this volume). The process is the same as that described above for the auction – selection, categorization, and only then valuation (Carman 1993).

The responsibility of coroners' inquests for declarations of Treasure Trove is covered by section 30 of the Coroners Act 1988. This provides that a coroner 'shall continue to have jurisdiction (a) to inquire into *any treasure* that is found in his district; and (b) to inquire who were, or are suspected of being, the finders' (emphasis added). The section limits the jurisdiction of the coroner to finds not of *possible* or *suspected* treasure but to *actual* treasure. In other words, the fact of the item constituting treasure for legal purposes is deemed to be established prior to the coroner's inquest. This is the process of selection as identified in the case of auctions.

Having confirmed that Treasure Trove relates only to finds of gold and silver, a distinguished legal counsel has pointed out that the doctrine has been applied as if each individual item should be considered separately (Sparrow 1982). By treating each find as an individual item, collections of finds are split. All such material is thus effectively decontextualized.

The main drive of the doctrine has been to acquire objects for museums. This relates closely to, and in a sense justifies, the decontextualization process. The effect of the law in decontextualizing the object serves to focus attention on the object alone and to allow its transfer into a new context: that of the museum case. Being also limited to items of silver and gold, such objects are ripe for display in the museum, less as items of specifically historic import than as valuable artworks.

This selection process, however, can have serious practical consequences for archaeology. The study of so-called 'structured depositions' seeks to challenge the idea that we can transfer into the past our modern distinction between 'rubbish disposal' and 'ritual deposit' and instead looks to the nature of deposits for some idea of the world-view of people in the past. Much of the material examined from this perspective is not given legal value and may suffer as a consequence of efforts to apply the law to a certain class of material.

The Snettisham hoards of Iron Age gold torcs were acquired for the British Museum through the Treasure Trove procedure in 1991. In the course of doing so, other features identified at the same location had to be relegated to the status of residuality: a more extensive excavation 'might have uncovered the bottoms of more Neolithic pits, but this was not the purpose of the exercise' (Stead 1991: 450); and other Iron Age material related to the hoards themselves had to be ignored (Stead 1991: 450). Here, the dismissal of relevant archaeological material is the logical consequence of the use of law. This is what always happens. If we continue to protect archaeological material under the law we are forced to recognize that we can only ever protect a part of it. It is the law that gives that protected material its value – and that law-given valuation then has inevitable consequences for archaeology.

The three processes of transformation from found object to Treasure Trove take place as part of the process of the coroner's inquest. The first two processes – selection and recategorization – are phases of progressive decontextualization, and the third – adding value – a phase of recontextualization.

This is the true meaning of the declaration of Treasure Trove. It serves to explain the great interest shown in such items by archaeologists, by the media and ultimately by the population at large. Treasure Trove items are tinged with an air of magic and mystery which makes them desirable. But they no longer belong exclusively to the king, as they did in the Middle Ages: by placing them on museum shelves they become, in a sense, owned by us all. This is the process of transition into the public domain (Figure 1.2).

The vertical axis represents measures of value – however defined; they may be monetary, informational, aesthetic. The horizontal axis represents social contexts, in this case two only: the realm of private property (including the economic marketplace) and the realm of public property (including the museum). The divergent curves represent different value gradients along which the object may be located. The hatched area is the realm of uncertainty between social contexts and, in the case of Treasure Trove, resides in the coroner's inquest in which the object is decontextualized. This is a realm of no-context. The place where the curves touch – within the area of uncertainty emphasized by the ellipse around it – is the realm of decision-making in which either the object is declared to be Treasure Trove or not. On declaration one way or another it leaves this realm and re-enters one or other social context.

The value gradients diverge as a result of the adversarial approach contained within the Treasure Trove procedure. Ownership is absolute and cannot be shared. Accordingly, neither claimant can be expected to give the object away unless its value to that claimant is relatively low. The

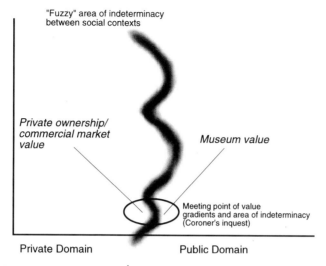

Figure 1.2   A Treasure Trove diagram

higher the object is placed on the value gradient, the greater the owner's resistance to parting with it, whether the owner is a private individual or a public museum. This is not to say that the measure of value for each is identical: the reason for two value gradients is that they measure different scales and types of value which are relevant to the social context in which they exist. The region between the two social contexts – the public and private realms – is a 'fuzzy' one and the two gradients do not meet neatly at a single point. Rather, it is an area of dispute and uncertainty – which is where the process of law comes into play, rather like the auction.

The Treasure Trove procedure, then, like the auction as described by Smith (1989), serves to resolve ambiguities and uncertainties, and to establish value, identity and ownership. First, a particular body of material is selected for processing, then it is placed in a new category, and finally it is given a value which is generally accepted by all concerned. The only difference between the auction and the Treasure Trove inquest – albeit a crucial one – is that whereas only ownership and cost are in dispute in the auction, in the inquest it is the kind of value to be ascribed to the item that is also in dispute. The reason for this is simply that in the auction the social context is already decided, but in the inquest it is the relevant context for the item that is really in question.

Here is the process of Rubbish Theory (Thompson 1979) in action. In Rubbish Theory nothing can change from its position on one value gradient to another without passing through the phase of 'rubbish'. By stripping components of the archaeological heritage of their context – phases one and two of the process – these items cease to belong on any value gradient. For a time they cease to have any cultural existence and it is this process of decontextualization which allows their re-emergence with new values and new meanings – as something we call the archaeological heritage.

CONCLUSIONS

This chapter has outlined some ideas about the relationship between archaeology and law. The focus has been not on law itself but on the effect of law on archaeological material. I have argued that the law in England acts on archaeological material, first, to give it a publicly recognized value. This promotion into the public domain was the intention behind the original passage of such law in the last century; since then legal coverage has been spread to other components of the heritage, both cultural and natural. This promotion remains a main purpose behind legislation to preserve archaeological material. Secondly, specific areas of law give specific bodies of material specific kinds of value. In the case of Treasure Trove, material is classed as 'treasure' suitable for display in a museum. The process is threefold: selection of specific items for treatment, then categorization, and finally placement on an appropriate value gradient.

In attempting to reveal the mechanism behind the application of law to archaeology, it is possible to glimpse the manner in which this application affects our understanding of the nature of the archaeological record. If what is archaeologically valuable is so because the law tells us so, then the law must also in some measure control our perception of what is 'archaeological'. Ultimately, the purpose of this line of research is to assist archaeologists to appreciate the nature of the phenomenon with which they have to deal.

ACKNOWLEDGEMENTS

Portions of this chapter were previously given in papers presented at TAG in 1991 and 1992 and in seminars in the Department of Archaeology at the University of Cambridge. I am grateful to all those who commented on these ideas. Particular thanks go to my supervisor, Dr Marie-Louise Sorensen, and to Professor Colin Renfrew and Dr Christopher Chippindale for helpful advice and comments. I owe an immense debt to my wife Patricia for all her support and help during the course of my research.

REFERENCES

Appadurai, A. (1986) 'Introduction: commodities and the politics of value', in A. Appadurai (ed.) *The Social Life of Things: Commodities in Cultural Perspective*, Cambridge: Cambridge University Press, 3–63.
Archaeological Journal, passim.

Benn, S. and Gaus, G. (1983a) 'The liberal conception of the public and the private', in S. Benn and G. Gaus (eds) *Public and Private in Social Life*, London: Croom Helm, 31–65.

Benn, S. and Gaus, G. (1983b) 'The public and the private: concepts and action', in S. Benn and G. Gaus (eds) *Public and Private in Social Life*, London, Croom Helm, 3–27.

Berger, P., Berger, B. and Kellner, H. (1973) *The Homeless Mind: Modernization and Consciousness*, Harmondsworth: Penguin.

Bourdieu, P. (1984) *Distinction: A Social Critique of the Judgment of Taste*, London: Routledge.

Carman, J. (1990) 'Commodities, rubbish and treasure: valuing archaeological objects', *Archaeological Review from Cambridge* 9, 2: 195–207.

Carman, J. (1991) 'Beating the bounds: archaeological heritage management as archaeology, archaeology as social science', *Archaeological Review from Cambridge* 10, 2: 175–84.

Carman, J. (1993) 'Valuing ancient things: archaeology and law in England', unpublished PhD dissertation, University of Cambridge, July 1993.

Carman, J. (in press) 'Wanted: archaeologists not bureaucrats', in H.F. Cleere and P. J. Fowler (eds), *Training Heritage Managers*, London: Routledge.

Chapman, W. (1989) 'The organizational context in the history of archaeology: Pitt Rivers and other British archaeologists in the 1860s', *The Antiquaries Journal* 69, 1: 23–42.

Chippindale, C. (1983) 'The making of the first Ancient Monuments Act, 1882, and its administration under General Pitt-Rivers', *Journal of the British Archaeological Association* 136: 1–55.

Douglas, M. (ed.) (1982) *Essays in the Sociology of Perception*, London: Routledge and Keegan Paul.

Douglas, M. and Isherwood, B. (1979) *The World of Goods: Towards an Anthropology of Consumption*, London: Allen Lane.

Edelman, M. (1967) *The Symbolic Uses of Politics*, Urbana, IL: University of Illinois Press.

Edelman, M. (1971) *Politics as Symbolic Action: Mass Arousal and Quiescence*, Institute for Research on Poverty Monograph, Chicago: Markham.

Giddens, A. (1984) *The Constitution of Society: Outline of the Theory of Structuration*, Cambridge: Polity Press.

Hill, Sir G. (1936) *Treasure Trove in Law and Practice from the Earliest Time to the Present Day*, Oxford: Clarendon.

Hodder, I. (1982) *Symbols in Action: Ethnoarchaeological Studies of Material Culture*, Cambridge: Cambridge University Press.

Kopytoff, I. (1986) 'The cultural biography of things: commoditization as process', in A. Appadurai (ed.) *The Social Life of Things: Commodities in Cultural Perspective*, Cambridge: Cambridge University Press, 64–91.

Lipe, W.D. (1984) 'Value and meaning in cultural resources', in H.F. Cleere (ed.) *Approaches to the Archaeological Heritage*, Cambridge: Cambridge University Press, 1–11.

McGimsey, C. (1972) *Public Archaeology*, New York: Seminar Press.

McGimsey, C. (1978) 'Cultural resource management – archaeology plus', in C.L. Redman *et al. Social Archaeology: Beyond Subsistence and Dating*, New York: Academic Press, 415–19.

McGimsey, C. and Davis, H. (1977) *The Management of Archaeological Resources: The Airlie House Report*, Washington, DC: Society for American Archaeology.

Merriman, N. (1991) *Beyond the Glass Case: The Past, the Heritage and the Public in Britain*, Leicester: Leicester University Press.

Murray, T. (1990) 'The history, philosophy and sociology of archaeology: the case of the Ancient Monuments Protection Act (1882)', in V. Pinsky and A. Wylie (eds) *Critical Traditions in Contemporary Archaeology*, Cambridge: Cambridge University Press.

Newton, C. (1851) 'On the study of archaeology', paper read at the Oxford Discourse of the Archaeological Institute, 18 June 1850, *Archaeological Journal* 8: 1–26.

Palmer, N.E. (1981) 'Treasure Trove and the protection of antiquities', *Modern Law Review* 44: 178–87.

Schiffer, M.B. (1972) 'Archaeological context and systemic context', *American Antiquity* 37: 156–65.

Schwarz, M. and Thompson, M. (1990) *Divided We Stand: Redefining Politics, Technology and Social Choice*, Hemel Hempstead: Harvester Wheatsheaf.

Smith, C.W. (1989) *Auctions: The Social Construction of Value*, Hemel Hempstead: Harvester Wheatsheaf.

Sparrow, C. (1982) 'Treasure Trove: a lawyer's view', *Antiquity* 56: 199–201.

Stead, I.M. (1991) 'The Snettisham Treasure: excavations in 1990', *Antiquity* 65: 447–65.

Stocking, G.W. (1987) *Victorian Anthropology*, New York: Free Press.

Thompson, M. (1979) *Rubbish Theory: The Creation and Destruction of Value*, Oxford: Oxford University Press.

Thompson, M. (1990) 'The management of hazardous wastes and the hazards of wasteful management', in H. Bradby, (ed.) *Dirty Words: Writings on the History and Culture of Pollution*, London: Earthscan Publications, 115–38.

Thompson, M., Ellis, R. and Wildavsky, A. (1990) *Cultural Theory*, Boulder, CO: Westview Press.

CHAPTER TWO

MARKETING NOSTALGIA

An exploration of heritage management and its relation to the human consciousness

MIM BOWER

In this chapter I wish to examine the control of the archaeological resource in terms of marketing and to examine the psychology behind this marketing of archaeology. I particularly wish to consider the archaeology which has become identified as our 'heritage'. The term 'heritage', as used here, refers to archaeological material which is immediately tangible – known sites, particularly excavated and published ones, ancient monuments, great houses, listed buildings, art galleries, plant and animal collections, museum collections and so on. If the consensus is that the material culture set labelled as 'heritage' or 'archaeology' must be preserved then it must be bound about with a conceptual and practical framework which can be used to protect it. This framework is used to manage archaeology and exists today in legislation, organizations and government bodies.

It is the use or abuse of this material culture resource within its present management structure, particularly in the shaping of public opinion, that I wish to address in this chapter. Public opinion may be seen as a powerful tool and weapon, particularly in countries where the media plays a large part in the lives of most individuals and contributes a great deal to the formation of views and values. If 'the media' can be defined as a medium by which information can be passed to a wide group of people then it is also possible to see the presentation of heritage through the medium of museums, exhibitions and ancient monuments as a form of media. If this is so, then the creators of museum displays, and heritage managers generally, can play a role in shaping the public's conception of heritage. Public opinion could greatly affect the preservation or otherwise of the archaeology which is yet to be discovered and uncovered.

As archaeology deals primarily with the preservation or control of a material base, part of which is heritage as we know it, it is paramount that archaeologists consider the manipulation of public opinion to further the cause of preservation of the record for the use and education of future generations. If, for whatever reason, people do not believe that the past is significant, preservation of the visible part of that past will not be an issue and public funding will evaporate.

MANAGEMENT AS MARKETING

The thought of marketing heritage as if it were a commodity is crude but not new. Marketing, though often confused with publicity and promotion, is borrowed directly from the business world (see Blockley, this volume). When heritage is viewed in marketing terms it is presented as a 'product' and the visitor to a museum or ancient monuments becomes a 'customer'. The customer lies at the centre of the activity, providing the energy to drive the reaction which generates revenue. It suggests a reflexive approach, including market research, identifying needs, desires and marketplaces, product development, selling, publicity and promotion, quality control and after-sales service.

Marketing is the process of finding or creating a need for a product, creating an image of a product in the consumer's mind and hoping that it will be desirable in such a way that people will want the product. We must ask how this principle can be applied to a material base as sensitive and, at first glance, as practically useless as heritage. How many times, in this customer-orientated and money-led phase of history, are we asked to justify ourselves in financial terms? Can heritage really be marketed as a need for the individual or the community, sold as if you cannot do without it? Can it be fitted in the same economic bracket as leisure products, fashion, beauty and sports goods – as things which are not essential for survival but which are still desirable?

However, heritage is undoubtedly being marketed already. The great changes in museum services and the presentation of ancient monuments that has come about under the auspices of the Museums and Galleries Commission, English Heritage and similar agencies, have brought heritage back into a state where it comes close to paying its costs. Attendances at heritage presentations have increased and continue to increase (Merriman 1991: 9). Museums and ancient monuments are being aimed at a wider consumer group, not just the educated and knowledgeable, and there is a greater emphasis on making the past interesting, attractive, accessible and educational. There is a product being marketed as heritage. How do we attempt to define this product?

On initial examination there may be a temptation to confuse the issue by thinking that it is the artefact, the heritage object, that is being marketed. This cannot be entirely true as the artefacts themselves are rarely sold. Nonetheless, it may be suggested that 'heritage shops', either at museums and monuments or on the High Street, are in fact pandering to this desire.

It may be better to approach the examination of the product from an entirely different angle. One may suggest that the thing which is marketed as heritage is not a material product but an emotional or perhaps even spiritual phenomenon. Certainly, it is a product that does not belong on the practical plane. It is plausible to suggest that it is the public's reaction to the artefact that is being sold rather than the artefact itself; it is the impact of the artefact on the consumer being sold, not the material object. It is an idea, an ideal, that we are selling (Greffe 1990).

What is this idea? The past as perfect perhaps, the past as a part of the present. We no longer look backwards to laugh at our predecessors as being clumsy and peculiar, different from us, savages. We look back and see things, deeds, actions, ideas, ways which are better than ours. We find skills that are admirable and lost. We appear tired of our 'we can make any-thing faster, cheaper, better than you' industrialized society. We see our environment being destroyed and look to the past believing that our ances-tors lived somehow in harmless equilibrium with their surroundings. We look to the past, our heritage, to answer the problems of the present and future.

This may seem a far cry from the reality of creating a museum display, or presenting an ancient monument which the public will find both attract-ive and informative, and yet I believe that it is relevant in so much as we need to identify, anticipate and meet the needs of the heritage-consuming community. In the system of management that exists at present, heritage must be manipulated to make it saleable. How is it made saleable? By creating or identifying an already-existing need, by making that which you are selling, desirable, and by appealing to the consumer.

Thus far it may be agreed that the thing which is presented to the public as heritage must be relevant both to the individual and to the present time. The consumer must be able to associate with or relate to the 'product'. So – what is the thing that the consumer relates to? Is it a leisure experience we seek? Do we lust after education? Or are we simply congenitally nosey and find the thought of scrutinizing the lives of the long dead quite delicious? I would suggest that it is a more complex and deeper need that generates enough public interest in heritage and makes museums a rel-evant part of our lives. There is a need that can support an enormous industry with not only museums and ancient monuments but also shops selling books and replicas, re-enactment groups selling ancient warfare and theatre. Interest in this small area is enough to support a number of magazines with national and international circulation. What is it that puts the re-enactment of the past on the front page of any local news-paper and in the pages of national newspapers? What is it that makes pubs and restaurants redecorate their interiors with 'Olde Worlde' fashions, fake beams and panelling, tiled floors, leaded windows and synthetic 'oak' doors?

NEED AS NOSTALGIA

Most people have a sense of history or, at the very least, of passing time. However, individuals feel a link with the past in different ways. The past and heritage can be categorized in many different ways; to some extent we use these varied categories when we are creating a museum display. For example a group of artefacts can be categorized as tools belonging to a specific craft process and be displayed along with the raw material and the completed product. This same group of artefacts can be displayed as the personal belongings of a particular artisan, so the artisan and their position in the community, or the position of that trade in society as a whole, becomes the focus of the display. The same group of artefacts can be displayed as the cultural markers of a particular socio-cultural group, reflecting their position in a regional context, a national context and perhaps even a world context. As individuals we seek to relate ourselves to these artefacts in their various categories; we seek to find these artefacts reflected in our own lives and to place onto these artefacts the importance and value we find in the present day artefacts that we see around us. We seek to see the ancient artefacts as reflections of their counterparts in use today – the fossilized lump of butter wrapped in leather is reflected in the supermarket foil-wrapped block – the Viking craftsman's tools and half-made bone combs are reflected in any hand-crafting process – the Roman matron's toiletry kit is reflected in carefully packaged lipstick and perfume – the Anglo-Saxon hut is reflected in our own home. We are deeply touched by the thumb-print signature on pottery or the child's hand print in the cave painting. We seek the human in the material object. We feel an empathy with the maker or past owner of the artefact through the medium of the silent object.

Empathy can be elicited in many ways but it is founded on the basis that one individual associates another individual's experience, reactions, emotional responses and so on, with corresponding parts of their own experience, reactions and emotional responses. One individual identifies with another. Individual identity can, just as heritage, be categorized in many ways. We see ourselves as members of a family, social group or club, or as members of a profession, ethnos or nationality. We may be identified as owners of a particular piece of material culture, for example a particularly expensive sports car or a strange pet. We are all multi-faceted and multi-layered. Thus also is heritage; it is personal property, a private past, it is the tools of a trade, it is a national treasure, it is a cultural symbol. We as individuals seize upon these multi-faceted layers and fit them to our own jigsaw-puzzle identities. Hence I suggest that humanity can be made to relate to its past through a series of self-images. For example: I am a member of this family, thus its history is my history; I am located in this locality, thus its history is related to mine; I am a member of this community, thus its history has affected mine; I am a part of this nation, thus I can call its history mine, and so on. Heritage from the basic heirloom to the World Heritage Site can be associated with and related to at various levels due to the myriad ways we see ourselves and the many contexts in which we can be seen to belong.

Perhaps the most accessible form of heritage is our close personal history and that of our family and our immediate spatial locality. Our feeling of the link we have with this past may be strong, lending us the feeling of belonging. It is often translated into the emotion which manifests itself as 'nostalgia'. Nostalgia, taken from the Greek, translates as a painful yearning to return home. We associate this feeling with the past. It is derived from the emotional feeling, the empathy, we feel from the close personal sense of the past. It expresses our close personal relationship with and to the past: 'the past is endowed with values which the respondent longs to enjoy but cannot find in the present' (Szacka 1972: 66).

Where this feeling comes from can only be guessed at. It may arise from a dissatisfaction with the present, or from a steady loss of identity due to the expansion of borders, growing population and increases in social and spatial mobility. Results from the interviews conducted by Nick Merriman, published in *Beyond the Glass Case* (1991), concerning the public's views on heritage in general show that many people recognized the advantages of modern technology while at the same time feeling that change was happening too fast and that people were losing their sense of place in the world. If clear continuity – a direct link between the present and the past – can be made through an heirloom or through a display in a museum it can be used by the individual to place themselves socially, culturally, and spatially. This is personal history as a form of emotional anchor; it suits me to see myself as belonging to this cultural group as I can point to their material culture in the museum. The interpretation of their artefacts helps me to define the group I wish to belong to and I can define myself in terms of surviving material culture. In this way I can trace my own identity back into my past to define my place in terms of belonging to a time-scale beyond my own lifetime.

THE RESPONSE OF ARCHAEOLOGY

The 'heritage industry', as it has been dubbed (Hewison 1987), has developed in response to this need for a tangible and relevant past. Heritage sites and museums are no longer seen as elitist and inaccessible. The managers of heritage pitch their material at a wider population and it is no longer necessary to have anything but the most basic level of knowledge about history or archaeology to be able to appreciate most of the heritage which is presented to the public. Displays with a heavy bias towards context and interpretation rather than the idea of artefact as being purely aesthetic form the basis of most heritage presentations. There is a growing emphasis on the evocative and didactic – education through interpretation – exemplified by such projects as the Archaeological Resource Centre in York and the long-established Science Museum in London. Communication of worth and relevance is as important as the artefact itself, if not more so. Artefacts are displayed in place, in a room situation; assemblages concerning a particular craft process are laid together with the products of the process or reproductions of them; stone tools are hafted onto handles, or laid out together with the debris discarded from their construction. Their use, function and significance in the past cultural arena or landscape is communicated. This form of display helps the individual make the mental leap between the artefact and what it means both to the original owner and to the individual themselves.

In the display and presentation of heritage, artefacts are made to appeal to us through basic concepts such as 'Hearth and Home', 'The Hunt', 'Pasture and Field', 'Artist or Artisan', 'Culture and Society', 'Poverty and Wealth', 'Social Relationships', 'Birth and Health', 'Death and Burial', 'Ritual and Religion'. These are simple and common social and cultural associations, they are relevant to us today in that to a great extent it is these basic aspects of life that preoccupy us in our daily lives. It is these associations that we, as those who present heritage, have learned to use. We have discovered, perhaps unconsciously, this need for roots in the past that many people share. This should be the key to our marketing strategy: 'Those who talk of the past as dead fail to recognize its organic nature and to appreciate that, despite its physical existence as monuments and muniments essentially it lives in the mind'(Fowler 1981:67).

CONCLUSIONS

When marketing archaeology as heritage, we sell nostalgia at a very basic level. It is this feeling that we use to make the first step of drawing in the public, attracting their interest. This allows the creation of the forum, by which we can make the general public understand the importance of heritage, its preservation and further support. The artefacts which the public sees are not silent and lifeless; they are brought to life by the interpretation communicated in the formation of the display. Heritage is made to speak to the individual in terms that are relevant to their present-day lives and their perceived identities. The context in which the artefacts are placed aids in communicating the value of heritage and the importance of preserving it for future times.

Our consciousness is channelled towards the associative pathways chosen by the interpreter to reflect that worth, so heritage gains a value reflected from the artefacts we find around us today. This can lead to the appreciation of the intrinsic value of heritage. It is our basic desire for a sense of belonging to an identifiable place in society and time that creates the initial need for the past. Nostalgia highlights the need for continuity in our lives, a desire to be identified with a deeper past that stretches beyond living memory. Those who market heritage have identified this need and learned to utilize it.

The clever management and marketing of heritage can be used as a tool to draw the 'consumer' into a position from which a deeper message can be delivered. As to what this message should be I will leave the reader to consider. Perhaps it is the need for the preservation and careful treatment of the known archaeological record. Perhaps it is the importance of excavation and recording, or the necessity to make all of archaeology available to all people. Perhaps it is the importance of decent funding. Maybe it is a less specific and more global message we should consider. Perhaps we should be using the knowledge gained from studying the past to formulate a better future, perhaps we should use this knowledge to show how damaging wars can be, how the lack of care for the environment can lead to disaster on a world scale. Archaeology can and has been used in many ways. Through marketing nostalgia perhaps we can turn its negative use into something more positive.

REFERENCES

Fowler, P.J. (1981) 'Archaeology, the public and the sense of the past', in D. Lowenthal and M. Binney (eds) *Our Past before Us: Why Do we Save it?*, London: Temple Smith, 56–69.

Greffe, X. (1990) *La Valeur économique du patrimoine: la demande et l'offre de monuments*, Paris, Anthropo-Economica.

Hewison, R. (1987) *The Heritage Industry: Britain in a Climate of Decline*, London: Methuen.

Merriman, N. (1991) *Beyond the Glass Case: The Past, the Heritage and the Public in Britain*, Leicester: Leicester University Press.

Szacka, B. (1972) 'Two kinds of past-time orientation', *Polish Sociological Bulletin* 1, 2: 63–75.

CHAPTER THREE

VALUE SYSTEMS IN ARCHAEOLOGY

TIMOTHY DARVILL

So often, when reflecting on the essential characteristics of the archaeological resource, great play is made of features such as rarity, fragility,
vulnerability, or the finite nature of the remains that we have to deal with.
These are the kind of characteristics that Planning Policy Guidance note
16 (Department of the Environment 1990) focuses our attention upon.
But there are other characteristics that must also be considered, among
them the matters of culturally attributed meaning and value. Both meaning and value subsist through socially contrived relationships between
understanding and social action. Both represent a basis for emotional commitment to the material that, as archaeologists, we are interested in. And
both have implications which carry through into comparative reflexes most
apparent during the decision-making that is an everyday experience in the
field of archaeological resource management.

   Against this background I would like briefly to touch on three themes.
First, the development of a general theoretical model of value systems and
what are termed value gradients as an aid to analysing the archaeological
material. Second, the definition of the value systems that can be discerned
with reference to archaeological resource management in Britain today.
Third, the implications of these defined systems for decision-making in
archaeological resource management.

VALUE SYSTEMS

The concept of shared social values and their importance to the understanding of social action can be traced back to the work of Durkheim,
Weber, and Marx, among others. At its most simple, a social value is gen-

erally taken to be a conception of the desirable, whether explicit or implicit, distinctive of an individual or characteristic of a group, which influences the selection and orientation of social action from available modes, means, and ends (Kluckholn 1951: 395). Values provide the basis for emotional commitment (Butterworth and Weir 1975: 428), and as such two interpenetrating but successive dimensions to the development of values can be identified. The first may be termed 'attitudinal' – that is the arrangements of standards and ideas which define goals and which form the basis of judgements. The second dimension is 'interest-based' and relates to objects and situations which are defined as desirable through the repetitious outcome of a succession of judgements. In this way things (material culture), acts, ways of behaving, goals of action can be set on a spectrum or continuum which ranges from approved (what is currently considered the most direct means of achieving the desired ends) at one end, to disapproved (what is currently considered least direct) at the other. These spectra of continuums may be called value gradients and they provide a useful tool with which to examine changing attitudes and value systems. Positioning along such gradients is not static but dynamic; what is acceptable between the extremes will vary over time according to a multitude of stimuli and experiences.

At the heart of any value system is a logical construct which is not directly observable but which can be understood through inference and abstraction from what is said and done through verbal and non-verbal behavioural events. The stimuli which create and update value systems are complicated, not least because values are held by individuals but shared (to a greater or lesser extent) by communities. Edelman (1992: 120–1), in his neurological explorations of mind, claims to have isolated a special value-category memory area in the human brain within which is what he calls primary consciousness, a kind of remembered present that reflects the result of the brain's capacity to continually correlate what is currently being perceived with feelings generated from previous perceptions. In this way, values often reveal themselves through 'means to ends' relationships (i.e. orientations of actions) and this contrasts with the more recognizable and familiar 'cause and effect' relationships characteristic of scientific inquiry.

Values are not received, for as Galbraith has pointed out (1958), values result from a persistent and never-ending competition for what is relevant and what is acceptable. The so-called 'conventional wisdom' is frequently neither long term nor universally accepted; its prevalence is more likely based on three principles:

1 that people in general associate truth with convenience;
2 that we find most acceptable that which contributes to self esteem; and
3 that people approve most of what they best understand or are most familiar with.

Knowledge both as a component of value formation, and as a stimulant to change in value systems, is critically important. Giddens (1990: 44) has argued that because there is no rational basis for the adoption of values, shifts in outlook deriving from inputs of knowledge have a mobile relation to changes in value orientations. Trust between members of society is a major feature of the way that values are shared between people, and in modern societies it must be recognized that expert knowledge is widely trusted and relied upon. Values and empirical knowledge are connected in a network of mutual influence (Giddens 1990: 54). For Habermas (1974: 272) this network creates a dialectical relationship between values that originate in specific configurations of interest and techniques for the satisfaction of value-oriented needs. This, he argues, has two implications. First, that over the course of time some values become depreciated as ideological and then become extinct. Second, that new techniques for the satisfaction of value-oriented needs can create new value systems within changed configuration of interests.

In turning now to look at the archaeological resource in relation to current value gradients relevant to it, these questions of expert knowledge and the formation and subsequent redundancy of value systems is highly relevant. Throughout the following discussion it has to be remembered that archaeologists are both participants in the application of value systems through being members of society, and generators of more widely adopted values because they are experts in their field (cf. Kristiansen 1993: 29).

VALUE GRADIENTS FOR THE ARCHAEOLOGICAL RESOURCE

Much of the discussion about 'value' in relation to archaeological remains has focused on simplistic functional arguments which tie interest in archaeological remains to other interests and define value more in terms of the number of such linkages rather than their social significance or relationship to underlying philosophies. Thus ideas of value for education, for research, for tourism, or as an economic resource often come to the fore both in the American and European literature (Green 1984; Lipe 1984; McGimsey 1984; Darvill 1987: 164–7). What is often being referred to might in fact be better seem as importance or relevance.

For a wider appreciation of value with reference to the archaeological resource it is necessary to take one step back from such analyses and try instead to identify value systems which can on the one hand be connected to attitudinal arrangements and on the other to interest-based arrangements; as it were the means and the ends. In so doing, the value systems which can be defined subsume and underpin some of the previously recognized ideas of importance and utility. The analysis also highlights diversity and contradiction within goal-orientation with the result that a series of different value systems can be seen to co-exist; this aspect is considered further in the next section. Only relatively rarely will such value systems be shared between societies.

In Britain it is possible to recognize the development of a series of value sets relating to archaeological remains since medieval times (Darvill 1993) but in present-day western society, three main value systems or value gradients can be identified with reference to the archaeological resource. These may be characterized as use value, option value, and existence value. Their definition is based on differences in attitudinal and interest-based orientations. The following subsections look briefly at each of these in turn.

USE VALUE

This value system is based upon the fact that demands or uses are placed upon the archaeological resource by contemporary society, as indeed they have been since at least medieval times. It is a set of values based on consumption, even though the act of consumption is also creative. Society's ability to use the archaeological resource depends on two things which are in practice contributions by experts with expert knowledge (cf. Giddens 1990: 54). First, the existence of some evidence, record or memory of things we are trying to draw upon. And second, our ability to attribute meaning to what we have. Such meanings are not necessarily right or wrong; they are attributed as part of the process of recognition, derivation, and renegotiation into a future state. The meanings which are created for aspects derived from our cultural heritage carry symbolic messages, and they are cast in a language which we hope others will understand.

The focus of this value set is the evidential nature of the resource as something which can be exploited to develop some kind of tangible return. Ancient things (here including structures and relationships as well as objects) are taken out of their original social context and given a new context and a new set of meanings within another society: history is used to make history (Giddens 1990: 50). The temporal context is essentially the present. Deliberate uncontrolled exploitation of whatever elements of the resource happen to command attention, with the concomitant destruction and loss that is likely to be entailed is one extreme of the gradient along which such values are likely to move. At the other end of the gradient is the highly controlled careful use of selected elements of the resource in such a way that their usefulness can be extended for as long as possible.

The attitudinal orientation of use value is set on a number of foundations, principal among which are the standards and expectations of academic, and in particular scientific, inquiry; and, increasingly, in the principle of resource exploitation as upheld in modern societies which allows individuals and groups to gain from the fortuitous and uneven distribution of natural and humanly produced resources.

The interest-based orientation of use value is very easy to identify, mainly because the ends or goals which reflect these values are clear enough and generally well known. A few are considered in the following subsection, but they are constantly changing and new uses of the past are constrained only by the limits of our imaginations to invent them.

Archaeological research

One of the most obvious uses we make of the archaeological resource is for archaeological research – the discovery of information or knowledge about the past. In this we draw on what is known or can be discovered to recreate pictures of various aspects of the past. The range of research objectives which inform the kinds of questions deemed relevant and acceptable to pursue is nowadays rather large, the research agenda rather long, and the theoretical frameworks within which interpretations are cast are both numerous and diverse.

Scientific research

Archaeologists are not the only users of the archaeological record for research purposes. Scientific research of many kinds uses data drawn from archaeological sites.

Creative arts

Artists, writers, poets and photographers draw inspiration from archaeological monuments and objects in their own translations and renegotiations of the material world into visual, literary, or oral images. Art historians also draw on archaeological material, and the uses of the aesthetic qualities of ancient objects are as numerous now as they ever have been.

Education

The archaeological resource plays a substantial role in the general education of children and adults. However, archaeology is a technical subject with a vast literature and there is still a long way to go before a wider public has a full grasp of the detail.

Recreation and tourism

Some of these same interests come out through the use of ancient monuments for recreation, tourism, and indeed entertainment. There is no disputing the fact that essentially archaeological monuments such as the Tower of London, Stonehenge, Roman and Georgian Bath, Hadrian's Wall, and Fountains Abbey are major visitor attractions, and many are being managed in a more visitor-orientated way. Away from the milling crowds of the honey-pot venues, many of the less publicized monuments are highly prized by visitors as attractions in their own right, as points of interest for walkers, hikers or pony trekkers, subjects for photographers and artists, and as themes for recreational enterprises.

Symbolic representation

Whether the popularity of archaeological sites with tourists is caused by, or gives rise to, abundant symbolic uses of images of archaeological sites is not really known. Stonehenge again comes to the fore as having been featured in many advertisements for things as diverse as lawn-mowers and cigarettes, computer consultancy services and photographic materials.

Legitimation of action

The ascription of meaning to archaeological evidence is not something that is always left to archaeological scientists to get on with under the conformable banner of academic freedom. Archaeological evidence is frequently used to support or legitimize particular propositions, especially politically motivated propositions (Ucko 1987; Fowler 1987, Layton 1989; Gathercole and Lowenthal 1990).

Probably the most well-known example of the way in which the archaeological resource was used to support a particular regime in Europe is the programme of archaeological research carried out to support the claims of supremacy by the leaders of Nationalist Socialist Germany (Arnold 1990). A more recent example is the work carried out in Romania under the Ceausescu regime (Chippindale 1989).

Social solidarity and integration

In a similar vein, we should not underestimate the use of archaeological remains to bolster social solidarity and promote integration. For Grahame Clark, this end alone justified the continuance of archaeological endeavour and its consequent costs (1957: 251).

Monetary and economic gain

The use of the archaeological resource for monetary gain is among the oldest known calls on the remains we have. Legitimate uses include the selling of books and publications about archaeological sites, guided tours, production of souvenirs, and so on. The illegitimate side of this use is the robbing of monuments and the sale of the antiquities so plundered.

OPTION VALUE

Turning now to the second value system, option value, something rather different is encountered. Here emphasis is on production rather than consumption, but the process of production is deferred because the temporal context of this value system is not the present but rather some unspecified time in the future. It shows a particular respect for those individuals and communities who will come after us and who might expect to use the resource in the future. The goal-orientation of this value system is the physical preservation of things (i.e. physical remains) in order to achieve the notional preservation of options.

Option values hinge on a projected understanding that future generations will both want to and be able to make some use of the resource or resources in question; the idea that we have a duty to those who follow. The main quality of the archaeological resource which is essential to the acceptance of this value is the question of potential. At one end of the value gradient is the idea of fossilizing of some or all of the resource; the 'don't do anything now because it might effect the future' argument. The overarching aim is to maintain the resource intact, in a virginal and unexploited state. At the other end of the gradient is the idea that everything is important but that some things are more important than others and that it would be better to lose the less important things than it would the most important things.

The attitudinal orientations of this value set are grounded in altruistic principles and selfless behaviour where the future is better than the present. Conservatism, conservationism, and traditionalism are the steering principles. New knowledge is rarely liberated and fed into the system; more often understandings change through the reworking of existing knowledge.

Identifying the interest base of these values is rather difficult, not least because specific uses cannot be predicted, although it is recognized that there will always be new questions about the past to be addressed, new data needed to renegotiate the future with, and there will undoubtedly be new techniques and methodologies through which to investigate the past. Certainly that has been the experience of the last few decades. The more fundamental interests related to these value sets are probably perceptual rather than functional.

Stability

Adherence to option values as the justification of action inhibits change and enhances the perception of stability, timelessness and tradition. Recreation and restoration of times past are an important dimension. Elements of the past become celebrated for what they might be rather than what they are.

Mystery and enigma

Not knowing about the past may be as important as knowing about it. The attraction of places such as Stonehenge is probably that fact that relatively little is known about their use and social context. Within a society in which knowledge is usually controlled and manipulated as a key element in the support of power relations the existence of knowledge gaps which are nonetheless human creations could be rather important.

Option value carries with it a contradiction, because whilst as a value set it stands in opposition to use value, the realization of option value involves the redefinition of the values themselves in order to realize the options being held up as supporting ends for the attitudinal stance.

EXISTENCE VALUE

The third and final value gradient relates simply to the existence of the resource. The temporal context is the present, although in this case the spatial context is not necessarily very clearly defined. Central to the realization of these values is the recognition of a set of feelings of well-being, contentment, and satisfaction; the so-called 'feelgood' factor. These feelings are triggered in people who may never expect to use or see the resource itself by knowing it exists. Analogies from the world of nature conservation abound and include the existence of the historic wilderness in Antarctica, the Blue Whale, the lady's slipper orchid, or the swallow-tail butterfly. Few of those people who contribute money or time to causes connected with the survival of these species will ever get to see them or have any direct dealing with them, but knowledge of their well-being is for them a tangible thing. For archaeology, the beauty of traditional forms of land use, skyline earthworks, and familiar landscapes and townscapes can draw similar emotions.

At one end of this value gradient is the elation of knowing that all is well because everything is safe, that viability and diversity are being maintained, and that existence is assured. At the other end is despondency because the resource is under great threat, viability and integrity are marginal, diversity is low, and continued existence endangered.

The interest base of these values is the psychological imperative in having a past, knowing of its well-being, without necessarily doing anything about it. Two interests stand out for special attention:

Cultural identity

There is an active reflection of feelings of belonging in the use of references to ancient monuments in place names and the periodic festivals and celebrations on anniversaries and 'special' occasions (Fowler 1992: 44–52).

Perhaps one of the most widespread and enduring celebrations of the heritage is the way that most historic towns tell visitors of the origin and depth of history of the place well before they get to see the evidence such as it might be for themselves. Identity is established and reinforced by knowledge of the existence of a past, albeit one that is not always fully understood or very well known (Lowenthal 1985).

Resistance to change

Every generation believes that the world is changing uncontrollably and at a more rapid pace than ever before. Maybe this is true. But a predominant theme of protests against change is the galvanising of interest in some previously almost unnoticed structure or institution. Such things are not recognized until they are threatened, but the force of the arguments for their retention is a reminder of the latent strength of existence value.

Closely related to this idea of resisting change is the idea of 'reaffirmation and validation' discussed by Lowenthal (1985:40). At the heart of this idea is the notion, often expressed, that historical precedent legitimates action on the assumption, explicit or implicit, that what has been should continue to be or be again.

VALUES IN ARCHAEOLOGICAL RESOURCE MANAGEMENT

Turning now to the third theme, the matter of values in archaeological resource management, we start from the position that each of the three sets of values just described (use values, option values, and existence values) are equally legitimate. In reality, of course, different individuals and organizations place slightly greater emphasis on some more than others.

The doctrine of protectionism, for example, naturally favours adherence to the realization of option values and existence values and at present this forms the main preferred option in archaeological resource management if only because it lies at the heart of the prevailing legislation.

It can also be argued, quite reasonably, that use value should be given priority: there are people who depend for their livelihood on archaeological remains through tourism and the existence of amenity interests; academic knowledge of the past would stagnate without fresh data and new questions to answer; there are probably more important uses of space in some cases than the preservation of buried remains; and there are undoubtedly always new philosophies and positions to be legitimated by further research.

Finally, I would like to touch on the question of 'importance'. This is a term I have avoided using hitherto with reference to the decision-making elements of value systems, not least because of the possible confusion that it causes. The determination of importance is crucial to the management of the archaeological resource (Darvill *et al.* 1987) and naturally the assessment of importance needs to be carried out in a systematic and coherent fashion. This is not what interests me here. Rather, one of the main implications of what I have discussed in this _chapter is that not only is there a series of potentially conflicting value systems being played out in archaeology but that within each system there will be different emphases on what is important. This is axiomatic to the proposition expressed at the start of this chapter on the role of value systems in decision-making. Thus exponents of option value or existence value may have a very different conception of what is important than exponents of use value.

CONCLUSIONS

In management terms a special difficulty arises when the same set of objects or materials are rated as important within conflicting value systems. This is one of the main areas that Archaeological Resource Management has to address in future, but for the time being I hope that in this short presentation I have adequately drawn attention to the complexity of value systems relating to the archaeological resource.

REFERENCES

Arnold, B. (1990) 'The past as propaganda in Nazi Germany', *Antiquity* 64: 464–79.

Butterworth, E. and Weir, D. (1975) 'Values', in E. Butterworth and D. Weir (eds) *The Sociology of Modern Britain*, London: Fontana/Collins, revised edition, 428–32.

Chippindale, C. (1989) 'Editorial', *Antiquity* 63, 416–7.

Clark, G. (1957) *Archaeology and Society*, London: Methuen, 3rd revised edition.

Darvill, T. (1987) *Ancient Monuments in the Countryside: An Archaeological Management Review*, London: English Heritage.

Darvill, T. (1993) 'Valuing Britain's archaeological resource', Inaugural Lecture, Bournemouth University.

Darvill, T., Saunders, A. and Startin, B. (1987) 'A question of national import-ance: approaches to the evaluation of ancient monuments for the Monuments Protection Programme in England', *Antiquity* 61: 393–408.

Department of the Environment (1990) *Planning Policy Guidance: Archaeology and Planning*, PPG 16, London: HMSO.

Edelman, G. (1992) *Bright Air, Brilliant Fire: On the Matter of the Mind*, London: Penguin.

Fowler, D.D. (1987) 'Uses of the past: archaeology in the service of the state', *American Antiquity* 52: 229–248.

Fowler, P. (1992) *Then, Now: The Past in Contemporary Society*, London: Routledge.

Galbraith, J.K. (1958) *The Affluent Society*, Boston: Houghton Mifflin.

Gathercole, P. and Lowenthal, D. (eds) (1990) *The Politics of the Past*, London: Routledge.

Giddens, A. (1990) *The Consequences of Modernity*, Cambridge: Polity Press.

Green, E.L. (ed.) (1984) *Ethics and Values in Archaeology*, New York: Free Press.

Habermas, J. (1974) *Theory and Practice*, London: Heinemann.

Kluckholn, C. (1951) 'Values and value-orientation in the theory of action: an exploration in definition and classification', in T. Parsons and E.A. Shils (eds) *Towards a General Theory of Action*, New York: Harper & Row, 388–433.

Kristiansen, K. (1993) 'The strength of the past and its great might: an essay on the use of the past', *Journal of European Archaeology* 1: 3–32.

Layton, P. (ed.) (1989) *Who Needs the Past? Indigenous Values and Archaeology*, London: Unwin Hyman.

Lipe, W.D. (1984) 'Value and meaning in cultural resources', in H.F. Cleere (ed.) *Approaches to the Archaeological Heritage*, Cambridge: Cambridge University Press, 1–10.

Lowenthal, D. (1985) *The Past Is a Foreign Country*, Cambridge: Cambridge University Press.

McGimsey, C.R. (1984) 'The value of archaeology', in E. L. Green (ed.) *Ethics and Values in Archaeology*, New York: Free Press, 171–4.

Ucko, P. (1987) *Academic Freedom and Apartheid: the story of the World Archaeological Congress*, London: Duckworth.

CHAPTER FOUR

GHOSTS IN THE MACHINE

ANTONY FIRTH

Individuals play a role in the transmission of values through archaeological activity by passing on both their own values and more general values at large in society. However, the mechanisms responsible for exposing archaeological activity to society's values are not wholly reducible to each individual's intentions; it is contended here that the institutional arrangements which are used to manage archaeology introduce values to the decision-making process which cannot be attributed solely to the individuals making the decisions. The arguments offered here suggest that rather than acting as simple tools or conduits of decision-making, institutions are hosts to values embedded within their substance, like ghosts in a machine.

The account of the institutionalization of management set out in this chapter parallels certain aspects of Giddens's theory of structuration (Giddens 1976, 1984) and Bourdieu's conception of *habitus* (Bourdieu 1990). Assimilation of the model presented below with such work has become a principal aim of the research from which this chapter arose (Firth forthcoming).

The term 'institution' is used in this chapter in a broad sense, referring both to organizations and to procedures. The chapter also adopts a wider conception of management than is usually associated with Cultural Resource Management or Archaeological Heritage Management, which often focus on the evaluation and treatment of material, considered as a 'resource' or 'heritage'. Instead, this chapter considers archaeology as an activity, manifested as a discipline, as a profession, as a service, and as a series of interest groups; the activity of archaeology is managed, and has institutional qualities, in all of these guises. The conception of management which underlies the following discussion is one of normative conflict resolution; that is to say that rather than conceive of management as a matching of costs and benefits through some rational, utilitarian, dialectical or other impartial algorithm, this chapter considers management as a process by which contested issues are resolved in favour of specific values.

Insofar as the frameworks through which management occurs are established by the state, it may be presupposed that some of the values which are transmitted through management are intimately related to values associated with the state. State values may extend beyond those of the specific population and regime which a named state represents to general values of statehood. Nationality and territoriality are essential value systems from which contemporary states derive legitimacy – that is to say, nationality and territoriality contribute to a relationship between rulers and ruled which both parties perceive to be 'just'. In the context of this chapter it is important to note that the current validity of nationality and territoriality is based partly on their apparent validity in the past. Hence, if either nationality or territoriality is questioned, then the legitimacy of statehood is also questioned. The discipline of archaeology is in a position where it may question the evidence for nationality and territoriality in the material record, but as archaeological activity takes place through management frameworks established by the state it is conceivable that implicit nationalism and territoriality within state institutions will tend to reinforce themselves. Consequently it might be suggested that archaeological activity managed through state institutions will be incapable of challenging contemporary values associated with the state, including conceptions of nationality and territoriality.

The above scenario is somewhat pessimistic, but an optimistic response can be offered. The state is not a static phenomenon; individual states, collections of states and statehood itself continue to evolve. In the above scenario, managed archaeology acts as a damper, legitimizing the state in its current conformation. It is equally conceivable, however, that understandings of the past gained through archaeological activity could play a more dynamic role in supporting the evolution of states, perhaps through questioning the role of nationality and territoriality as essential bases of state formation. This chapter suggests that by engaging the character of management explicitly, it is possible to manipulate its institutional characteristics to favour critical research which can contribute to such debates.

This chapter presents a model which is being developed to facilitate the identification of institutional effects upon archaeology arising from management. The model is still under development by the author (Firth in preparation) and makes use of a number of freshly defined concepts which categorize the influences on management. The model has been developed in the course of an attempt to understand the management of archaeology underwater, though it is apparent that it might be applied fruitfully to other aspects of archaeology. Early development of the model was based on empirical material arising from a detailed comparative study of the management of archaeology underwater in a number of European countries and the model has also been used in attempting to understand the evolution of management of archaeology underwater in the UK.

The model hinges on distinguishing between the context, values, functions and form of management (Figures 4.1 and 4.2). Context is used in this chapter to refer to the circumstances – including the types of material discovered, threats, working conditions and research interests – which harbour

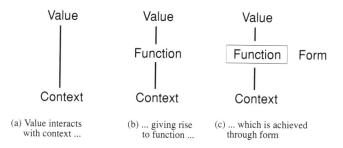

(a) Value interacts with context ...

(b) ... giving rise to function ...

(c) ... which is achieved through form

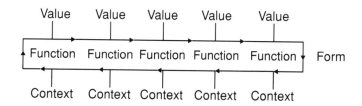

(d) The forms used to achieve various functions act as a link across value-context combinations. This link permits the transmission, through form, of effects attributable to values and contexts elsewhere in the system

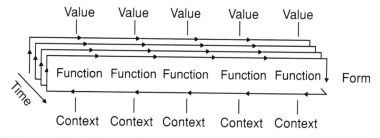

(e) Form acts through time, transmitting effects attributable to previous values and contexts

Figure 4.1   A model distinguishing between the context, values, functions and form of management

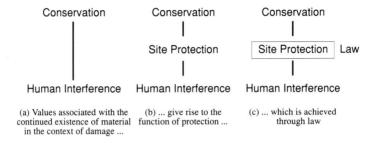

(a) Values associated with the continued existence of material in the context of damage ...

(b) ... give rise to the function of protection ...

(c) ... which is achieved through law

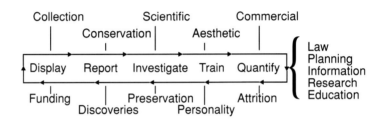

(d) Many values, contexts, functions and forms generate complex interrelationships in managing archaeology

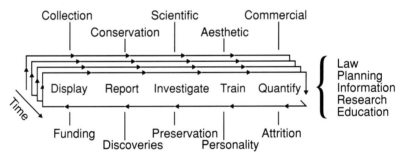

(e) These interrelationships must be considered historically

Figure 4.2 The model applied to archaeology

the conflicts which management attempts to resolve. As noted above, the management of archaeology is regarded here as a normative pursuit, hence the importance of identifying the values which are applied, through management, to context (Figure 4.1a). In this model, the attempt to apply values to context results in management emerging as a series of functions such as protection, investigation, quantification and dissemination (Figure 4.1b). These functions are implemented through a number of forms (Figure 4.1c), for example the function of site protection can be pursued through regulation, through education, or through financial incentives, among others.

It should be noted from the outset that this description of the model is, in effect, a suggestion as to a set of relationships between the concepts which are 'ideal'; the association of context with value generates functions which, in turn, give rise to form. The early paragraphs of this chapter proposed, however, that the relationship between form and the other three concepts is far more complex than the ideal implies. Consequently, the following sections are intended not only to demonstrate the utility of trying to break management down in this way, but also to indicate the presence of relationships in which the context, values and functions of archaeology respond to the formal characteristics of the institutions through which archaeology is managed.

FORM

The concept of form is central to the model presented. Form is considered here to be the concrete manifestation of an intention being carried out through a decision, a procedure, an organization and so on. Hence form *consists of* decisions, procedures and organizations, in contrast to abstract ideas about what ought to take place, referred to in this chapter as functions.

The various forms adopted in the management of archaeology have different characteristics. This can be seen in that although a function such as reporting may be encouraged to equal effect by, for example, education or financial incentive, the formal characteristics (i.e. the decisions, procedures and organizations) associated with reporting will differ according to whether an educational or financial approach is in fact adopted. Insofar as values are embedded within formal characteristics, the embedded values differ from form to form.

The recognition of form is essential because it is so closely related to the institutionalization of management. Form has an evolutionary character, arising from the aggregation of many thousands of decisions as people attempt to 'manage'. As initial decisions are repeated and adapted to new circumstances management moves away from *ad hoc* solutions to regular, repeatable systems which ease the decision-making process and generate a degree of predictability for those concerned. Form will encounter various value systems and contexts as it is evolving and the results of these encounters will be incorporated into its institutional structure (Figures 4.1d, 4.2d). However, as institutionalization proceeds the propensity to take on new values and to address new contexts will decrease. Hence approaches to management acquire organizational and procedural patterns, and management becomes institutionalised at the expense of evolutionary flexibility. It is useful to maintain a distinction between the concept of form and the process of institutionalization as this makes it possible to refer to certain forms of management as being more or less institutionalized than others.

The process of institutionalization is well advanced in many forms of management, including those which the management of archaeology makes use of most frequently, including the law. Forms in which institutionalization is well advanced already have qualities which predate the first encounter with archaeology. Hence when archaeological managers adopt forms such as protective legislation or grants for maintaining sites they introduce values pertaining to the use of legislation or grants which predate such use in relation to archaeological material. It follows that these values are somewhat 'alien' to archaeology, and they may confound the intentions of the people who make use of these forms of management.

VALUES

In this chapter values are characterized as being 'archaeological' and 'non-archaeological', though it may be more accurate to regard them in terms of a continuum of varying compatibility. It is worth emphasizing that this chapter is concerned with the juxtaposition of different value systems rather than relative values within a single value system (compare Carman, this volume; Darvill, this volume). Although other authors have recognized that material may be subject to different value systems, less attention has been paid to how archaeologists themselves accommodate different values systems simultaneously, and how such value systems are incorporated institutionally in management.

Examination of management in a number of countries by the author suggests that several distinct archaeological values systems have been pursued within management, and can be abbrieviated under the following headings: 'collection'; 'science'; and 'conservation'. It is probable that these headings camouflage more complexities than they reveal, and elaboration will follow (Firth in preparation), but they serve here to emphasize that the motivations of archaeologists cannot be assumed to be coherent, consistent or compatible. Early archaeological activity in the countries considered might be regarded as having collection as its primary value, both through assembling objects in museums (see Pearce 1992) and by compiling lists of what are collectively termed 'monuments'. Collecting might be said to have been displaced by a 'scientific' value system which concentrates on the information which can be derived from material about the past. The scientific value system appears to have been dominant for much of the past hundred years. When scientific values predominate, emphasis is placed on the quantification of objects and sites rather than the material itself. Pursuit of scientific values often entails exploitation of sites, which has become of increasing concern as 'conservation' values have come to the fore (Lipe 1977). Conservation values are marked by the idea that archaeological material cannot be reduced to information by scientific method, however advanced that may be, and the conservation value system is typified by interest in preservation *in situ*.

Several points are worth making about this simplified description of value systems in the management of archaeology. First, management need not be associated with a single archaeological value system. Second, the dominant value systems within archaeology may have changed through time. Third, although any one value system may be dominant, other value systems may co-exist with it and exert a subordinate, but observable, influence. Hence this rough progression must be tempered with the recognition that these values systems overlap and that their influence may be concurrent in contemporary management. Given our understanding of form, it can be suggested that the management of archaeology has been shaped by different archaeological value systems in the course of becoming institutionalized, and that provisions which date back to a period when certain values were prominent will encourage the persistence of that value today, even though managers may think that the older value system has been superseded. An example of this would be the frustration of the efforts of a manager to preserve a site *in situ* because the available legislation favours either the acquisition of material through collecting, or destructive investigation in the name of science.

Non-archaeological value systems include commercial systems operating on the basis of exchange, aesthetic values which are closely related to the visual qualities of material, and value systems derived from faith, as well as those associated with the state such as nationality and territoriality, and so on (Lipe 1984, Schiffer and Gumerman 1977: 241–8). The value systems which archaeologists encounter amongst treasure hunters, art collectors, indigenous peoples and politicians are often far from their own, yet they all have to co-exist in day-to-day life. As with the various archaeological value systems, non-archaeological values may reside in the institutions which managers make use of, frustrating the intentions of their decision-making to various degrees.

Although a number of different value systems are apparent in the management of archaeology, many of them appear to have been prominent in each country where management is practised. Hence evidence of 'collection', 'science' and 'conservation' are visible in the management of many of the countries studied in the course of the research from which this model derives. This feature is important in understanding the degree of homogeneity in management of archaeology from country to country.

CONTEXT

Context is used here to refer to the material and cognitive circumstances of archaeology, some of which management has to address. It includes the archaeological record (actual and perceived), archaeological knowledge, methods and theory, and the characteristics of the people involved. The presumption that context is the dominant factor affecting management is implicit in statements such as 'management reacts to discoveries of archaeological material', 'changes in our understanding of the past result in changes in management', and 'effective management depends on the abilities of managers'. While not disputing that these matters can be significant, management does not always respond to them. Hence other reasons must be sought which explain why in some cases context is significant whereas in others it is not. Moreover, although appreciable similarities are observable in the context of archaeology from country to country, management as a whole varies appreciably, suggesting that the factors identified here as context play a limited role.

Within the terms of the model proposed in this paper, the physical aspects of context are less problematic than those concerning cognition, knowledge and theoretical orientation. Insofar as the study of archaeology attempts to restrict itself to material evidence, it can be argued that some aspects of context are unavoidably physical. Working conditions and the physical, chemical and biological processes which affect the preservation of material are not susceptible to alteration solely as a result of interpretation. However, difficulties are encountered in trying to extend this immutability to matters where recognition is required; for example it is hard to maintain that if a site, or type of site, does not exist, then it cannot be discovered; if someone is inclined to find something then their interpretation of material will tend to accord with their desire. Hence the aspects of context in which perception are involved are effectively infused with value at such an early stage that the context/value division pursued in this paper becomes less helpful. Nevertheless, the division remains tenable as a heuristic device.

FUNCTIONS

The relative homogeneity of context across state boundaries is paralleled by a general uniformity apparent in the functions of management from state to state. This arises partly from contextual similarities, but also from similarities in the archaeological values underlying management, mentioned above. The homogeneity of the functions apparent in management among the countries considered was sufficient to allow the construction of a standardized scheme by the author (Firth in preparation) of seven 'archaeological' functions (location, quantification, control of activities, investigation, conservation, dissemination and instruction) and five 'relational' functions (assertion of control, division of responsibility, determination of ownership, compliance and international co-operation), where the former were associated with the pursuit of archaeological values and the latter with reconciling attempts to apply both archaeological and non-archaeological value systems to the same contextual circumstances. For example the function of determining ownership of archaeological material arises because the discovery of an object is both an archaeological event and a proprietary event, as ownership must be ascribed to the object if it is to be accommodated within current distributive regimes. The dozen principal functions could be subdivided into more specific functions, such as provision for reporting discoveries, control of archaeological prospecting, participation by volunteers in fieldwork and so on. This ability to draw up standardized schemes, indicative of the relative homogeneity of the functions of managing archaeology internationally, is also implicit in the work of O'Keefe and Prott (1984), for example.

While these functions are discernible in many countries it is equally clear that the way in which each function is carried out (ie. form) varies widely from state to state. The relative heterogeneity of form is understandable in that the evolution of decision-making which results in form will have reflected the specific details of the development of each state's system. Hence Cleere observes 'The form of any cultural resource management system is determined by the administrative and legislative framework of the country in which it operates' (1984: 125). Some countries have made greater use of some forms of management than of others; some may, for instance, emphasize public education rather than regulation, or favour financial incentives over development control. The details of each general form – for example the legal, educational or taxation system – will tend to be very specific to the country concerned. Consequently, even where the archaeological context is the same, and the same archaeological values have been pursued, management may differ significantly, as might be seen where a contemporary jurisdictional boundary cuts across an archaeological 'region'. The net result is that an appreciation of management which focuses on functions is unlikely to provide much insight into management, though it will not be 'futile' (Cleere 1984: 130) if it is used as a first stage in analysing the institutional characteristics, and the archaeological consequences, of the forms through which management takes place.

MANAGEMENT ENVIRONMENTS

So far the chapter has concentrated on an analytical division of the factors affecting management which provides insight into the effect of institutions on archaeology. However, the difficulties of teasing these factors apart into conceptual categories has already been remarked upon, notably with respect to 'context' and 'value'. Before proceeding to a case study it is worth floating another concept which allows for the collective appreciation of factors which have been disconnected for analytical purposes, namely the concept of management environment. The notion of management environment arises from a softening of the division between 'concept', 'value', 'function' and 'form' which encourages a holistic appreciation of the relationships in management which their identification facilitates. In particular it is worth identifying management environments applicable to specific areas of the management where the circumstances are relatively homogeneous and yet collectively distinct from the circumstances applicable to other aspects of management. Archaeology underwater, which is the area in which this model has been developed, presents a case where it is necessary to recognize differences in circumstances which distinguish it from archaeology on land. The invisibility of material, public perceptions of 'treasure', the unpredictability of working conditions, the need for specialized equipment, the predominance of ship-related material, the intimate interaction between sites and their aquatic surroundings and the persistence of distinct legal regimes can all be said to constitute a distinct management environment for archaeology underwater.

Similarly, specific management environments might be identified in considering wetland, urban, upland and Palaeolithic (see Wenban-Smith, this volume) archaeology, among others. Importantly, 'management environments' do not equate to jurisdictional boundaries, hence the managers of archaeology underwater in one country may recognize close parallels with the situation in another country, while at the same time experiencing considerable detachment from archaeology on land in their own country. This may be so even where institutional matters contribute to the management environment, notwithstanding the general comments made above regarding the heterogeneity of form from country to country. This possibility is illustrated by legal regimes which address the sea – such as the regime dealing with salvage – which are closer in their details to equivalent regimes overseas than to the domestic regime applicable on land; i.e. the parallels between salvage law in, for example, the UK and France may be greater than those between the law affecting discoveries in the sea and on the land in the the UK alone. In sum, reconstitution of the freshly divided factors through the concept of management environment facilitates the recognition of boundaries in management which reflect the circumstances with which archaeologists have to deal rather than the archaeologically abritrary ones of district, county or state.

A CASE STUDY: THE PROTECTION OF WRECKS ACT 1973

The management of archaeology underwater in the UK has, until recently, focused largely on implementation of the Protection of Wrecks Act 1973. Administration of the Merchant Shipping Act 1894, which regulates the salvage and disposal of wreck, is also relevant but it is not central to this discussion. Management using the 1973 Act has been limited to the essentially archaeological functions of controlling damaging activities and fieldwork on sites. These functions might be assumed to arise from the attempt to apply 'archaeological' value systems in the context of archaeology underwater in the UK.

Evidence of archaeological values can certainly be discerned in the provisions of the 1973 Act. For example it might be said that the ability to license competent persons is evidence that the Act is intended to facilitate the realization of the scientific values of shipwrecks. The prohibition on tampering with, damaging or removing material from areas restricted under the Act, however, indicates the presence of values associated with preservation *in situ* and conservation. On the other hand, reference to 'diving or salvage operations' (rather than 'investigation') seems distinctly 'non-archaeological'. It might imply that the underlying value is one of conflict avoidance in the context of competition for space and resources, rather than anything more positive. Even this superficial analysis suggests that alternative and not necessarily complementary values are evident in apparently archaeological functions. It also demonstrates that unambiguous values cannot be derived by reference to the Act alone. It follows from the discussion above that a consideration of the formal attributes of management should provide greater insight into the value systems which are present.

Recognition of the importance of form draws attention to the fact that the 1973 Act is a manifestation of criminal law. This fact is inconsequentially self-evident, unless it is accepted that criminal law is only one form available to management among numerous others, and that the law is host to many other 'subforms' associated with the different branches of law, such as Admiralty Law or Environmental Law. For instance, criminal law contrasts with planning law in formal terms as although they both make use of a statutory framework; the first is characterized by deterring and resolving mischief on the basis of offences actually occurring, whereas the second emphasizes resolution by early and continuing discourse. Similarly, the existence of laws on schooling, copyright and taxation does not mean that education, information technology and financial incentives have the same formal, and consequently institutional, characteristics (Firth in preparation).

Law is a pervasive form of management which has developed through the centuries. Only in recent times has it been used to manage archaeology; although legislation referring to antiquities stretches back to the fifteenth century (O'Keefe and Prott 1984: 34), practices that would be recognized as management of archaeology are rare prior to the nineteenth century. Law has only been used to manage archaeology underwater in the UK since the late 1960s. There is an intriguing relationship between the introduction of antiquities law and the evolution of the modern state, hinting at an apparent wish by sovereigns and élites in some countries to be seen as guardians of the past in order to bolster their own legitimacy. This adds a further dimension to the close relationship between the development of antiquities law and the development of the discipline of archaeology itself noted by Carman (this volume). If the relationship between antiquities law and the state is as intimate as is suggested here, then the introduction of antiquities law at an early stage of the development of the legal system may shape law on later, unrelated matters. In general terms, however, it appears that many of the characteristics of law, including its institutional qualities, had their origins prior to introduction of antiquities law. The 1973 Act itself owes much to existing laws affecting salvage, to the extent that it appears as a statutory variant of the common law concept of 'salvor in possession'. The provisions of the 1973 Act appear to reflect values and contexts associated with centuries of saving things from the sea rather than with the management of antiquities.

Appreciation of form encourages a dynamic perspective which addresses institutionalization, hence the effects of this law on archaeology might be understood by considering the origins of the Act and its consequent implementation. Insofar as law is shaped by its origins, the understanding of statute law is enhanced by the study of the legislative process. The Protection of Wrecks Act 1973 was enacted as a result of lobbying which generated a Bill sponsored by a Member of Parliament and supported by the government. It was introduced as an interim measure to protect a small number of specific wreck sites from the destructive effects of competitive looting, pending the results of a review which was expected to result in amendment of the salvage provisions of the Merchant Shipping Act 1894 in favour of archaeological material (Dromgoole 1989a: 37). Consequently the 1973 Act was neither comprehensive with respect to the material it applied to, nor to the options which it presented. A further characteristic of UK statute law in particular is the inability to extend its principles to matters which Parliament neglected to make specific in the statute at the time it was enacted. As a result, nothing short of amendment could allow the 1973 Act to be applied to archaeological material other than wrecks and their contents. The difficulties arising from the permitted limits of interpretation are compounded by pressure on parliamentary time, which has several effects. First, it does not favour frequent reappraisal of statutes, especially less 'essential' ones; second, even where amendments are proposed, the time available may evaporate; third, less essential statutes tend to be passed at speed when a fortuitous opportunity arises. The Protection of Wrecks Act 1973 was subject to such pressures, and successive governments have, not surprisingly, tended to consider the replacement of the interim 1973 Act as a low priority. The government's interest in amending the Merchant Shipping Act 1894, which appeared strong in 1970, had waned by 1976, as explained by Mr Clinton Davis, Secretary of State for Trade: 'I have carefully considered the recommendations of the Committee on Wreck but consider it premature to enact a change in the law at present' (Official Report HC 906 707–708w). Government interest in amending the 1894 Act enjoyed a brief show of strength in the early 1980s when 'Proposals for legislation on marine wreck: A consultative document' was issued by the Marine Directorate of the Department of Transport, containing proposals which were thwarted by lack of parliamentary time (Dromgoole 1989b: 101). Major heritage legislation was passed as the Ancient Monuments and Archaeological Areas Act in 1979, including new provisions on vessels and on monuments in the territorial sea (s. 61(7)(c) and s. 53 respectively). However, such was the speed at which the Bill passed through the House of Commons that there was little opportunity to question or debate the government's statement of the relationship which the new act should have to the 1973 Act (Official Journal HC 965 1360–1375, notably 1363). Notwithstanding its specific and temporary origins, the Protection of Wrecks Act has applied generally for twenty years now. As this section has sketched out, this has more to do with the relics of parliamentary procedure than the relics which it was supposed to protect.

Institutionalization, and further effects of form, become evident in considering how implementation changes through time. Unlike heritage laws in many countries, the 1973 Act did not create its own administrative structure. Nevertheless a specific system grew up, under the authority of the Secretary of State for Trade (later Transport, Environment and currently National Heritage (see Dromgoole 1992)), consisting of day-to-day administration by civil servants of the corresponding department, a nominally consultative (but effectively executive) role by the Advisory Committee on Historic Wreck Sites and, since 1986, provision of advice and information based on fieldwork by the Archaeological Diving Unit. Implementation was largely in the hands of the people licensed to do work on the protected wrecks, including licensees, diving teams, archaeological directors and archaeological advisors. These distinct roles have their origins not in the legislation but in its administration; although the 1973 Act refers to 'the licensee' (s1(5)(b)) this does not equate to the role of 'licensee' as it arose in practice in the ensuing years. The development of such roles presents an example of how form sees the translation of early decisions into relatively rigid institutions, which has the effect of further limiting the ability of management to adapt to new contextual circumstances or to the introduction of fresh values. Hence the interpretation of the 1973 Act is no longer a matter of the meaning of its provisions, but of the meaning which its provisions have acquired in the course of its administration. Such meaning may be more restrictive than the legislation itself. The meaning of the law may be subject to scrutiny in the event of prosecution and appeal through the courts, at which points some of the administrative baggage may be stripped away. However, there have only been two instances of prosecution under the 1973 Act which were resolved by summary conviction at a magistrates' court, without legal debate (Anon. 1991).

The case of the 1973 Act illustrates the complexities of the role of form in relation to context and value. While specific material and cognitive circumstances and certain value systems combined to give rise to the Act, it can be argued that they have had a minimal role in the consequent evolution of management. It may not be too much of an exaggeration to say that the form of management has overwhelmed the factors that gave rise to management. Where contextual circumstances and values do have an effect, they appear to be relics of their original impulses, rather than new circumstances or values. Beyond this, it might be suggested that the context and the values of management through the Protection of Wrecks Act are actually a creation of that regime. Put simply, one effect of form on management is to perpetuate the circumstances which it can deal with. Because the 1973 Act as implemented to date can only deal with isolated, recognizable ship wrecks under pressure from recreational diving activity, such sites became the sole concern of management and, arguably, the sum of what was perceived to require management. From the arguments presented above it may be concluded that it is the characteristics of form, rather than value, context and function, which must be addressed in order to break out of such self-perpetuating processes.

Appreciation of the value systems, both archaeological and non-archaeological, which have operated in archaeology underwater in the UK in the past twenty years is difficult, not least because of the opacity of the decision-making process and the lack of published material. Management through agencies separated from those which deal with archaeology on land appears to have resulted in excessive concentration on technical aspects of diving and on nautical aspects of the subject matter, with virtually no contact with terrestrial archaeology or archaeologists. It is arguable that the degree of separation between land and sea exceeds that which might be warranted by differences in the management environments concerned. It is difficult to say what it was hoped would be achieved through use of the Act. Certainly, lack of support for investigation, analysis or publication suggests that the presence of 'scientific' values has not been overwhelming. The uneasy relationship between the 1973 Act and salvage law has tended to disperse material recovered, rather than facilitate the maintenance of assemblages, and the list of wrecks protected can hardly be regarded as a representative sample of the UK's maritime heritage, so on neither score can 'collection' be identified as a dominant value. Even an observable reduction in intrusive investigation is more likely to be a result of lack of resources than of the operation of a conservation ethic. While it would be naive to suggest that management of archaeology through the 1973 Act has played an influential role in maintaining the legitimacy of the nation-state set within terrestrial boundaries, it does appear that it has done little to challenge anything.

GENERATING CHANGE

It is clear that all is not well in the management of archaeology underwater in the UK. Moreover, it appears that improvements are unlikely to arise from the 1973 Act because of the formal attributes of the legislation, the legislative process, and its subsequent administration. There are, however, two possible sources of change. First, other forms, with different formal characteristics, may be adopted. This already appears to be happening insofar as planning approaches (including environmental assessment and the preparation of sympathetic development and management plans) are beginning to be applied to archaeology underwater, as are information-based approaches through the work of the Royal Commission on the Historic Monuments of England and increasing numbers of local authority Sites and Monuments Records (see Firth 1993). Second, the formal attributes of the existing regime could be altered. Despite its conservative tendencies, form continues to be an aggregation of decisions. As the decisions change, so does form. This may be cataclysmic, in that a new policy, a new organization or a new statute may be introduced, or it may be gradual. The success of any change will depend on the propensity of the given form to allow change, and on the directions that form will impress upon change, but change may occur nevertheless. With respect to the 1973 Act is arguable that its formal characteristics are such that the success of any attempt to change its use will have to address not only the interpretation of the statute but also the circumstances which surrounded its enactment, its implementation, and the institutions (i.e. organizations and procedures) which have grown up around it.

While the model advanced in this paper may have appeared to marginalize the role of the individual it can be seen on reflection that this role is significant nonetheless. Decisions are made by individuals, and although managers may be bound by the forms they adopt, their own decisions will affect the future constitution of the form. Individual decision-making raises several opportunities: first, it may be possible to recognize and then counteract the embedded values which tend to impede the manager's intentions; second, it may allow managers to compensate for distortions arising from the previous effects of form; third, it should enable managers to introduce fresh agendas into the heart of management. The third possibility is particularly exciting as it suggests a means of encouraging management which attends to administrative necessities in such a way as to generate new research.

CONCLUSIONS

This paper has presented a model of management in terms of relationships between values, context, functions and forms. In particular it has looked at how the notion of form encourages an appreciation of the mechanics and effects of institutionalization in management. The most significant assertion is that unintended values can reside within form. While the characteristics of form may affect values, contexts and functions, curtailing management's ability to respond to new circumstances, decision-making which addresses the institutional qualities of management may permit the manipulation of the system of management as a whole. The concept of management environment was introduced to allow a holistic appreciation of management to coincide with the otherwise divisive analytical framework.

The utility of the model in offering insights into management was illustrated by reference to use of the Protection of Wrecks Act 1973. The concepts outlined in the model were used to draw attention to the ambiguity of the values apparent in the provisions of the Act itself, the qualities of the Act as criminal law, the consequent effect of circumstances which predate the management of archaeology on the Act, and the Act's specific legislative background. Concern for management as a dynamic phenomenon extended to a consideration of the addition of formal characteristics to management of archaeology underwater through implementation of the Act, concluding with the suggestion that the formal characteristics of management using the 1973 Act have shaped perceptions of the archaeological record.

It was also suggested, however, that the processes involved are susceptible to influence, as form consists of the aggregation of decisions made by individuals. It was proposed that attention to the influence of institutions in management could give rise to changes which might be cataclysmic or gradual, depending on the precise formal characteristics of the institutions to which change is addressed. Moreover, it was suggested that conscious manipulation of institutions might permit the incorporation of archaeological research into management at a fundamental level.

ACKNOWLEDGEMENTS

This chapter has been written in the course of research in the Faculty of Law, University of Southampton, funded by the Economic and Social Research Council. In addition I wish to express my gratitude to the postgraduates and staff of the Department of Archaeology for their incalculable support.

REFERENCES

Anon (1991) 'Heavy fines for dives on banned wreck', *Diver* 36, 3: 53.

Bourdieu, P. (1990) *The Logic of Practice*, Cambridge, Polity Press.

Cleere, H.D. (1984) 'World cultural resource management: problems and perspectives', in H.F. Cleere (ed.) *Approaches to the Archaeological Heritage*, Cambridge: Cambridge University Press, 125–31.

Department of the Environment/Welsh Office (1992) *Planning Policy Guidance: Coastal Planning*, PPG 20, London: HMSO.

Dromgoole, S. (1989a) 'Protection of historic wreck: the UK approach part I: the present legal framework', *International Journal of Estuarine and Coastal Law*, 4, 1: 26–51.

Dromgoole, S. (1989b) 'Protection of historic wreck: the UK approach part II: towards reform', *International Journal of Estuarine and Coastal Law* 4, 2: 95–116.

Dromgoole, S. (1992) 'Transfer of administrative responsibility for historic wrecks', *International Journal of Estuarine and Coastal Law* 7, 1: 68–74.

Firth, A. (1993) 'The management of archaeology underwater', in J. Hunter and I. Ralston (eds) *Archaeological Resource Management in the UK: An Introduction*, Stroud: Alan Sutton Publishing.

Firth, A. (in preparation) 'Managing archaeology underwater', University of Southampton.

Giddens, A. (1976) *New Rules of Sociological Method: A Positive Critique of Interpretative Sociologies*, Cambridge: Polity Press.

Giddens, A. (1984) *The Constitution of Society: Outline of the Theory of Structuration*, Cambridge: Polity Press.

Lipe, W.D. (1977) 'A conservation model for American archaeology' in M.B. Schiffer, and G.J. Gumerman, *Conservation Archaeology: A Guide for Cultural Resource Management Studies*, New York: Academic Press.

Lipe, W.D. (1984) 'Value and meaning in cultural resources', in H.F. Cleere (ed.) *Approaches to the Archaeological Heritage*, Cambridge: Cambridge University Press, 1–11.

Official Report (4 March 1976), House of Commons (Hansard) Fifth Series, vol. 906, cols 707–8 Written Answers.

Official Report (4 April 1979), House of Commons (Hansard) Fifth Series, vol. 965, cols 1360–75.

O'Keefe, P.J. and Prott, L.V. (1984) *Law and the Cultural Heritage*, vol. 1, *Discovery and Excavation*, London: Professional Books.

Pearce, S. (1992) *Museums, Objects and Collections: A Cultural Study*, London: Leicester University Press.

Schiffer, M.B., and Gumerman, G.J., (1977) *Conservation Archaeology: A Guide for Cultural Resource Management Studies*, New York: Academic Press.

PART II

GENERAL MANAGEMENT THEORY

CHAPTER FIVE

THE ARCHAEOLOGICAL MANAGER

Applying management models to archaeology

MALCOLM A. COOPER

If it happen that something hard or impossible be laid upon any brother, let him receive the command of his superior with all docility and obedience. But if he see that the weight of the burden altogether exceeds the measure of his strength, let him explain the reasons of his incapacity to his superior calmly and in due season, without pride, obstinacy, or contentiousness. If after his representations the superior still persist in his decision and command, let the subject know that it is expedient for him, and let him obey out of love, trusting in the assistance of God.

Rule of St Benedict, Ch. 68 (McCann 1976)

One of the most significant changes in British archaeology in the past thirty years has been the change in the relationship of the discipline to the society in which it exists. This change – for there has unquestionably been a change – has been reflected in a wide exploration of the discipline's relevance, value and meaning by those outside the discipline, and by attempts either to explain what archaeologists believe these are, or to question more widely what society wants and to tailor more of the output of archaeological research in this direction. The more sceptical reader might suggest that these activities reflect the desire for archaeologists to carry on their practice unchanged while offering token products to society to keep it happy. However, the reality is perhaps rather better balanced and less cynical. As archaeologists have come to better understand their resource and as they have developed more complex goals and methodologies, they have recognized the need to influence government and society in order to improve the framework in which the discipline is practised. This has involved influencing the direction of planning legislation to enable better protection of the resource base and improving the nature of the funding base to better provide adequate support. However, such implicit and explicit strategies have a cost. To change the ways things are done often involves detailed explanation of what is actually done and why it is valuable to those groups in society who have the power to effect change. This inevitably leads to a critical exploration of what that 'value' is to those groups *by those groups*. And with understanding and such questioning comes the opportunity for those groups to influence the practice in return. In Britain, the change in the nature of the funding base of archaeology and the increased placement of professional archaeologists in local and national government has involved the profession and its professionals in wider developments in British society, especially in relation to concepts such as accountability, value-for-money, and marketing.

The change in the relationship between the archaeological profession and society as a whole necessitates a far more detailed exploration of the role of managers in British archaeology, whether managers of archaeological organizations, managers of particular archaeological projects, or managers of particular specialisms and services. While many archaeological professionals would identify themselves as managers and spend increasing amounts of time on management activities, there is little discussion of what an archaeological manager actually does – or should do – and very little published guidance on the application of management techniques to archaeology as a whole (Cooper 1993).

While there have been a large number of publications on field techniques, analytical methods, theory development, the management of the archaeological resource, and on the presentation of archaeology to the public, little exists on more general management techniques written specifically by and for archaeologists. One explanation for this may be the belief that relevant publications exist in the management field and therefore there is no need for archaeologists to reinvent these particular wheels. While this belief may appear reasonable, it is arguably a short-sighted approach. In the early days of archaeology, many of its practitioners undertook their work using skills and techniques learned while involved in other professions, particularly the army (see McAdam, this volume). However, the profession is made up of an increasing number of archaeologists who have spent their entire working lives in archaeology, having studied the subject at university. In comparison to their predecessors, therefore, their exposure to management theory and practice has been relatively restricted. The limited attention currently paid to management theory and practice on archaeological courses in British universities, in combination with the lack of professional development courses in such techniques, severely limits the ability of archaeologists to explore, understand and apply well-founded approaches. Ironically the lack of recognition of the importance of this area to archaeology leads to a lack of published discussion and this in turn discourages consideration of the area as central to the profession and as a core part of taught courses.

The wheel turns full circle in a self-reinforcing manner (but see Darvill, this volume).

For any archaeologist wishing both to research and apply management theory there is a bewildering variety of publications on other disciplines' bookshelves offering a variety of perspectives on theory and practice, from do-it-yourself guides to detailed academic volumes. These are, however, frequently applied in a way which may be seen as not only irrelevant to the archaeological discipline but in opposition to some commonly held philosophical principles. Topics such as value-for-money commonly get side-tracked into debates over whether heritage and arts should be 'profit-making' and there is an inherent danger that the management baby is thrown out with the political and philosophical bathwater.

Archaeologists are facing a choice: to leave management to external professionals, or to bring management techniques explicitly within the profession. A well-known example of the former in Britain is that of the Health Service (Mays 1991) which since the 1980s has seen an increasingly heated debate and conflict between the local managers and the professional staff over topics such as goal-setting and service-targeting. While the evolution of a parallel system of professional managers and specialist staff in archaeology may be seen as an anathema to many, such a system is likely to develop increasingly within our profession unless the professional archaeologists explicitly develop and use management techniques and include them within formalised training itineraries both in educational institutions and in the workplace.

Whilst archaeological projects and other activities such as cultural resource management have increased in complexity both in terms of their size and in terms of more ambitious goals and programmes, the development of the management techniques to drive them has not occurred at the same rate – or if they have then there is little or no published material on which to base this conclusion. This lack of public discussion makes it extremely difficult to assess whether the techniques being used are based on valid models and approaches, and to share learning and experience in a positive manner.

Given the above, this paper has been written to investigate the usefulness of management theory and practice to our profession, to assess the development of the theory and applications by archaeologists themselves, and to raise issues regarding the nature of management itself.

MANAGEMENT FRAMEWORKS

There is a wide variety of general textbooks which investigate the development of particular management ideas (e.g. Butler 1986; Handy 1985; Kakabadse et al. 1988; Morgan 1986) and a number of schools have been identified. In a thought-provoking investigation of the reasons behind the popularity of certain management writers in the twentieth century, for example, Huczynski (1993) identifies a series of 'families of management ideas' or schools of thought: bureaucracy, scientific management, administrative management, human relations, neo-human relations, and guru theory. Underlying these families of ideas are a series of particular themes or models which served to act as a basis for conceptualizing organizations and their activities. While each of the above schools would seem to have relevance to practising archaeologists, it is not the intention to investigate these in detail within the confines of this chapter. However, as particular management approaches seem to be given undue emphasis within the archaeological profession while others appear briefly or not at all, it is useful to explore particular themes which run through the management literature and which have had a somewhat variable impact on our profession.

SPECIALIZATION, MEASUREMENT AND MONITORING

As is discussed elsewhere in this volume (see Andrews and Thomas) one of the few areas in British archaeology which has seen published discussion of management theory is project management. The specific nature of archaeological projects in terms of task identification, programming, financial management and accountability to external sponsors is directly paralleled in the business and construction industry where it has received much attention in the post-war period (Lock 1992; Reiss 1992; Andersen *et al.* 1987). Project management techniques can be applied not only to projects external to organizations such as the construction of new buildings and roads but also to particular activities which occur within organizations such as the installation of new computer systems. The literature varies in scope from evaluating the financial risk of such projects through to techniques of organising and controlling projects once underway (see, for example, *Harvard Business Review* 1989).

Techniques of project management can be seen to have developed from the work of two influential writers, the first of whom was Frederick Taylor. Taylor was an engineer by training who followed a career in the American steel industry before becoming a consultant and writing widely on work-measurement and time-and-motion studies (1911). His influential ideas, which have seen continued development to the present day, have been brought together under the title of scientific management.

Fundamental to the application of scientific management was the detailed analysis of particular repetitive tasks and the design of the optimum methods by which they could be undertaken. This detailed and explicit development of specialization still has wide-scale application. However, other conclusions he reached were less well-founded and enduring. He strongly believed that there should be a clear division between managers who would design activities and monitor performance and the workers who would be selected to ensure that they possessed the appropriate physical and intellectual qualities. The application of this latter approach in a government arsenal led to the creation of an American House of Representatives' Special Committee to investigate the resultant labour problems (Aitken 1960)!

Specialization has a particular impact on the way in which organizations are structured and on the roles which are given to particular members. These ideas were developed by a French mining engineer, Henri Fayol. Fayol explored the concepts of specialization and hierarchy within organizations with the aim of identifying principles which when applied would lead to optimization of the efficiency of organizations. He identified five elements as comprising management: forecasting and planning, organizing, commanding, coordinating, and controlling (Fayol 1949).

The ideas raised by Taylor and Fayol and subsequently developed by a variety of others can be seen to underlie general project management techniques. The movement in British archaeology towards specifically defined projects and project-funding has encouraged the adoption of these philosophies and techniques. Andrews and Thomas (this volume) have discussed in detail the application of such techniques to archaeological project management. The clear definition of project goals, the breaking down of projects into particular stages and activities, the measurement of performance against predetermined targets, and the use of graphical charts to aid in project management each have their roots in the scientific school of management.

When looking at the impact that the scientific management philosophy had on British archaeology – together with the related theories developed from the work of Weber which are grouped under the term classical management theories (see, for example, Cooper 1993) – one cannot ignore the context within which archaeological excavation was taking place. Of particular importance was the positivist approach espoused by the New Archaeologists and which was having an increasing influence on European and particularly British archaeology (Binford, 1972, 1983; Binford and Binford 1968; Gibbon 1989). The stress of the positivist view, among others, was that anti-speculative attitudes were to be avoided and that observation could lead to objective recording of data on which theories could be tested (see, for example, Gibbon 1989; Hodder 1992). This philosophical approach reinforced the classical and scientific management approach to organizational structures and roles in British field archaeology. In the 1980s it became increasingly common to divide excavation sites into discrete areas with explicit management structures and clearly laid-out chains of command. Archaeological activities were carefully broken down and roles specifically allocated to individuals such as area excavators, recorders, and photographers. At the same time there was a growth in the use of 'single context recording systems' involving proforma recording sheets to be filled out by nominated recorders who would compile an 'objective' record of the deposits. Indeed at its most extreme it was stated publicly by at least one senior British archaeologist in the 1980s that to ensure an objective record and to avoid this 'primary data' being biased by subjective impressions during the subsequent stages of the project he would prefer to use a completely different team of staff during post-excavation and analysis. The debate over the validity of the positivist approach in science is not the subject of this chapter, but it is interesting to note that both positivism and classical and scientific management were already the subject of intense scrutiny and criticism elsewhere when they were being adopted by archaeologists.

One of the fundamental criticisms of the scientific and classical management schools approaches was that they had the potential to depersonalize the individuals undertaking the particular roles and responsibilities allocated to them. The machine-like analogy which these management schools developed and used encouraged the view that staff were simply resources similar to the machinery also employed which were to be installed and used to produce output. The impact of such systems in the archaeological profession remains relatively unexplored. However, in the 1980s there was a general complaint of those working in the middle ranks of archaeological projects in Britain that excavation, recording and interpretation had become too mechanical and lacked inspiration. Indeed the effect of the hard-structuring of the roles and responsibilities on field projects, the use of pro-forma recording, and the removal of 'subjective' interpretation on site could be highly demotivating. In some cases it is arguable that such processes may have been used to meet the power needs of the supervisors and directors of such projects rather than the needs of other team members.

PEOPLE NOT MACHINES

The Rule of St Benedict, from which the quotation at the beginning of this paper is taken, represents an early example of a management text about running a large organization. The recommended approach given in Chapter 68, while perhaps less acceptable in the 1990s, shows a certain recognition that human factors are a significant concern within bureaucratic organizations and that a consideration of the methods of communication are also important. However, the management approaches referred to earlier in this chapter, while having wide and continued application, had the effect of conceptualizing the staff as 'cogs in a machine' rather than as people, with the inherent and frequently experienced dangers of depersonalization and demotivation. As Taylor was to find out, the application of scientific and classical management principles, while perhaps leading to the design of efficent organizations on paper, led to problems if they did not include consideration of the people in whom the roles and responsibilities were vested. The lesson was that people were human beings rather than machines or elements of machines and were likely to act in ways which if unrecognized could undermine the successful application of the classical and scientific management techniques (Doray 1988).

The recognition that the study of the behaviour of people in organizations was as important to the achievement of organizational goals as their defined tasks and activities developed out of a series of studies undertaken in the 1920s and 1930s by Elton Mayo, Professor of Industrial Research at Harvard University. Mayo was particularly interested in the study of the human elements in organizations and he investigated a variety of phenomena such as worker fatigue and labour turnover. His most famous and often quoted study was that undertaken over a period of five years at the Hawthorne Works of the Western Electric Company in Chicago. Here Mayo and his team experimented with working conditions, varying factors such as lighting, rest pauses, payment schemes, refreshments, and working hours. Whilst the application of scientific management principles would have suggested that output would have been directly correlated with these factors in a predictable fashion, the results of the experiments showed the relationship to be less clear. Mayo and his team concluded that other factors were also at play which complicated the relationship between working conditions and organizational output. The results of the study led ultimately to the recognition that concepts such as motivation were a fundamental consideration in the management process as were the importance of group norms (values, attitudes, needs and expectations) in the workplace (Mayo 1933, 1949; Roethlisberger and Dickson 1949). The subsequent development of these ideas and concepts can be grouped under the heading of the 'human relations' school of management and underpinned the development of industrial sociology. Subsequent development of ideas from these initial concepts led to the exploration of a variety of approaches which could be used to enrich the role of members of organizations at all levels and which to some extent challenged the conventional wisdom of the then current organizational management philosophies. If account was taken of employees' needs for acceptance, _status and recognition then a natural development was the exploration of how traditional structures and activities in the workplace constrained the fulfilment of these needs and how such structures and roles could be altered.

A variety of researchers developed approaches regarding the nature of particular aspects of human needs and motivation in relation to the workplace (Argyris 1970; Maslow 1943; Margulies and Raia 1973) and these were subsequently grouped together under the heading 'neo-human relations'. The resultant development of these ideas included concepts such as quality circles, job enrichment and personal development (Sisson 1989).

The implications of the human relations and neo-human relations ideas, while relevant to archaeologists, have seen little critical assessment in the archaeological literature. As McAdam outlines (this volume) much of the earlier archaeological literature which includes mention of project structures tends to emphasise hierarchical approaches with clear divisions between the skilled director and assistants and the unskilled workforce. The location of many archaeological organizations in Britain within larger bureaucratic organizations such as local authorities has also tended to re-inforce organizational thinking in terms of hierarchies, roles and authority both implicitly through working in such structures and through the nature of in-house training. The few archaeological papers on management such as *Management of Archaeological Projects* (MAP2) (English Heritage 1991) may, through their application of scientific management methods to pro-ject management, have implicitly reinforced the view that the classical and scientific management approaches shed the most appropriate perspectives on archaeology and management approaches. To redress this balance – which exists in the literature if not in actual practice – there is a clear need to encourage discussion of the ways in which archaeological organizations and projects are actually structured. The use of matrix structures for pro-ject teams, for example, implies a differing philosophy towards the nature and structuring of organizations (see, for example, Locock, this volume; Nixon, this volume).

Whilst the exploration of alternative forms of organizational structure has somewhat ironically been encouraged by the change in archaeological funding in Britain to more structured and accountable systems of project-funding, another area exhibiting a surprising lack of discussion is that of prevalent cultures in archaeological organizations. The impact of organiz-ational culture on work practice has seen much general discussion (e.g. Schein 1988 and works cited). In investigating the effect of hidden aspects of group culture on organizational goals, Gerard Egan defined a particu-lar concept, the 'shadow side' as

> those things that substantially and consistently affect the productivity and qual-ity of the working life of a business, for better or for worse, but which are not found on organizational charts, in company manuals, or in the discussions that take place informal meetings.
>
> (Egan 1993: 33)

He continues:

> The shadow-side activities of the business . . . have two distinct character-istics. They are outside the ordinary management processes because they are covert, informal, or even undiscussable; and they are economically significant, that is they add value or, very often, add direct or indirect costs, that escape ordinary accounting procedures. In other words, although these activities are elusive, they need to be tracked down and managed because of their poten-tially enormous economic consequences.
>
> (Egan 1993: 33)

In his article, Egan explores the impact of such concepts as organizational stupidities, organizational messiness, idiosyncrasies of individuals, vagaries of the social system, organizational politics and culture, and concludes not only that such things exist, but they do so with regularity in any organization. The prevalent organizational cultures are likely to vary in each case, and their study would seem as relevant for the manager as is the consideration of the more traditionally recognized management areas.

The usefulness of developing perspectives on culture in archaeological organizations has been explored in a paper on the impact of the introduction of computer technology on an archaeological organization in Britain (Cooper and Dinn 1995). Perhaps more accurately the paper explores the impact of the organizational culture on the planned introduction and implementation of the computer systems. Over a period of five years the authors recognized a series of unexpected outcomes on staff and organizational activities which occurred as a result of particular hardware and software systems being introduced. These included the informal 'osmosis' of computer applications from one archaeological project and project team to another, the impact of this osmosis on staff roles and job activities, and also the effect of this osmosis on the overall resourcing within the organization as a whole. The authors concluded that one of the underlying factors causing this unexpected impact of the technology on the organization as a whole was not predictable from a traditional analysis of the organization but could more reasonably be explained by looking instead to the prevalent organizational culture, which in turn was influenced by the nature of the structure and funding of British archaeology.

The values, attitudes, needs and expectations of archaeologists, their motivation, job-security and career progression are perhaps the most poorly discussed subjects in print within the archaeological profession in Britain. Ironically, while changes in legislation and government guidance in the early 1990s led to archaeologists having a greater control of development and its impact on the archaeological resource, it also led to a movement away from large-scale excavation projects to shorter and arguably more limited 'evaluation' projects which are specifically designed to provide information for the design of development schemes which leave archaeological remains *in situ*, either underneath or in the open space allocation of development projects. Concern among archaeologists about this change has focused on sites rather than archaeologists (e.g. papers presented at the 'To Dig or Not to Dig' session of the Archaeology in Britain Conference 1992; Startin 1993). The undiscussed and underplayed effect has been twofold: firstly to change the nature of archaeological projects towards shorter and more limited works (with less funding per project) and also to restrict archaeological works in many cases to merely locating significant archaeology rather than excavating it. While successful in terms of the aims of preserving the archaeological resource for future generations it has had a significant impact on archaeologists themselves by making their projects shorter, funding for their posts in many cases more insecure, and by limiting the opportunities for them to contribute significantly to the wider questions regarding the development of human society as a whole. Such changes are likely to affect significantly the nature of archaeological organizations in terms of the people who work in them and their motivation. Yet little exists in the way of discussion of these effects or indeed ways of reducing the dysfunctional impact of these external changes.

Any consideration of organizations, human motivation and culture should also take into account the dynamics of teams working and interacting in the pursuit of particular goals (see, for example, Blumberg and Golembiewski 1976; de Board 1978). However closely one defines the goals of projects, the structures of project teams and the roles of its members, and however closely one characterizes the organizational culture and individual motivational factors of the team members, the dynamics of group behaviour which result can make-or-break the project. While traditional management approaches tend to negate the impact of individual needs and expectations on any defined activity, problematic behaviour is often seen in terms of one individual rather than as a function of the group dynamics as a whole. The key underlying concept here is that particular combinations of people with particular forms of behaviour often lead to dysfunction which is not the result of one member alone and which may not appear in other groupings which have members in common. The development of 'T-groups' in the 1960s and 1970s (Bion 1991; Yalom 1985) isolated the importance of group dynamics which team members needed to be skilled in understanding if teams were to develop towards their full potential. When attempting to identify and reduce dysfunction, the approach of focusing not on individual behaviour but on the dynamics of the group in which that dysfunctional behaviour is occurring also lies at the base of psychodynamic approaches to therapy. An extremely valuable literature of wider relevance to organizational management exists in this field (eg. Barker 1986; Burnham 1986; Pines 1992).

ARCHAEOLOGY AND ITS CONTEXT

The previous discussion has concentrated to a great extent on the nature of archaeological organizations in terms of their internal structures and the people within them. However, in the same way that archaeologists and historians have explored the relationship of their discipline to those outside it and its contribution to society as a whole (eg. Fowler 1992; Hodder 1992) so the focus of organizational research has also explored the relationship between organizations and their external environment. As with many disciplines, part of the driving force for studies of organizational environments can be traced to the development and subsequent impact of general systems theory and systems modelling (von Bertalanffy 1968). A systems perspective was adopted by a series of industrial sociologists in the 1960s who took issue with the underlying philosophies of other management schools which suggested that there was an 'ideal' form of organization for any particular activity. Instead they adopted an open systems perspective in which it was argued that the environment of an organization would not only influence organizational goals but also its internal structure, and the roles and relationships of the people within the organization. One of the most influential studies in this area was that undertaken by Paul Lawrence and Jay Lorsch based at the Harvard Business School. Their seminal work *Organization and Environment* (1967) was based on the detailed study of ten organizations and clearly identified that decisions on the structuring of organizations frequently took account of the organization's external environment. One of the conclusions of their studies was that where an organization was placed within a relatively stable external environment, conventional bureaucratic structures appeared to be common and appropriate. However, the more turbulent the external environment, the more likely that more flexible internal structures would be successful. Where the latter conditions existed, it was also likely that new roles and relationships within the organization would develop – such as particular groups or departments being set up to buffer the core activity of the organization from the outside world.

The Lawrence and Lorsch study suggested that an organization's internal structure would also vary in reaction to other aspects of the external environment. This was reflected in segmentation within the organization in order to deal with specific and significant aspects of the external environment. This differentiation of internal structures of sections of the organization led, perhaps more importantly, to differences in the values and attitudes of the members of individual units. While such differentiation can be of benefit to an organization, there was clearly a need for the organization to have integrating mechanisms to avoid inter-unit conflict. Interestingly, the use of multi-disciplinary teams which cross-cut departments is one mechanism which has developed and which underlies the idea of matrix management referred to above.

Lawrence and Lorsch's work is deserving of detailed study for the impact it had on the development of management theory and to the development of contingency theory. Their conclusions have continued relevance for managers of archaeological organizations. By way of example, in any medium-sized archaeological field unit in Britain the complexity of the discipline and the degree of knowledge necessary to fulfil its defined functions leads to specialist roles for many members of staff. These roles may include specialisms in cultural resource management, excavation, survey, building analysis, conservation, artefactual analysis, environmental analysis, illustration, and computing (the Institute of Field Archaeologists in Britain have recognized these skills as 'areas of competence' for registration). Within an organization these skills may be organized into specific departments or services. The particular people undertaking these specialist responsibilities are likely to have come from differing backgrounds, have different training, be influenced by different elements of the organization's external environment and be responsible for satisfying the differing demands of their particular area of the external environment. Arguably, such differentiation is inevitable within organizations undertaking a complex activity such as archaeology. However, differentiation is also likely to lead to differing goals, approaches and priorities existing in different places within the organization. Although this may be entirely healthy, considerable thought must be given to the appropriate integration structures and processes – a role frequently falling to the manager of an organization or the director of a particular project.

Given the increasingly turbulent external environment of archaeological organizations in Britain, the trend towards hard-structuring of archaeological organizations must be viewed with a certain amount of suspicion in terms of its theoretical basis. In reality the move towards creating more flexible organizations and the need to provide training to develop staff experience in terms of flexibility and responsiveness deserve detailed consideration and development in our profession.

The systems perspective can be applied to the archaeological discipline as a whole with interesting results. Perhaps the clearest example of this is the perceived division between academic organizations and field units in Britain. Tension between the values, goals and approaches of each of these areas can be frequently witnessed at national conferences such as the Institute of Field Archaeologist's annual conference and the annual Theoretical Archaeology Group conference with each 'side' attacking the other's practices and questioning their relevance to the discipline as a whole. The reality is that each perspective is as valid as the other if one views the development of the discipline in terms of its relationship with its external environment. If any criticism can be raised, it reflects not that such differing views and approaches exist, but that not enough effort has yet been placed on the processes and methods of integrating these seemingly contradictory views into a complementary whole.

MANAGING THE STRATEGIC PROCESS

One complaint that is frequently heard in archaeological corridors if not in the lecture rooms themselves is that both archaeology and archaeological organizations in Britain appear to be reactive in nature and that many changes which come about are in reaction to changes in the external environment over which archaeologists have little influence. As the above discussion has indicated, the complexities of the management process mean that the archaeological manager needs to take account of scientific and classical approaches, human relations approaches, and analysis of the relationship with the external environment. When looking at the causes of change within our profession, while many are derived from within the discipline as a whole – changes in technique, in methodologies, in research strategies and the like – the context of archaeology, its funding and its customers suggest that it is perhaps to the external environment that our attention should be directed when discussing strategic planning and the future of our discipline and profession as a whole. Many of the approaches adopted by management theoretists on strategic planning can be seen to have derived from the systems approach as discussed above and it is to this that we can now turn.

Many discussions of the environment of archaeology tend to approach it in a relatively crude fashion visualizing it as having one or perhaps two main areas (such as 'the discipline' and 'the general public'). However, it can be argued that such a conceptualization is overly simplistic and therefore of limited use for the archaeological manager. The identification and grouping of 'customers' (the people who use our products) and 'stakeholders' (the people who can influence our activities) is perhaps one approach which can add refinement to such an analysis. For an archaeological field unit based in an English County Council, for example, one can identify at least five identifiable environments – archaeology service, local authority, archaeological, non-archaeological (specific), non-archaeological (general) – the each characterized by the differing needs of its customers and its stakeholders (Figure 5.1).

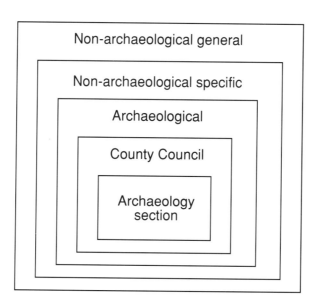

Figure 5.1   Five environments of an archaeological field unit

Such an approach can also include the internal environment as a relevant one for study. While the internal environment may not appear to be 'external' in the previously used sense of the word, a fundamental concern of organizations is that they must serve the needs of their employees (see Brooke, this volume). Lawrence and Lorsch (1967) highlighted three key elements in organizational behaviour: it is people who have purposes, not organizations; people have come together to coordinate their different activities into an organization; and the effectiveness of the organization is judged by the adequacy with which the members' needs are satisfied through planned transactions with the environment (Pugh and Hickson 1989: 45). As we have seen in the earlier discussions, the prevalent culture of an organization, the values, attitudes, needs and expectations of the employees, and the shadow side issues, each influence the organization and its activities. As customers of the organization, the employees' needs are likely to include financial needs, career development needs, social needs, and a desire to contribute to the development of the discipline, to mention but a few.

In this example, the archaeology service, as part of a local authority, will to a greater or lesser extent be influenced by the authority itself, through the desires and wishes of the senior management teams, and by the elected members who people the council's committees and who are responsible for the adoption of the authority's policies. It would be unusual for the members of this environment to have the same needs as the archaeological community. Instead their desires may include, for example, the provision of a visible local service to the community, the generation of good publicity, the attraction of external finance into the organization, and the development of the historic pedigree of the area to enhance tourism and employment.

The archaeological environment would comprise those organizations and individuals who can be seen to belong to the profession by other professionals, themselves located in central and local government organizations, universities, field units, consultancies, and many other organizations. Here the desire of these individuals may be for academically sound publication, development of methodologies and approaches of wider application, and the timely publication of results.

The non-archaeological (specific) environment will comprise those organizations and individuals which while not professional archaeologists come directly into contact with archaeologists during their professional work or in their leisure time. The first of these would include developers, landowners and planners seeking to identify archaeological constraints in proposed developments, or commissioning archaeological excavation as a result of proposed development. Additional areas of potential product for developers and landowners may include displays and good publicity in relation to their development (see, for example, Cooper and Mundy 1991). This environment will also include people and organizations exploiting the

heritage in their leisure activities, whether passively through visiting excavations, museums, historic buildings and the like (e.g. Lowenthal 1985), or
more actively through, for example, membership of local history and
archaeology groups or metal-detector clubs.

The final environment in this simplified model would be that of the
non-archaeological (general) environment. This represents the environment which while not directly involved with archaeology, will nonetheless affect it indirectly. Activities and phenomena such as European and
central government legislation, recession, population growth, general
demographic trends and the like will affect the other environments defined
above and through that will affect the discipline as a whole.

The above is undoubtedly a simplistic model and the reader may choose
to define a different number of environments on the basis of different criteria. Similarly the inclusion of particular groups of organizations within
each environment is likely to be based on both personal experience
and personal life-views. However, once defined a model of analysis such
as given in Figure 5.2, allows that environment to be characterized and
explicitly defines a set of needs (or products) which the organization either
chooses to meet or not. The crucial point here is, however, not so much
how one chooses to model the external environment, but to recognize that
depending upon that model and the nature of the organization, the
'world-view' is likely to be different, and the placement of of the organization in terms of these environments is likely to be different (see Carman,
this volume; Firth, this volume). Using a contingency perspective, the
defined organizational activities and goals, and thus the organization's
internal structures are likely to be different, and so they should be! The
role of a good manager is to create a model of these environments and,
having assessed the total possible demand, to select the most appropriate
set of objectives to be met and to design the organization on the basis of
the form which best allows the achievements of these.

The subject of strategic management in archaeology falls outside the
confines of this paper. There are however a variety of highly relevant text-
books on the subject to which the reader is addressed (e.g., Johnson and
Scholes 1989; Asch and Bowman 1989; Mintzberg and Quinn 1991;
Kotler 1991). However, the model outlined above can also be used to provide a useful starting point for exploration of more general strategic
management issues. Figure 5.2 provides a second model which can be used
to explore these differentiated environments in terms of a more general
marketing and strategic management approach.

CONCLUSIONS

Given the width of the management field and the lack of published debate
noted above, this discussion has been inevitably general, partial and
personal in its approach. However, the themes and perspectives raised

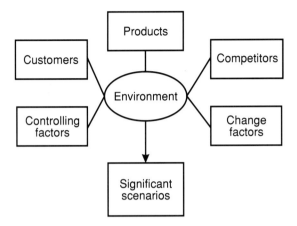

Figure 5.2 A model of the external environment

would seem relevant to both our profession and our professionals. The archaeological manager is not a mythical figure who exists in theory but not in practice. Nor is the archaeological manager likely to be found exclusively in the upper echelons of organizations. The reality is that there are elements of management in every archaeological task and at every level of an organization and this should be recognized and reflected in our training and development activities. The above discussion has highlighted a few of the approaches and concepts which may be of relevance and use though many more exist and continue to be developed. While our discipline exists in a state of flux and in a turbulent environment – and this is likely to continue – it may not be possible to predict the relevant skills which the next generation will need. However, the richness and variety of management approaches being developed in many other professions should give us the confidence both to develop our own explicit approaches and techniques in the management field and to teach and publish our discussions for the benefit of the discipline as a whole.

REFERENCES

Aitken, H.G.J. (1960) *Taylorism at Watertown Arsenal, Harvard*, Cambridge, MA: Harvard University Press.

Andersen, E.S., Grude, K.V., Haug, T. and Turner, J.R. (1987) *Goal Directed Project Management*, London: Kogan Page.

Argyris, C. (1972) *The Applicability of Organizational Sociology*, London: Cambridge University Press.

Asch, D. and Bowman, C. (1989) *Readings on Strategic Management*, London: Macmillan.

Barker, P. (1986) *Basic Family Therapy*, Oxford: Granada.

Binford, L.R. (1972) *An Archaeological Perspective*, London: Seminar Press.

Binford, L.R. (1983) *Working at Archaeology*, London: Academic Press.

Binford, S. and Binford, L.R. (eds) (1968) *New Perspectives in Archaeology*, Chicago, IL: Aldine.

Bion, W.R. (1991) *Learning from Experience*, London: Heinemann.

Blumberg, A. and Golembiewski, R.T. (1976) *Learning and Change in Groups*, Harmondsworth, Penguin.

de Board, R. (1978) *The Psychoanalysis of Organizations*, London: Tavistock.

Burnham, J.B. (1986) *Family Therapy*, London: Routledge.

Butler, G.V. (1986) *Organization and Management*, London: Prentice-Hall.

Cooper, M.A. (1993) 'Archaeology and management perspectives', *The Field Archaeologist* 18: 346–50.

Cooper, M.A. and Dinn, J. (1995) 'Computers and the evolution of archaeological organizations' in J.D. Wilcock and Lockyear, K. (eds) *Proceedings of the Computer Applications and Quantitative Methods in Archaeology Conference 1993*, BAR International Series 598: 89–94.

Cooper, M.A. and Mundy, C.F. (1991) 'The art of digging', *Bulletin of the Centre for Environmental Interpretation* June 1991: 6–8.

Doray, B. (1988) *From Taylorism to Fordism: A Rational Madness*, London: Free Association Books.

Egan, G. (1993) 'The shadow side', *Management Today* September 1993: 33–8.

English Heritage (1991) *Management of Archaeological Projects*, London: Historic Buildings and Monuments Commission for England.

Fayol, H. (1949) *General and Industrial Management*, London: Pitman.

Fowler, P.J. (1992) *The Past in Contemporary Society: Then, Now*, London: Routledge.

Gibbon, G. (1989) *Explanation in Archaeology*, Oxford: Blackwell.

Handy, C.B. (1985) *Understanding Organizations*, Harmondsworth: Penguin.

Harvard Business Review (1989) *Managing Projects and Programs*, Boston, MA: Harvard Business School Press.

Hodder, I. (1992) *Theory and Practice in Archaeology*, London: Routledge.

Huczynski, A.A. (1993) *Management Gurus*, London: Routledge.

Johnson, G. and Scholes, J. (1989) *Exploring Corporate Strategy*, London: Routledge.

Kakabadse, A., Ludlow, R., and Vinnicombe, S. (1988) *Working in Organizations*, London: Penguin.

Kotler, P. (1991) *Marketing Management*, London: Prentice Hall, 7th edn.

Lawrence, P.R. and Lorsch, J.W. (1967) *Organization and Environment*, Boston, MA: Harvard Business School Press.

Lock, D. (1992) *Project Management*, Aldershot: Gower, 5th edn.

Lowenthal, D. (1985) *The Past Is a Foreign Country*, Cambridge: Cambridge University Press.

McCann, J. (1976) *The Rule of St Benedict*, London: Sheed & Ward.

Margulies, N. and Raia, A.P. (1973) *Organization Development: Values, Processes and Technology*, New York: McGraw Hill.

Maslow, A.H. (1943) 'A theory of human motivation', *Psychological Review* 50, 4: 370–96.

Mayo, E. (1933) *The Human Problem of an Industrial Civilization*, London:

Macmillan.

Mayo, E. (1949) *The Social Problems of an Industrial Civilization*, London: Routledge & Kegan Paul.

Mays, N. (1991) 'Origins and development of the National Health Service' In E. Scambler (ed.) *Sociology as Applied to Medicine*, London: Balliere Tindall 199–200.

Minzberg, H. and Quinn, J.B. (1991) *The Strategy Process*, London: Prentice-Hall.

Morgan, G. (1986) *Images of Organization*, London: Sage.

Pines, M. (ed.) (1992) *Bion and Group Psychotherapy*, London: Routledge.

Pugh, D.S. and Hickson, D.J. (1989) *Writers on Organizations*, Harmondsworth: Penguin.

Reiss, G. (1992) *Project Management Demystified*, London: Spon.

Roethlisberger, F.J. and Dickson, W.J. (1949) *Management and the Worker*, Cambridge, MA: Harvard University Press.

Schein, E.H. (1988) *Organizational Psychology*, London: Prentice-Hall.

Sisson, N. (ed.) (1989) *Personnel Management in Britain*, Oxford: Blackwell.

Startin, B. (1993) 'Preservation and the academically viable sample', *Antiquity* 67: 421–6.

Taylor, F.W. (1911) *Principles of Scientific Management*, New York: Harper.

von Bertalanffy, L. (1968) *General Systems Theory: Foundations, Development, Applications*, New York: Braziller.

Yalom, I.D. (1985) *The Theory and Practice of Group Psychotherapy*, New York: Basic Books, 3rd edn.

CHAPTER SIX

TRYING TO MAKE IT HAPPEN

ELLEN MCADAM

This chapter is a partial and personal account of the history of archaeology as a profession, and is not intended as an exhaustive scholarly survey. The underlying motive is a desire to examine how management techniques in archaeology have developed, and whether the divergence between historical and current practice has any bearing on the question of why, despite the dedication of those working in the field, so many projects fail to reach publication and so much unofficial discontentment is expressed. If it encourages serious debate it will have served a useful purpose.

MYSTICS AND SAVANTS

The antiquarian and amateur origins of archaeology as a subject are well known and were elegantly documented by an earlier generation of archaeological scholars (for example, Piggott 1950; Daniel 1967). From the Renaissance onwards, the study of the physical remains of the past took two different forms; on the one hand there were the travellers and collectors whose classical learning or Biblical research took them to the Mediterranean, Egypt and the Near East, and on the other the local antiquaries, concerned with the antiquities of their own country. It can be argued that modern professional archaeology in Britain developed out of the efforts of the latter, a fascinating group of polymaths and eccentrics who included Camden, Aubrey, Lhwyd, Rowlands and Stukeley. It can also be argued that the distinction between the two areas of interest prevails to this day, with surprisingly little communication between those archaeologists who work under the aegis of the British Schools abroad and those employed in British archaeology.

Throughout the seventeenth and eighteenth centuries the relics of antiquity continued to receive the attentions of madmen and geniuses, showmen and mountebanks. Their approaches were as diverse as their personalities, by turns learned, anecdotal, mystical, mythological, romantic or literary, according to the spirit of their times, sometimes preserving and brilliantly illuminating the archaeological record, elsewhere falsifying it or destroying it for ever. Some, like the flamboyant Giovanni Belzoni, made a profession out of tomb-robbing and antiquities-dealing, but for the more studiously inclined there were no career prospects; the antiquary was a gentleman.

The Age of Reason saw the beginnings of more rational discourse; as the mysteries of Ancient Egypt and the Near East were revealed by the decipherment of hieroglyphic and cuneiform scripts, the principles of stratigraphic deposition and typological classification were being applied to the antiquities of the British Isles.

VICTORIAN RESPECTABILITY

In the course of the nineteenth century archaeology acquired a certain respectability, with mixed consequences. Opening barrows was an amusement for gentlemen, hiring a few navvies or farm labourers for the day and pausing at noon for a visit by the house-party and a light luncheon of cold pheasant and hock. Sometimes there is a charming sketch, showing an efflorescence of umbrellas sheltering in the cut from a sudden rainstorm (Wheeler 1954: 7 and Plate 1), sometimes a steel engraving of an urn and three flint arrowheads accompanied by a perfunctory account of the central burial in which 'the bones crumbled to dust as soon as they were exposed to the air', a common phenomenon according to nineteenth-century accounts (McAdam 1974), but one never apparently encountered in the last quarter of the twentieth century. Otherwise the deliberate opening of many monuments on a scale which would now be regarded as major research excavation went completely unrecorded.

The contemporary equivalent of rescue archaeology fared rather better. Queen Victoria's reign was distinguished by a boundless energy and curiosity, in private as well as in public enterprises. Amateur societies were founded in many counties, supported by the professional classes and minor gentry, and these enthusiastic and educated amateurs made great advances in recording their local archaeology. Entries in the journals of these societies testify to an increasingly systematic and scientific approach to recording the chance finds which the galloping progress of the day uncovered in railway cuttings, quarries, drainage works and agricultural improvements. Many of the best recorders were retired military men or local doctors, the interests of the former often revealed in accurately surveyed plans and sections and of the latter in an extensive literature on physical anthropology and the determination of racial characteristics.

If archaeology was becoming a subject of wider interest, however, and sufficiently popular to be regularly reported in the pages of the *Illustrated London News*, it was still an occasional pursuit for the gentry and upper middle classes, not a full-time career. Projects were tackled on an *ad hoc* basis, with one more or less knowledgeable figure directing the efforts of volunteer or unskilled labour. Finds were still of paramount importance, although there was a growing interest in survey and the study of monument types; methodology was rarely, if ever, considered. It is perhaps fortunate for the history of archaeology in Britain that its monuments are on the whole tastefully understated and its finds sparse and intrinsically unattractive, unlike the spectacular remains to be found elsewhere; had the Home Counties been scattered with Near Eastern-sized tells and the Scottish Highlands adorned with the summer palaces of ancient kings, the gentle paternalism with which investigations into British archaeology were run might have been replaced by excavations on an industrial scale, with huge workforces labouring under the conditions of the Victorian factory.

The modest charms of the Bronze Age barrow and the Roman fort did not tempt the mill-owners of Birmingham or Manchester. Instead they attracted the attention of that *doyen* of retired military men, General Augustus Henry Lane Fox Pitt Rivers, whose calm and ordered approach not only to the results of his fieldwork but to the practical organization of both excavation and publication puts many of his successors, as well as his contemporaries, to shame. Here is his own lucid account:

It only remains to say something of the way in which the work has been carried out. I saw clearly that it was more than I could accomplish without assistance in the brief space of time allotted to me at my period of life. I therefore determined to organize a regular staff of assistants, and to train them to their respective functions after establishing a proper division of work. It was necessary they should all have some capacity for drawing in order that the relics discovered might be sketched as soon as found, instead of entrusting the drawings to inexperienced lithographers and artists who had little feeling for the subject . . . The work of superintending the digging – though I never allowed it to be carried on in my absence, always visiting the excavations at least three times a day, and arranging to be sent for whenever anything of importance was found – was more than I could undertake single-handed, with the management of a property and other social duties to attend to, since I had by ample experience been taught that no excavation ought ever to be permitted except under the immediate eye of a responsible and trustworthy superintendent.

Reserving, therefore, to my share of the work the entire supervision of everything, the description and arrangement of the plates, the writing of the record, checking the calculations and the measurements of every relic discovered in the diggings, and all the bones, I have, after some changes and preliminary trials, been able to engage the following assistants with suitable salaries, viz.:-

Assistant	..	..	Mr. F. James
Sub-Assistants	..	..	Mr. W. S. Tomkin
			Mr. F. W. Reader

. . . Some if the workmen, of whom I employed from eight to fifteen constantly, have acquired much skill in digging and detecting the relics in the several villages and tumuli that have been examined, so as to entitle them to be regarded as skilled workmen, upon which no small share of the success of an investigation of this kind depends.

(Pitt Rivers 1887: xviii–xix)

Sir William Flinders Petrie, one of the great but idiosyncratic figures of archaeology, took a rather different view of man management. His expeditions were notoriously spartan; one visitor to his excavations was entertained to a dinner consisting of tinned peas, eaten cold out of the can (C. Aldred, personal communication). Writing in 1904 on the aims and methods of archaeology, Petrie provides comprehensive and detailed advice for the would-be excavator under headings such as: 'the excavator'; 'discrimination'; 'the labourers'; 'arrangement of work'; 'recording in the field'; 'copying'; 'photographing'; 'preservation of objects'; 'packing'; 'publication'; 'systematic archaeology'; 'archaeological evidence'; 'ethics of archaeology'; and 'the fascination of history'. Much of his practical advice (particularly on publishing) is full of common sense and it is difficult to disagree in principle with his ethical views. His attitude to the management and supervision of excavation, on the other hand, is chilling. Writing mainly about digging in Egypt, Petrie recommended having two or three dozen well-trained men each overseeing half a dozen new hands in a gang of 150 or 200 (Petrie 1904: 20–37). He advises paying by the day 'where minute valuables may be scattered anywhere in the soil . . . or where the work is very irregular, and time needs to be spent on moving stones' (Petrie 1904: 27). Otherwise Petrie paid by the volume of soil shifted, with differing rates for differing hardnesses (Petrie 1904: 20–37). On top of this, men were rewarded for finding objects by the *bakhshish* system, of which he says 'the actual amount given should be as much as a travelling dealer would pay to the peasant, were he buying the object'(Petrie 1904: 34).

Petrie seems to have worked without assistants, at least as far as supervision and recording were concerned. Here is his advice on how to maintain regular and continuous digging when working by the day:

It is impossible to be known to be away, as then no work will go on effectively. An air of vigilant surprises has to be kept up. A sunk approach to the work behind higher ground is essential; and, if possible, an access to a commanding view without being seen going to and fro. A telescope is very useful to watch if distant work is regular. At Tanis the girls in a big pit were kept by the men walking up and tipping baskets at the top; but the telescope showed that the baskets were all the time empty. . . A telescope will also show if a boy is put up to watch for the master's coming. Various approaches should be arranged from different directions and the course of work so planned that no men can give notice to others. . . The need of thus acting as mainspring. . . is wearing and time-wasting; and it leaves no chance of doing writing, etc., during work hours.

(Petrie 1904: 28)

According to Petrie, the need for all this exhausting subterfuge could be obviated by piecework.

ANIMAL, VEGETABLE, MINERAL?

Fortunately for British archaeology, General Pitt Rivers proved a more powerful and lasting influence on British archaeology in the twentieth century than Flinders Petrie. In the period up to World War II, archaeology became established as an academic discipline, with university positions held by such eminent figures as Gordon Childe and Mortimer Wheeler, and outside the universities, posts in archaeology also began to appear. In the Ordnance Survey, for example, which had been systematically including antiquities on maps since the mid-nineteenth century, O.G.S. Crawford was appointed as Archaeology Officer in 1920 (Harley 1975: 145), and other archaeologists were working in the Royal Commissions on Ancient and Historic Monuments or in museums. It was now possible to have a paid career in archaeology.

Sir Leonard Woolley and Sir Mortimer Wheeler, very disparate characters but giants in their fields, both acknowledged the influence of Pitt Rivers. Like Wheeler, although in a different way, Woolley was a gifted populariser, and his books of reminiscence are still worth reading. He worked in several areas of the Near East before embarking on a programme of excavations at Ur in southern Iraq, and his publication of the results of many seasons there, including the Early Dynastic 'Royal tombs', stands as a monumental and unique achievement, particularly in view of the conditions in which it was achieved. According to the memoirs of his assistant, Sir Max Mallowan, Woolley employed 200–250 men each season during his excavations at Ur in the 1920s and 30s (Mallowan 1977: 33–67). The workmen were organized in gangs consisting of a pickman, a spademan and four to six basketmen, and Woolley employed as foreman Hamoudi ibn Sheikh Ibrahim, who had worked with him at Carchemish in Syria before World War I, and who brought with him his three sons. Like Petrie, Woolley relied on paying *bakhshish* for small finds, and the system seems to have worked well. In addition to Woolley and Mallowan, the European staff included an epigraphist and an architect.

In later seasons, Woolley was accompanied by his wife, the redoubtable Katharine Woolley, described by Gertrude Bell herself as 'dangerous' and capable, according to Mallowan, of ending a battle among the workmen merely by putting in an appearance (Mallowan 1977: 36). For further details of her personality, the reader is referred to the autobiography of Agatha Christie, who met Max Mallowan while visiting Ur and subsequently married him, and to her novel, *Murder in Mesopotamia*. Agatha Christie was a notable contributor to a class of literature which seems unfortunately to be missing in British archaeology, the 'book of the dig', an account (usually by the director's wife, and entertaining in direct proportion to its frankness) of the personalities of the team and the vicissitudes of coping with workmen and cockroaches. Christie's book on digging with her husband in the 1930s in Syria, *Come Tell Me How you Live*, is one of the best of the genre.

During most of Woolley's time at Ur, Iraq was under British administration. It is disconcerting, reading contemporary literature, to realize to how great an extent attitudes which would now be considered grossly and offensively racist were taken for granted as part of the Imperial ethos. The opposite extreme is sometimes observable among Europeans working in Near Eastern archaeology today, in the form of a cloying romanticism about the host culture. Woolley avoided both racism and romanticism: Mallowan and Woolley write of their workmen with sympathy and respect, and certainly in a less patronising vein than Petrie. According to Mallowan the workmen, who 'were desperately poor and lived next door to starvation . . . could hardly be expected to have any surplus energy and had to be driven along by exhortation and encouragement' (Mallowan 1977: 42). Nevertheless, the work was much coveted and over four or five years a considerable *esprit de corps* developed. Slightly less *esprit de corps* seems to have prevailed among the European members of the expedition; according to Mallowan, Woolley's assistants rarely went to bed before midnight, and were expected to be on the dig not later than half an hour after sunrise, which during the winter in southern Iraq would be around 6 or 7 a.m. Woolley himself worked until two or three o'clock in the morning, which provides some justification for the episode in which Mallowan, having started a game of cards with the epigraphist, was told that if he had insufficient energy to work he had better go to bed. In other words, if Woolley ran his local workforce with the liberal paternalism of the best colonial administrators, not very different from the way in which the General writes of his labourers in Cranborne Chase, his treatment of his European assistants was rather on the lines of a Victorian counting-house. Nevertheless, there must have been something exceptional about Woolley's ability to create and motivate a team in such unpromising conditions: he himself says: 'the work was team-work throughout . . . that is the highest praise I can give to a staff which deserves all my praise and gratitude; they did not do this job or that – they were the Expedition, and its success was the measure of their devotion' (Woolley 1929: 17).

Woolley's younger contemporary, Mortimer Wheeler, gives the precepts of General Pitt Rivers a rather different gloss in his enormously influential textbook on excavation techniques, *Archaeology from the Earth* (1954). This work is peppered with military metaphors, as becomes a military man; thus, the problem of training excavation staff 'is almost exactly that of a commanding officer with a bevy of young subalterns' (Wheeler 1954: 130), site supervisors are platoon commanders, the foreman is the Sergeant Major and so on.

The staff structure of an excavation as described by Wheeler in the 1950s was not essentially different from that used by Woolley at Ur in the 1920s, or indeed by Pitt Rivers in Dorset in the 1880s, consisting of a handful of trained or semi-trained staff supervising a workforce of professional labourers and volunteers, and it is worth considering his version of the system in some detail. Then as now every excavation had a director who was an experienced excavator, usually with academic qualifications, and possibly a deputy director, also an experienced field archaeologist. Site supervisors (in charge of recording an area) were usually students with some previous experience of excavation. In addition, a foreman might be taken on to supervise the labourers, if any were employed. Wheeler has this to say on the subject of labourers:

> Digging is a skilled craft, and many years ago I began a note on this subject with the words 'Abjure voluntary labour'. Today, in 1955, voluntary labour is Hobson's choice. The old-fashioned British labourer survives only in a few odd corners of the land. . . A drawback to the kind of labour that usually comes to the field-archaeologist today in Great Britain is that it is often unacquainted with pick and shovel and has to be taught *ab initio*; it consists of unemployed or unemployable invalids, garage-hands, drapers' assistants, university students and the like . . . to be just, the university student, if he is of the right sort, can usually be trained without undue delay to a fair measure of technical competence; only, he could usually be better employed in more detailed and specialized work and is largely wasted in the basic task of digging.
>
> (Wheeler 1954: 148)

Finds processing usually took place on site in a draughty garden shed, and on large excavations there would be a pottery assistant. On exceptionally well funded digs there might also be a photographer, a surveyor, a conservator and a draughtsman. Since the excavation team came together only for the duration of the dig, usually during the summer vacation, as much processing as possible – bulk and small finds recording, marking and packing – was done on site.

Generations of archaeologists were weaned on *Archaeology from the Earth* (1954), and it is regrettable that although Wheeler has much to say that is sensible about publication he did not perceive the post-excavation analysis phase of a project as requiring the same rigorous military organization as fieldwork. His approach to the process of writing up results could be described as intuitive, and because he was a man of great energy and intelligence he succeeded. Despite his good advice on illustration and literary style, many lesser others failed.

Wheeler was by no means alone in his attitude to the 'basic task of digging'. Dame Kathleen Kenyon, who began her digging career in Britain with the Wheelers before moving on to Near Eastern archaeology, also proffered advice to would-be archaeologists. Her book, published a few years earlier than Wheeler's, reveals a great deal about the organization of archaeology in the post-war years:

> Comparatively recent developments have brought about the creation of a number of full time posts, whose holders can devote all their attention to archaeology, and who can thus be called professional archaeologists. But the subject has grown up on an amateur basis, through the labours of people to whom it was a hobby or a part-time occupation, and it will always be largely dependent on them. It is most unlikely, and most undesirable, that there will ever be enough full-time archaeologists to do all the work . . . because of the fact that vacancies only occur rather sporadically, it may be necessary to wait for a time, after training is completed, before a vacancy occurs. Therefore, anyone who is completely dependent on his earnings must consider the matter seriously and decide whether he is prepared to take the risk. . . . There are in fact no paid full-time excavation posts. Almost all digs in Britain are seasonal affairs. While the dig is in progress, the director and the senior assistants may get some pay. . . But for the intervening periods there is no pay, even though work on the finds [i.e. the whole of what would now be known as the post-excavation process] often has to be carried out during them.
>
> (Kenyon 1952: 54–8)

> [F]unds at the disposal of most excavation committees do not cover more than the expenses of navvy labour for heavy work. . . . The work of volunteers is mainly the careful excavation of archaeological levels, usually with a small tool such as a trowel. If a thick and unproductive level has to be removed with pick and shovel, most directors prefer to use a professional navvy if they can afford to employ one, as they do such work very much better than someone not trained to use these tools. The equipment with which a volunteer who is going to dig should arrive on a site is simple. The principal requisite is old clothes which can be allowed to get dirty without a qualm. Strong shoes are necessary in most seasons, though in fine weather sandals or plimsolls may be all right. Gum-boots are a great help, for even in fine seasons morning dew may be quite enough to soak one's feet. An old mackintosh is essential. . . . Beginners are strongly advised to provide themselves with a pair of old leather gloves, unless they are already pretty horny-handed, as working with a trowel can easily produce blisters at first. . . . A useful accessory is a rubber kneeling mat such as gardeners use, as there are seldom enough on a dig to go round.
>
> (Kenyon 1952: 65–6)

It is a measure of how rapidly archaeology has developed in the last twenty years that although this view of excavation prevailed at least until the early 1970s (see, for example, Alexander 1970), it now seems unimaginably quaint. What happened to change and professionalise this pursuit of amateurs and young men of independent means?

Archaeologists had more reason than most to be grateful for the air forces of World War II, which obligingly created opportunities for large-scale urban excavations. In the wake of the bombers came the town planners, who (as has often been remarked) proved considerably more destructive. In most countries in Europe the devastated centres of historic towns and cities were lovingly and faithfully reconstructed. In Britain the destruction of large areas of inner city was seized on as an opportunity to destroy still more, partly because access for cars was seen as of paramount importance and partly in the name of modernity. Half-timbered cottages and market crosses were out and concrete shopping centres and flyovers were in. As Jones relates (1984), at the same time as redevelopment was destroying historic buildings and archaeology on a massive scale in the centres of Britain's towns and cities, motorways, deep ploughing, forestry and gravel extraction were laying waste vast tracts of archaeology in the countryside.

THE GOLDEN AGE

The detailed history of how British archaeology met this challenge and evolved into a profession deserves to be written, and only a very incomplete account based on hazy memories and anecdotal evidence can be offered here. By the time the author was an undergraduate in the early 1970s the problem of rescue archaeology had already been recognized; RESCUE – The Trust for British Archaeology – had been founded, many of the excavation committees which formed the nuclei of the later county units had been in existence for some time, and the first Sites and Monuments Record was being assembled. The memories of those who were working in archaeology at this time are now slightly vague about the sources of finance, although clear that it was never lavish; indeed, discussions of the early funding structure are all too liable to become bogged down in competitively spartan anecdotes. It appears to have come from a variety of sources – the Department of the Environment, local councils, and some business sponsorship. Certainly from the late 1960s onwards it became possible to earn a living as a digger, moving on the circuit from one excavation to another, and although volunteer labour and amateur involvement remained significant the importance of a workforce of skilled diggers was established. It would never again be felt that intelligence was wasted on digging. This development was concurrent with a more formal and theoretical approach to data collection and analysis and a move (by no means rapid or universal) towards the standardization of site recording, of which the most noticeable effect for most workers in the field was the replacement of the green site notebook with the context sheet.

In the later 1970s and 1980s, archaeology, then as always starved of funds, took advantage of a series of schemes devised by successive governments to alleviate unemployment. The most archaeologically useful of these was the Community Programme run by the Manpower Services Commission, which allowed archaeological units to offer continuous paid employment as a digger or supervisor and provided a way into archaeology for many. Whatever the drawbacks of undertaking excavation with this sort of funding – not the least of which was the difficulty of funding post-excavation – it allowed units to survive and even to grow.

THE COMING OF MAMMON

All things must pass, and as the economic miracle of the 1980s began to reveal itself as a rather inept conjuring trick this source of finance began to run out; in 1988, the Community Programme was replaced by a scheme known as Employment Training, whose structure and bureaucratic requirements were inimical to archaeology. Its loss was palliated by the introduction of competitive tendering in archaeology, a development which at the time was seen as most shocking, with county units working outside their own areas. With the enshrinement in PPG 16 of the principle that the polluter pays, however, and the advent of developer funding policed by curatorial County Archaeologists, competitive tendering was an inevitable development. The move to more formal systems of management and accountability, particularly in post-excavation, has also been greatly stimulated by the production by English Heritage of the two editions of *Management of Archaeological Projects* (see Andrews and Thomas, this volume).

TRYING TO MAKE IT HAPPEN, OR WHAT YOU WILL

This review of the historical development of archaeology (with apologies to Sir John Harvey Jones) shows that the current preoccupation with management techniques is a relative novelty. The writers quoted here clearly devoted some thought to the organization of their work, but they were essentially adapting the normal working practices of the time and place to the demands, as they perceived them, of the capture and analysis of the archaeological data in which they were interested. Their preoccupation with fieldwork reflects the fact that it involved visible expenditure on labour, transport, accommodation and tools. Post-excavation involved fewer people, typically the director, his assistants (often his students) and an illustrator, and salary, equipment and overhead costs were either absorbed by the institution for which the director worked, or subsidised in whole or in part from the private incomes of the individuals involved. Less formal planning was therefore required.

The past is indeed a foreign country, and they did things differently there. It is difficult to imagine General Pitt Rivers, Sir Mortimer Wheeler or Dame Kathleen Kenyon accepting the description of 'manager', and the

General might even have jibbed at 'archaeologist', but all would surely have conceded 'scholar'. Other chapters in this volume deal with the current state of management in archaeology and the difficulties of reconciling commercial, academic and professional demands. These problems no doubt reflect our time and our place, but in our collective anxiety we have perhaps overlooked something. Whether one describes archaeology as a business, a discipline or a profession, its stock in trade is information in some form. There is concern that new techniques and procedures have not been designed with the data in mind. Project planning has become increasingly sophisticated; considerable skill has been acquired in identifying and estimating the tasks involved in recording, analysing and interpreting a given body of data, and the focus of archaeological management is on increasingly tight monitoring and control of these tasks.

Unfortunately, our growing ability to recognize and plan these activities has not been accompanied by a commensurate growth in formal understanding of how the data are transformed and manipulated during the process that leads from excavation to publication. The process is understood by some individuals intuitively, but the quality and scope of individual intuition vary, as the quality and quantity of archaeological publication demonstrate. We should accord the data that primacy which our distinguished predecessors gave it. If as much effort were expended on analysing and documenting the operations to be performed on data in order to arrive at reliable interpretations as has been devoted to adapting the techniques of management, we might achieve a marked improvement not only in the quality and successful outcome of archaeological projects, but in the morale of archaeologists and the level of public interest and support. If we knew more about managing the data, in other words, we might be better at managing ourselves.

REFERENCES

Alexander, J. (1970) *The Directing of Archaeological Excavations*, London: John Baker.

Daniel, G. (1967) *The Origins and Growth of Archaeology*, Harmondsworth: Penguin.

Harley, J.B. (1975) *Ordnance Survey Maps: A Descriptive Manual*, Southampton: Ordnance Survey.

Harvey-Jones, J. (1988) *Making it Happen*, London: Fontana.

Jones, G.D.B. (1984) *Past Imperfect*, London: Heinemann.

Kenyon, K.M. (1952) *Beginning in Archaeology*, London.

McAdam, E. (1974) 'Bronze Age cists in Scotland containing datable grave goods', unpublished MA dissertation, University of Edinburgh.

Mallowan, M. (1977) *Mallowan's Memoirs*, London: Collins.

Petrie, Flinders W.M. (1904). *Methods and Aims in Archaeology*, London: Macmillan.

Piggott, S. (1950) *William Stukeley: An Eighteenth-Century Antiquary*, Oxford:

Clarendon Press.

Pitt Rivers, A.H.L.F. (1887) *Excavations in Cranborne Chase near Rushmore*, vol. 1, London: Privately published by the author.

Wheeler, R.E.M. (1954) *Archaeology from the Earth*, Oxford: Clarendon Press.

Woolley, L. (1929) *Ur of the Chaldees*, revised and updated by P.R.S. Moorey (1982), London: The Herbert Press.

CHAPTER SEVEN

ARCHAEOLOGISTS IN THE MARKETPLACE

MARION BLOCKLEY

Marketing is more than just advertising and promotion, and so far has been under-valued as a management tool for archaeologists. Marketing is a corporate philosophy, a set of tools and techniques, and a systematic approach to problem solving in a rapidly changing market (Houston 1986). In the realm of organizational planning, marketing is a relatively recent (post-World War II) development (Ford 1976). Within the Heritage sector its principles have only been adopted over the last ten years (Anderson and Sprouse 1984; Dimaggio 1985; Middleton 1990; Bower, this volume).

An organization recognizes the value of marketing when it begins to ask 'What line of business are we actually in?' This may seem rather simplistic and obvious, but many archaeologists when questioned closely would probably define their basic purpose too restrictively. The marketing approach links the line of business to customer benefits, and seeks to define what benefits the customer is seeking. The majority of archaeologists recognize that clients (other than English Heritage) rarely request their services to add to the sum of archaeological knowledge. Archaeological intervention is usually carried out to provide information for planners, developers or engineers as part of an Environmental Assessment, or to provide a resource for leisure and recreation.

Archaeologists have to find the best way of reconciling their own objectives with those of potential customers, in order to survive in a changing funding environment, whilst not abandoning professional standards and integrity (Institute of Field Archaeologists 1990). Marketing planning techniques can help to resolve this dilemma and make decision-making and forward planning less random. Marketing theory, like all management theory, can seem unnecessarily complex but its basic principles are simple

(Cowell 1990; Kotler and Andreasen 1987). There are a number of key concepts that can be usefully transferred to the archaeological sector to help guide decision-making at a time of bewildering change.

Over the last decade there have been major changes in the practice of archaeology brought about by factors such as the decline in large scale Manpower Services Commission (MSC) funded projects (Drake and Fahy 1987; Lawson 1993: 150–2, Figure 14.2), and changes in the philosophy of English Heritage funding (English Heritage 1986, 1991; see also Andrews and Thomas, this volume). The revision of central government policy on the environment, enshrined in the White Paper *This Common Inheritance* (Department of the Environment 1990a) and the recognition of archaeology as a material consideration in the planning process (Department of the Environment 1990b) have had a major impact on work-load. Further, the current review of the structure of local government and the proposed formation of unitary authorities has far reaching implications for the future funding and management of metropolitan, district and county archaeology services.

The widespread introduction of compulsory competitive tendering (English Heritage 1991; Swain 1991), the market testing of local authority services and the increasing separation of local authorities into enabler and provider divisions have effectively imposed market forces on local authority archaeologists (Davies 1992: 20). Successful organizations anticipate change in order to survive and local authority archaeologists can respond to competition from the private sector by adopting aspects of the marketing approach.

Marketing strategy guides the direction an organization will pursue within its chosen area of work, and assists in the allocation of resources. Marketing objectives (e.g., 'to be the most successful unit in the South of England') are translated into strategy by analysing market opportunities (e.g., 'The Blankshire Unit is suffering from a withdrawal of funding – The *X* Archaeological Unit is about to close down after 18 years funding from *XDC*') and researching and selecting target markets. The analysis of market opportunities in the process of strategic planning is an essential element of marketing, and removes the guesswork from decision making. The Jorvik Viking Centre and Archaeological Resource Centre in York are successful examples of the transfer of thoroughly tested ideas from American theme parks and science museums to the UK archaeological market. Within the realm of interpretive planning the low-cost trialling of exhibitions, leaflets and panels before final production is a valuable technique 'borrowed' from market research and market testing. However, organizations' forward planning should not be totally market-led. Marketing should always be driven by, and help define, the organization's overall objectives. The concern voiced over English Heritage's recent forward strategy document *Managing England's Heritage – Setting our Priorities for the 1990s* (English Heritage 1992) neatly illustrates this point (Evans 1992; Keen 1992).

The marketing concept should also be addressed to employees as well as to customers. This is particularly so in the field of archaeology, which is geared towards providing a service. Human performance shapes the quality of the service provided, therefore there has to be a commitment towards training staff, to improving management style, and to the delivery of services with an emphasis on quality and action. The market influence is already permeating local authorities following the introduction of the Citizen's Charter in 1991–2, which emphasizes the importance of achieving positive new relationships with customers, clients and stakeholders (Davies 1992: 20). Will the 'archetypal' local government officer (I write here as a recent local government employee) – unhelpful, unreasonable and slow to respond – be re-educated through customer-awareness training or replaced through a programme of positive recruitment, or is this stereotype already outdated?

THE MARKETING PLAN

Within the area of corporate planning, the marketing plan has great value, and should enable archaeologists to be more outward-looking. The outline of the marketing plan (Figure 7.1) should include a definition of corporate objectives (the mission statement) and an assessment of the external environment (the political, social and economic threats and opportunities),

What business are we in, and where do we want to go?	MISSION STATEMENT
How do we get there?	CORPORATE OBJECTIVES
Who are our customers, and what benefits are they seeking?	MARKETING RESEARCH
How is our working environment changing?	AUDIT OF EXTERNAL ENVIRONMENT
What do we we have work with?	ANALYSIS OF STRENGTHS AND WEAKNESSES
How do we match objectives and goals with resources and market opportunities?	STRATEGIC MARKETING PLANNING
When will we achieve our objectives and goals? Who will make this happen?	ACTION PLAN
Are we meeting our objectives? What needs to be changed?	MONITORING AND REVIEW

Figure 7.1 Elements of the marketing plan

including the potential impact of these on the organization. The marketing plan should evaluate current and potential resources and skills, such as a skilled workforce, detailed knowledge of a particular region, period, or technique and, for instance, access to specialist equipment for geophysics or survey. Having defined the strengths it should outline marketing objectives and specific goals to be achieved in a set time (Cowell 1990: 43–76).

THE MISSION STATEMENT: WHAT BUSINESS ARE WE IN, AND WHERE DO WE WANT TO GO?

The mission statement specifies the chief function of the organization. In essence it is a vision of what the organization is or is striving to become. The mission statement is the starting point in the marketing planning process since it sets the broad parameters within which marketing objectives are established, strategies developed and programmes implemented. The statement should denote the broader purpose of the organization as reflected in its corporate policies; it should be succinct, distinctive and wide in scope: *To be a leading organization for archaeological research, providing a comprehensive range of quality services to both public and private sectors* (Northamptonshire Archaeology 1993).

CORPORATE OBJECTIVES: HOW DO WE GET THERE?

The corporate objectives translate the vision of the mission statement into quantifiable and achievable goals. They are usually more concrete than the vision and should be viewed as targets which can be achieved in a specified time and can also be used to measure performance. Corporate objectives usually identify major variables such as:

REPUTATION
Establish and maintain a high reputation for:
- academic ability and integrity;
- economic, efficient and effective working.

MARKET SHARE
- Increase involvement in cultural resource management, e.g.: strategic enhancement of Sites and Monuments Records, or in education, presentation and interpretation;
- Develop expertise in geographical information systems;
- Expand building survey and recording projects.

PROFITABILITY
- Achieve growth in project turnover;
- Implement quality working procedures;
- Reduce operating costs and overheads;.

- Deliver quality services at competitive prices;
- Maintain a surplus of income over expenditure to permit continuing investment.

MARKETING RESEARCH: WHO ARE OUR CUSTOMERS AND WHAT BENEFITS ARE THEY SEEKING?

Marketing research is the planned, systematic collection and analysis of data designed to help managers reach decisions about operations and to help monitor the results of these decisions. This research provides information on potential customers' preferences, asking questions such as: 'Who wants to buy our services? What services do people want and what benefits are they looking for? When will they buy these services? Why will people buy these services and not those of our competitors?' (Kotler and Andreasen 1987: 200–34). The answers to these questions enable managers to apply an analytical approach to decision-making.

Marketing research can help archaeologists to develop their optimum client base in order to undertake work of research value rather than merely carry out clearance of sites prior to development. Archaeologists have the potential to engage in work for a wide range of public and private developers, research bodies, planning authorities and heritage organizations such as Cadw, Historic Scotland, English Heritage and the Royal Commissions.

Once the organization's corporate objectives have been defined (e.g., to carry out regional studies, prepare urban databases, to provide advice on planning matters, to carry out topographical surveys or to produce management proposals and mitigation strategies) then marketing research will help to identify clients who require these services. At its simplest level marketing research might involve managers keeping themselves informed of RCHME and English Heritage policy statements and research priorities.

National and local government departments already rely on marketing research for data to help create policies such as the planning of local education, social services and transport strategies. These same methods should be applied to help formulate heritage strategies. Archaeologists already use systematic analytical techniques for the definition of the cultural resource. They could easily extend this approach to the acquisition of information about the needs and wishes of local communities when preparing local management plans for sites and monuments. Money spent on the guardianship and presentation of monuments and properties in care can be allocated on the basis of rather superficial assumptions about the 'needs' and 'wants' of a rather loosely defined 'public'. Funds for the conservation of the historic environment are limited; how do we decide where best to allocate them (see National ·Audit Office 1992)? Do people want the creation of sterile green deserts? How do we reconcile the needs of the natural environment and archaeology (see Macinnes and Wickham-

Jones 1992)? Providing a better service to the community involves testing assumptions. One assumes that the principle of free access to museums and country parks and the landscape is sacrosanct, yet people appear to have accepted admission charges for certain classes of monument, museum and historic house. What impact would the introduction of admission charges have? What level of consumer resistance would there be? Are people happy to make a small charge to conserve 'their' local heritage? Are they aware how much of their local rate is spent on safeguarding 'their' heritage? Are the users of sites and monuments records happy with the service they are provided? Is it organized in a user-friendly way? These types of question can only be answered through marketing research.

THE MARKETING AUDIT: HOW IS OUR WORKING ENVIRONMENT CHANGING?

To function in a competitive environment it is critical to know the organization's current position in the market(s), and to be aware of the social, political and economic environment in which the organization is struggling to survive. Successful organizations achieve this through their marketing audit. The audit takes the form of a review of the way in which market research is carried out (Kotler and Andreasen 1987: 235–58).

The marketing environment consists of all the external factors which affect the relationship with customers. Social factors might include levels of unemployment or the fall in demand for housing and the decline of local industry. Shifts in cultural factors such as the rise of the 'green' movement, the decline of 1980s corporate values, the increase in cultural tourism and the increasing significance of 'a sense of place' to displaced communities, all affect the level of importance given to archaeology and heritage within society today (Fowler 1987). Economic factors such as the recession of the early 1990s clearly have a significant effect on the non-statutory functions of archaeology. During a recession, spending on longer-term capital items diminishes, there is a downturn in the national economy, local authority expenditure is capped and all levels of archaeological activity come under threat. Many archaeological contractors were helped to survive the recession of the early 1990s largely by the buoyant state of the government's road-building programme – which seemed to be the only recession-proof form of development.

Knowledge of competitors is obviously fundamental to the way in which organizations operate. Each public sector has to compete with each other sector for funds, and each institution has to compete with other institutions in the same sector for their share of funding. Differences can be offset by developing a good image and a reputation for effectiveness, and by concentrating on those aspects which are attractive to clients. The difficulty is in balancing the conflicting demands of stakeholders, employees, clients and the community. Many field archaeologists have sought to ease the competitive pressures upon them by combining with their colleagues in conservation of the built and natural environment to create a 'heritage' lobby which is more powerful as a whole.

Definition of the market in which archaeologists function is a critical process, and the definition should not be drawn too tightly. The geographical limits are an obvious starting point. However, even for public sector archaeologists the long-held perception of the local authority providing a service to the community within its boundary is rapidly changing (Lambrick 1991: 23–4). Trade practice is undergoing alteration and local authority archaeologists are working outside the traditional boundaries, in open competition with the private sector. With the introduction of Compulsory Competitive Tendering and the system of free trade, the catchment area of an archaeological unit is only limited by the ability of its staff to travel.

As competition increases with new organizations entering the market, so the need to consider an overall marketing strategy becomes increasingly important. Where marketing demand is low or negative, when potential clients actively avoid the service (e.g., dentistry) there is need for positive promotion. The archaeological analogy would be the positive promotion of archaeology to farmers, landowners and developers using the glossy brochure *Farming, Historic Landscapes and People* (English Heritage/Ministry of Agriculture, Fisheries and Food, n. d.). Where no obvious demand exists at present it may be possible to stimulate this by linking the service to individual needs. For example the benefits of the interpretation and management grants available through the Countryside Stewardship Scheme (Countryside Commission 1991, 1992) could be pointed out to landowners. Grant aid provides an opportunity to combine commercial farming and land management with public access and management of historic landscapes. When demand is irregular it is possible to control it and redistribute it more evenly, perhaps through alterations in pricing policy. Marketing techniques are regularly used by the National Trust and the National Parks Authorities to protect vulnerable historic buildings and landscapes (English Tourist Board *et al.* 1991a; English Tourist Board/Department of National Heritage 1993); 'de-marketing' involves increasing admission charges at sites which are close to their carrying capacity to reduce the impact of visitors when they cannot be excluded altogether (English Tourist Board/Employment Department Group 1991b; English Tourist Board *et al.* 1991c).

ANALYSIS OF STRENGTHS AND WEAKNESSES: WHAT DO WE HAVE TO WORK WITH?

Of equal importance to an archaeological organization is knowledge of its own strengths, weaknesses, opportunities and threats (SWOT). The SWOT analysis is a summary of the internal marketing audit. It helps to focus on key organizational areas that need to be taken into account when producing a marketing plan.

Strengths

The list of strengths ranked in order of significance can help to identify those aspects of the organization which can be built upon. Strengths might include location, strong management teams, skilled specialists, expert local knowledge, committed staff, workable procedures, well organized services and high-quality equipment. More abstract strengths might include the image and reputation of the organization and its standing in relation to its competitors.

Weaknesses

Organizational weaknesses will be the opposite of the strengths, including poor reputation, difficult communication links, badly organized services, poorly motivated staff and lack of expertise in a particular period or technique. If weaknesses such as insufficient commercial awareness can be identified, it may be possible to correct them. If the organization is pressurised to be more marketing-orientated and the management team has few marketing skills it might be possible to appoint a marketing professional (if the organization is large enough) or to undertake staff training. If the organizational goal-posts shift, in that the organization's environment changes, weaknesses may be exposed and skills shortages identified. For example the separation of local authority units into curator and contractor divisions has meant that inexperienced junior archaeologists are suddenly having to acquire skills in development control procedures, planning legislation and a whole range of new archaeological specialities in order to write briefs and specifications for archaeological assessments and field evaluations. In addition, the separation of units into curator and contractor divisions may have resulted in a loss of goodwill and the breakdown of long-established networks of collaboration.

Opportunities

The exposure of weaknesses due to organizational change can also be viewed as an opportunity to develop. There is clearly a market for fast-track training for many curatorial archaeologists in customer care, the concept of 'reasonableness' within the planning process and for specific archaeological skills among those with responsibility for monitoring fieldwork. Skills gaps can also be filled by forming collaborative consortia, or by providing specialist services to competitors under contract. The rapidly changing external environment provides the opportunity to develop new client bases, whilst restructuring within local authorities may provide greater autonomy.

Threats

The public sector archaeological services are continually threatened by reductions in core funding due to policy changes about levels of public expenditure. Internal struggles within organizations can be eased if management policy encourages a corporate view of cooperation rather than competition. Group responsibility for reductions in expenditure or income should be borne across the whole organization. However, this approach runs counter to the situation of strong competition that exists in the external marketplace.

STRATEGIC MARKETING PLANNING AND THE 'MARKETING MIX': HOW DO WE MATCH OBJECTIVES AND GOALS WITH RESOURCES AND MARKET OPPORTUNITIES?

Having established the organization's position in the market and identified customer needs, the next step is to develop a marketing strategy. In traditional marketing theory there are four major variables which can be controlled to produce the strategy. These are the product (or service) provided, its price, the way it is promoted, and the place or places through which it is delivered to clients. These variables – the four Ps – make up the 'marketing mix'. Within the service sector, however , where most archaeologists are firmly rooted, there is a fifth variable – 'people'.

The optimum marketing mix is the most appropriate combination of Ps to meet a particular set of circumstances. If the balance is wrong the marketing strategy is likely to fail. Successful organizations manipulate the balance of their marketing mix to retain their competitive edge. The guiding principle of the marketing mix is that of synergy, i.e.: that the total combined effect of the variables is greater than the sum of their parts.

Product

The product of archaeology is a service; most archaeological units provide a service which is less tangible than a manufactured product. To improve the performance of a service the quality has to be raised. This will add to the cost and will be passed on to the client as an increase in price. However, if the service is improved, it could be more acceptable, leading to higher uptake, economies of scale and lower unit costs and prices (Cowell 1990: 99–110). An example of this might be investing in new surveying equipment such as a Total Station to provide more effective landscape and building surveys.

Most service providers emphasize the quality they provide, since they rely on word of mouth recommendation to establish their reputation. Low price is not necessarily a substitute for quality in a competitive situation. This should be of some comfort to all those in the archaeological profession who are concerned about the perceived decline in professional standards brought about by 'cowboy contractors'. Where the product is a service, the single most important activity in marketing is getting the service right. If the customer is satisfied with the service, then demand is likely to be maintained, other services may be demanded, and the service may be recommended to other organizations.

The essential role of marketing is to identify those benefits which an organization offers that are not provided by the competition – the Unique Selling Proposition (USP). These benefits will include intangibles such as customer satisfaction, staff attitudes and levels, service reliability and the ability to meet deadlines. The quality of the service provided will depend on the expectations of individual clients. However, most will assume that the organization should meet standards of professional practice (Association of County Archaeological Officers 1993; Institute of Field Archaeologists 1990). Overall, corporate image and reputation are a major influence on the level of demand for a service and a key factor in positioning an organization in relation to its competitors.

Many public sector organizations are being forced to take on board the lessons of total quality, not only having the technical ability to deliver a service but also the right staff with the right approach and motivation (Cowell 1990: 202–25; Dimaggio 1985; see Brooke, this volume). The staff who provide the service are part of the product. This makes it difficult to guarantee the quality of the service unless there is investment in staff through training, motivation and continued professional development (see Darvill on training, this volume). Typically when mistakes occur – for example a pipe burst during machining leads to a cut in water supply – the efforts taken by staff to repair the damage can create more goodwill than if nothing had gone wrong in the first place. The mistake can provide staff with the opportunity to show a caring professional attitude to clients.

Price

Pricing policies should always be influenced by the marketing environment in which the organization operates. For political or social reasons it may be decided that a local authority service is provided at a subsidized price or at a full commercial profitable price. The provision of a 'free' or subsidized service such as free admission to a museum or country park involves the same strategic marketing decisions as would the provision of a service at profit within the commercial sector. Nowadays local authorities need to know the true cost of providing a service in order to demonstrate that they are delivering value for money and are functioning economically, efficiently and effectively (National Audit Office 1992).

The cost of a service has to be met, even if it is not charged for at the point of sale. Clearly archaeologists functioning within the local authority sector are constrained by local and national policies and regulations that reflect the prevailing political and social ideas about how services should be made available to clients. At present the imposed change from cost centres to profit centres makes it essential that all archaeologists whether in the public or commercial sector are aware of the principles of pricing policy (Kotler and Andreasen 1987: 449–70).

Decisions on price are based on four main factors:
- those under the control of the organization itself;
- those that operate in the chosen market;
- those influenced by customers' needs;
- those determined by changes in the marketing environment.

Pricing policy should always be linked to marketing objectives. It may be essential to keep prices low to encourage the use of a particular service in order to make best use of the available resources. Alternatively, the strategy might be to raise cash for investment in expansion. The price of a service is also influenced by the other services in the portfolio of the organization. For example, a large unit might be able to provide a low-cost geophysics service if the specialist technicians can be employed in other areas of work such as desk-based evaluations, report preparation or field walking when not engaged in geophysical survey; a small specialist geophysics consultancy would need to keep its prices high to retain staff over the shoulder months when demand is low. A decision may be taken to sell a service at a loss in order to develop or penetrate the market. Such 'loss leaders' might include an evaluation which coincides with the period research interests of the organization, or be within an area where they have a long track record of achievement on which to build. A low-cost evaluation could ultimately lead to full recording action and provide valuable data for the unit's research strategy (Cowell 1990: 151–61).

Correct positioning within the market is of importance, since if too low a price is charged the organization will not be taken seriously. It is difficult to determine an appropriate price when competitors guard their trade information. The simplest solution is the cost-plus process, since there is more certainty about costs than there is about demand. The drawback of the price based on costs is that it does not take into account changes in the market, or it does not vary enough to take account of the wide range of market segments. In a very competitive market it is not realistic to charge over the odds, since customers will go elsewhere. In a truly competitive market there are many buyers and sellers with a homogeneous service and one price. Despite the confidentiality of trade information there appears to be a consistency of price amongst the main players in the field of contract archaeology. In effect market forces appear to have come into play and the market has found its own level.

The influence of the customer on price is critical as ultimately the client decides whether the price is set at the correct level. In arriving at a price it is important to consider the clients' perceptions of price and how this affects their decision to buy. The perceived cost for a client is any negative outcome – not just the price charged – including the difficulties encountered in having to obtain a service, such as time spent waiting or a bad working relationship.

Consumer resistance to the introduction of charges or an imposed increase is a significant factor to consider and complicates the simplistic view that increased charge equals greater profit. There has been a long tradition of free access to our national and local museums, which are perceived by many to be part of their birthright. When the government imposed charges on the national museums there was a 40 per cent decline in admissions to the Science Museum (Besterman and Bott 1982; Museum Professionals Group 1985). Significantly the recent Policy Studies Institute report has highlighted the fact that those national museums which charge for admission actually generate less gross income from their shops and cafes than those which are free (Eckstein 1992: 48–54, Table 40).

Place

In marketing terms 'place' is where a service is delivered to the client. It can also refer to the marketing channels used by organizations to reach their customers. It can be a physical location such as an office, shop, visitor centre or excavation site, or a system of communications such as a report, leaflet, video, Geographic Information System, talk or interpretation panel (Cowen 1990: 182–201).

Management of these channels of distribution is particularly important since the client has to know about the service, and know where it will be delivered. The length of the channel and its complexity will depend on the size of the market. One of the most radical changes in the archaeological market place has been the lengthening of existing channels of distribution with the introduction of the curator, enabler and contractor divisions within local authorities (Figure 7.2).

The breadth of the channel depends on the number of retailers/ contractors available to deliver the service. A direct channel is where the organ-ization deals directly with its clients; an indirect channel is one in which the organization deals through intermediaries. Most organizations prefer to deal with their customers directly, since in this way they gain a

Figure 7.2   Channel length

better understanding of their needs and a rapid awareness of any problems. If any problems arise they can respond quickly to changes in the market and the particular needs of market segments. One of the great marketing problems created by the creation of the curator/contractor role within local authorities has been the introduction of greater 'distance' in channels, both between different sectors of the archaeological profession and between them and their clients.

Promotion

Promotion – the fourth 'P' – is what many mistakenly assume is the sole function of marketing. Promotion is just one important aspect – communication with customers and potential customers. People cannot use your services if they have never heard of you, or do not know where to contact you. The promotional mix is the range of media used to remain 'visible' in the marketplace, such as corporate brochures, articles in the trade press, and ultimately paid-for advertising. Successful promotion requires the ability to target consumers through the appropriate media. Care must be taken to convey the right image for the organization. Often the image can be conflicting or ambiguous and convey unintended meanings.

Effective promotion to stakeholders such as public bodies can be important when an organization is trying to maintain or increase its levels of funding. Similarly, attention to internal communications systems is a key factor in staff motivation and team building. Employees need to feel they are working for a caring organization that values their input and, above all, internal communication should be seen as a two-way process.

Archaeologists are less likely to resort to one of the most expensive tools in the promotional mix, that of paid advertising, although there are occasions when low-cost advertising could be effective to remain visible in the trade press. Before committing money to an advertising budget it is important to define the target audience and to ask 'When and where is the best time and place to advertise?' Although there might be value to specialist contractors or to educational establishments offering courses in Continuing Professional Development promoting themselves at the Institute of Field Archaeologists' Conference, is there much point in an archaeological unit advertising its services to its peers?

The most effective form of promotion that archaeologists are used to employing is that of public relations and free publicity. Archaeologists have the great advantage of a discipline which is newsworthy. With the aid of a small promotional budget it is possible to obtain and manage good quality editorial coverage through a variety of media to raise the profile of the organization. However, good publicity does not occur randomly and is usually the result of a planned and sustained effort by the organization, a lesson which English Heritage learned to its cost in November 1992 (Keys 1992; Renfrew 1992; Fowler 1992).

Market Segmentation

A market segment is a group of customers with needs that are distinctive from those of other groups for the same product or service. Typical segments of the archaeological market might include:

Property developers;
Education;
Leisure and recreation;
The heritage industry;
Extractive industry;
Major landowners;
Consultancies;
Local authorities;
Central government organizations;
Non-governmental organizations;
Public utilities.

Targeting specific segments of the market enables organizations to find the best opportunities for the organization's talents and advantages so that its strengths are maximised and its weaknesses minimised. The organization may not be large enough to control a large share of the whole market, but it could be a major contender in a particular segment such as urban archaeology, geophysics, documentary survey, field walking, building recording, maritime archaeology or industrial archaeology. It is important that organizations do not try to provide too many services in too many segments, otherwise they will lose economies of scale. The achievement of the right balance of services to offer is critical. However, there are various constraints within which organizations work which can help to define their market segments. These might include the influence of existing heavy users of their services, such as English Heritage. Should organizations continue to concentrate on a market segment dominated by a single heavy user? What happens, for example, if funding criteria change?

ACTION PLAN: WHEN WILL WE ACHIEVE OUR OBJECTIVES AND GOALS? WHO WILL MAKE THIS HAPPEN?

Strategies identified in an overall strategic marketing plan, based upon a three-year schedule, are implemented through the one-year marketing action plan (see Figure 7.3). The strategies are costed out in terms of staff and finance and if found not to be practicable alternatives are proposed and costed until a satisfactory solution can be reached. It is essential that all the stated objectives are prioritized according to their impact on the organization and that resources are allocated effectively. There should be a set of written procedures and a well-argued common format for marketing planning so that all key issues are systematically considered. Above all it is

Tactical Action Plan (one year)	**Strategic Marketing Plan** (three years)
March	
Planning tean meet line managers to discuss overall guidelines for three-year planning period.	
March–May	May
Managers carry out marketing audits, identify problems and solutions and agree with planning team.	• Mission statement • Summary of last year's business performance
May	• Summary of financial projections for next three years
Planning team discuss three-year business plan with line managers and amend as necessary.	• Market overview • SWOT Analysis • Marketing mix • Marketing objectives and strategies for next three years • Financial projections for next three years
September–October	
Prepare detailed one-year operational plan with forecast and budgets.	
November	
Present three year plan and detailed one-year plan.	
December	
Consolidate one-year and three-year plans.	

Figure 7.3   The one-year planning cycle

critical that the staff responsible for marketing have the necessary marketing knowledge and skills for the job.

MONITORING AND REVIEW: ARE WE MEETING OUR OBJECTIVES? WHAT NEEDS TO BE CHANGED?

Monitoring and review are essential to all marketing strategies and plans. The planning and control process requires a regular marketing audit. This should take the form of a comprehensive, systematic review of the organization's marketing environment, its strategies and activities, so that problems and opportunities can be identified and a plan of action proposed to improve its marketing performance. Levels of customer satisfaction are the most obvious measures of successful marketing, but they are difficult to quantify. Both qualitative and quantitative measures of performance should be involved. There are no absolute standards, just varying degrees of client satisfaction. Increasing the satisfaction of one client group could reduce the satisfaction of another.

The one-year tactical plan should also identify the critical success factors. These might include key areas such as:

- the internal market;
- tendering and other project opportunties;
- overhead costs;
- continued competitiveness and ability to win tenders;
- completion of projects within forecast timescale and budget allocation;
- academic research fulfilment.

Marketplace success might be judged on such criteria as responsiveness, delivery, quality, project variety, innovation, continuity of provision and academic value. The systems for monitoring marketing performance should be built into existing project management procedures and management reviews such as project evaluations, staff appraisals and strategic assessments.

CONCLUSIONS

On the whole the local authorities within which many archaeologists work have tended to be product-oriented, rather than marketing-oriented. The local authority culture was dominated by the necessity of the service rather than the requirements of the customer, whether they be external in the form of the local community or property developers, or internal divisions of the local authority. The 'culture of professionalism' is still prevalent in many places, so that some local authority officers believe they have the knowledge and skills to the exclusion of others in their service, as well as the public or the client. Traditionally, local authorities have been bureaucratic organizations based on the hierarchy of command and often the needs of the public and those of its employees have had to be fitted into these constraints.

The marketing approach can encourage organizations to help rather than hinder clients by developing appropriate procedures. To do this archaeologists have to find out what their clients think of the service they provide. Is the Sites and Monuments Record user-friendly? Do the clients understand the need for archaeological intervention within the Development Control process? Is the popular publication readable and interesting, or is it merely the hobby of the curator?

Ultimately, the style adopted by any archaeological organization will depend on its priorities and objectives. The culture of the organization could be pro-active or inert, democratic or autocratic, traditional or radical, expansionist or relatively passive, aggressive or defensive. However, there will be aspects of the marketing approach that will be of benefit to all styles. In today's competitive world all archaeologists whether in the public or private sector have to demonstrate that they carry out their jobs efficiently, economically and effectively.

REFERENCES

Anderson, W.R. and Sprouse, H. (1984) 'Museums in the market place', *Museum News* October 1984: 59–67.

Association of County Archaeological Officers (1993) *Model Briefs and Specifications for Archaeological Assessments and Field Evaluations*, Bedford: Association of County Archaeological Officers.

Bestermann, T. and Bott, V. (1982) 'To pay or not to pay?', *Museums Journal* September 1982, 2: 118–19.

Countryside Commission (1991) *The Countryside Stewardship Initiative*, Cheltenham: Countryside Commission.

Countryside Commission (1992) *Action for the Countryside: Historic Landscapes, Old Meadows and Pasture,* Cheltenham: Countryside Commission.

Cowell, D.W. (1990) *The Marketing of Services*, (2nd edition) Oxford: Heinemann/Chartered Institute of Marketing.

Davies, S. (1992) 'Citizens, Customers and Curators', *Museums Journal* 92, 9: 20–1.

Department of the Environment (1990a) *This Common Inheritance*, London: HMSO.

Department of the Environment (1990b) *Planning Policy Guidance: Archaeology and Planning*, PPG 16, London: HMSO.

Dimaggio, P.J. (1985) 'When the Profit is Quality', *Museum News* June 1985, 28–35.

Drake, J. and Fahy, A. (1987) *Guide to Archaeology on Community Programmes*, (Institute of Field Archaeologists Occasional Paper 2), Birmingham: IFA.

Eckstein, J. (1992) *Cultural Trends 14: Museums and Galleries Funding and Finance*, London: Policy Studies Institute.

English Heritage (1986) *Rescue Archaeology Funding: A Policy Statement*, London: English Heritage.

English Heritage (1991) 'Competitive tendering for archaeology projects', *The Field Archaeologist* 13: 2–6.

English Heritage (1992) *Managing England's Heritage. Setting our Priorities for the 1990s*, London: English Heritage.

English Heritage/Ministry of Agriculture, Fisheries and Food (n. d.) *Farming, Historic Landscapes and People*, London: English Heritage.

English Tourist Board, Countryside Commission, Countryside Council for Wales, Rural Development Commission, Wales Tourist Board (1991a) *Tourism in National Parks: A Guide to Good Practice*, London: English Tourist Board.

English Tourist Board/Employment Department Group (1991b) *Tourism and the Environment: Maintaining the Balance*, London: English Tourist Board.

English Tourist Board, Rural Development Commission, Countryside Commission (1991c) *The Green Light: A Guide to Sustainable Tourism*, London: English Tourist Board.

English Tourist Board/Department of National Heritage (1993) *Tourism and the Environment Challenges and Choices for the 90s*, privately circulated proceedings of a conference held in London, 16–19 November 1992.

Evans, N. (1992) 'Our heritage, lost to the free market', *Independent* 28 October 1992.

Ford, D. (1976) 'The marketing of non-profit making organizations', *European Journal of Marketing* 10, 5: 266–79.

Fowler, P.J. (1987) 'What price the man-made heritage?', *Antiquity* 61: 409–23.

Fowler, P.J. (1992) *The Past in Contemporary Society: Then, Now.*, London: Routledge.

Houston, F.S. (1986) 'The marketing concept: what it is and what it is not' *Journal of Marketing*, 50, 2: 81–7.

Hunter, J. and Ralston, I. (eds) (1993) *Archaeological Heritage Management in the UK: An Introduction,* Stroud: Alan Sutton Publishing.

Institute of Field Archaeologists (1990) *By-laws of the Institute of Field Archaeologists: Code of Approved Practice for the Regulation of Contractual Arrangements in Field Archaeology*, Birmingham: Institute of Field Archaeologists.

Keen, L. (1992) 'English Heritage plan is "foolish and irresponsible"', *Independent* 5 November 1992.

Keys, D. (1992) 'English Heritage set to privatise 200 major sites', *Independent* 26 October 1992.

Kotler, P. and Andreasen, A.R. (1987) *Strategic Marketing for Non-Profit Organizations*, 3rd Edition, Englewood Cliffs, NJ: Prentice-Hall.

Lambrick, G. (1991) 'Competitive tendering and archaeological research: the development of a CBA view', in H. Swain (ed.) *Competitive Tendering in Archaeology*, Hertford: RESCUE Publications/Standing Conference of Archaeology Unit Managers, 149–57.

Lawson, A. (1993) 'English archaeological units as contractors', in J. Hunter and I. Ralston (eds) *Archaeological Resource Management in the UK*, Stroud: Alan Sutton Publishing.

Macinness, L. and Wickham-Jones, C.R. (eds) (1992) *All Natural Things: Archaeology and the Green Debate,* Oxbow Monograph 21, Oxford: Oxbow.

Middleton, V. (1990) *New Visions of Independent Museums in the UK,* Chichester: Association of Independent Museums.

Museums Professionals Group (1985) *Admission Charges at National Museums,* Transactions 21, London: Museum Professionals Group.

National Audit Office (1992) *Protecting and Managing England's Heritage Property*, London: HMSO.

Northamptonshire Archaeology (1993) *Business Plan, December 1993*, Northamptonshire County Council Planning and Transportation Department Consultation Document 6.

Renfrew, C. (1992) 'Elusive ways of English Heritage', *Independent* 3 November 1992.

Stevens, T. (1989) 'The visitor – who cares? Interpretation and customer relations', in D. Uzzell (ed.) *Heritage Interpretation* Vol. 2, *The Visitor Experience*, London: Belhaven, 103–7.

Swain H. (ed.) (1991) *Competitive Tendering in Archaeology*, Hertford: RESCUE Publications/Standing Conference of Archaeology Unit Managers.

CHAPTER EIGHT

THE BAD, THE GOOD AND THE UGLY:

Archaeology and the management discipline

CAROLE BROOKE

Archaeology is coming under increasing pressure of forces of change. The nature of these forces was indicated by Cooper in his paper 'Archaeology and management perspectives' (Cooper 1993). Consequently, people in the discipline are becoming anxious. This anxiety can be viewed as the product of, on the one hand, fear of the known (experiences at the Victoria and Albert or Natural History museums in London, for example, where new forms of management structure, redundancies and entrance charges accompanied cuts in public funding, under the dictum of 'value for money', sending shockwaves through the profession); and, on the other, fear of the unknown. Negative responses are triggered by a belief that management is largely uncharted water as far as archaeology is concerned and is somehow intrinsically and ethically dubious. The purpose of this paper is not to extol the virtues of management, but to challenge the justification for such anxiety and to consider whether archaeology does have anything to learn from the discipline of management or, indeed, whether management has anything to learn from the discipline of archaeology.

The author was trained in archaeology, moved into business studies, and now lectures within a business school, and therefore had the opportunity to view archaeology's current situation from 'both sides of the fence'. Having crossed the archaeology/management boundary with relative ease, it would appear that the divide is neither as concrete nor as wide as some might believe. This chapter is based on that premise.

THE BAD

Cooper (1993) suggests that archaeology should look to management theory for guidance. He has noted that a gap exists between archaeology's theoreticians (academics) and its 'practising professionals'. Whilst acknowledging that someone can, in fact, be both, if there is a gap between theory and practice then looking to the management discipline for guidance will not be productive. The reason for this is that management suffers from the same symptoms! Responses to the current management concept of Total Quality Management (TQM) are a classic example of the gap between espoused organizational philosophy and actual management practice.

During 1989 and 1990 the author conducted fieldwork within the Information Technology departments of two large service sector companies in the UK (Brooke 1992). In both cases, organization-wide structural and cultural changes were taking place designed to improve overall efficiency, responsiveness to customer need, and increase competitive edge in an aggressive marketplace. The top management of each company believed that TQM (described below) was an appropriate way to implement these changes. Research indicated, however, that attempts had been unsuccessful and that the TQM philosophy engendered by the companies was not borne out by experiences of their staff in the workplace. Examples taken from the research demonstrate this mismatch. First, though, a few words on the concept of TQM.

TQM is one of a number of 'methods' for introducing quality into the workplace. Its basic tenet is that quality is the responsibility of *everyone* within an organization (Collard and Sivyer 1990). A 'customer' is anyone for whom a service is provided, both internal and external to the company. This means that quality is a people issue and that only through the commitment of all employees can an organization achieve 'true' TQM. Clearly, this requires attention to the needs and values of employees; indeed, to human resource issues in general. Unfortunately, the empirical evidence suggests that this did not happen in the two companies researched.

Both case-study organizations had chosen to introduce change through the vehicle of TQM and their strategic objectives reflected this. Each company had the following major TQM-based objectives in common:

- introduce the notion of quality as a continuous process of improvement;
- encourage employee participation in achieving company goals;
- encourage communication between customer and supplier in the pursuit of customer satisfaction;
- enable staff to perform effectively and develop their potential;
- improve employee commitment at all levels.

Both companies had also publicized their intention to introduce TQM within a certain time-scale. This struck a note of discord, and not just because it contradicted a stated objective. Another basic principle of TQM, as the objective suggested, is the continuous nature of quality improvement. What the organizations were proposing was more of a definable programme of change. This was not the only contradictory aspect (see Figure 8.1). The TQM programmes had taken up to three years to reach review stage and staff felt that this diluted any beneficial impact which they might have had. Both organizations were seen as hierarchical and reactive and staff identified their top management with this culture, too. The TQM idea had been launched as something which broke with past traditions – yet membership of the respective boards had not changed. Staff, therefore, remained unconvinced of board commitment to TQM.

The programmes of change were implemented in a top-down way, characterized by change by control rather than change by commitment at the individual level. Management directives had been issued with virtually no prior staff consultation. A few seminars and open forums had been held by senior managers to spread the TQM message but these were too formal and too brief to allow staff much opportunity for interaction. These events were geared more towards communicating a decision than to discussion and debate. In other words, there was little evidence of staff participation.

Implementation was typified by a distinct focus on formalised and documented procedures. The heavy reliance on manuals, distributed to staff impersonally, gave the impression that TQM was a set of procedures to manage procedures. There was little employee involvement and attention was to process issues rather than people issues. This was particularly evident within the IT departments where formal methodologies were introduced into the software development life-cycle. In the second company, a project management methodology was introduced, too. All methodologies were document-based and staff were expected to read the numerous handbooks associated with them. Unsurprisingly, many did not, and in some cases the old methods of working were still being used in preference to the new. To complicate the matter further, within the second organization there was an unclear relationship between the project management

COMPANY OBJECTIVES	STAFF EXPERIENCES
• Continuous quality	• Three-year roll-out
	• Top-down implementation Lack of consultation
• Employee participation	
• Customer–supplier relations	• Intermediaries
• Maximize staff potential	• Lack of training Skills undermined by detail
• Employee commitment	• Processes not people

Figure 8.1   The gap between theory and practice

methodology and the formal software methods. This gave the impression of a fragmented rather than an integrated strategy. It also led to confusion.

Perhaps the most blatant example of this was where a software product was being produced for their own marketing department. (In TQM terms it was, therefore, a good example of service provision for an internal customer.) According to the project management methodology, the technical team were not obliged to communicate directly with the department. Instead, an intermediary was appointed to take overall responsibility on behalf of the target users, and translated dialogues between the parties concerned. Project staff complained on a number of occasions that this led to misinterpretation and a decreased ability to produce something which met with customer expectations. This situation was in direct opposition to their management's stated objectives as well as the notion of TQM.

For staff of both companies, one side effect of the new methodologies was the proliferation of documentation which had to be produced as part of the job. This resulted in extended time-scales which were viewed as a distinct disadvantage. This problem could have been overcome if the longer term benefits of TQM had been explained more clearly. Staff would then have been able to see that some sacrifices in the short term could produce bigger benefits in the future. This lack of awareness was a symptom of the general paucity of training for TQM. In some cases, one-day workshops had been held to introduce staff to the concept of TQM. Most staff found this to be extremely useful and interesting, but the lack of follow-up training meant that they failed to put what they had learnt into practice. Once back on project, it was often difficult for staff to get support in their new skills. There were very few fully trained people on site, and those who existed were in heavy demand. Sitting with Nellie (training on the job) methods can be very effective, especially on busy projects where removing staff from their work context is problematic. However, the constraints on human resources meant that almost none of this was provided. The lack of training augmented a feeling that some analysts and programmers had of being de-skilled. The detailed procedures and documentation attached to the TQM methods provoked frustration in the most experienced employees. Some felt patronized, others constrained or even bored. What had previously been part of the craft of their work had now been formalized and subsumed under the 'drudge'. There are a number of arguments which can be presented in defence of formal methods, such as that it prevents a 'creative' programmer designing something that is difficult to modify and maintain. These arguments are well rehearsed in the software development literature. The main point in respect of this research paper is that the employees were neither being developed to their full potential nor were they committed at the personal level.

Clearly, then, there was dissatisfaction amongst staff and extensive divergence from both organizations' original TQM objectives. Many of the problems could be categorized as failures in communication. Ullah (1991) highlighted the importance of communications in shaping quality conscious behaviour when he said that it 'entails individualized communication to the actual tasks people perform, rather than the mass communication of a philosophy. It is in this sense that TQM, if it is to work, must involve everyone within the organization. . . . One way of increasing acceptance is to set goals participatively rather than imposing them from above.' (Ullah 1991: 79).

The techniques employed by the two case study organizations did not resemble this TQM approach.

For those archaeologists who identify with some of these experiences, this story is not offered merely as cold comfort. As the next section suggests, there are aspects of the archaeological discipline which serve as a basis for a more positive management profile.

THE GOOD

Picture of a quality organization

Whilst interpreting the fieldwork, a statement came to mind which had appeared in one of the organizations' TQM guides. Previously it had seemed a very ordinary quality statement, similar to the sort of message which appears in many such texts. On reflection, it acquired a new and more revealing character. The statement was:

> Our primary goal is to serve our *customers* well in every respect. That means identifying their specific requirements and then meeting them – first time, every time. This is what Total Quality Management is all about.

The word 'customers' is highlighted to draw the reader's attention to the earlier description of what TQM is all about. Remember that within a TQM framework everyone is considered to be a potential customer, whether internal or external to the organization. That means employees, too. If the statement is refocused to take account of this point, an interesting change in emphasis occurs:

> Our primary goal is to serve our employees well in every respect. That means identifying their specific requirements and then meeting them – first time, every time. This is what Total Quality Management is all about.

The stress, once again, is that TQM is about employee participation, commitment and development. Yet the focus in both companies had been on monitoring procedures and not identifying the needs of individuals. The second statement represents another shift in perspective, fundamental but more subtle. It is an *emic* philosophy – that is, an 'insider's' view rather than an 'outsider's' view. It is particularly important to bear this in mind when reading the rest of the chapter. At this point in the research, however, the main concern was to make sense of the empirical work and to attempt a synthesis. The way in which the organizations had implemented TQM was clearly influenced by their respective hierarchical and reactive cultures and indications were that this did not effectively promote TQM.

In taking an overview of the fieldwork (only a tiny part of which appears here), a picture gradually emerged of the hierarchical and reactive organization, closely followed by a contrasting vision of a 'quality' organization. These pictures came in analogical form. The analogy which suggested itself as appropriate for the hierarchical organization was a volcano. For the 'quality' company it was a tree. A summary of each analogy follows. For the purpose of this discussion, the emphasis will be on points of general management. The reader is asked to compare their personal experiences with the two scenarios presented.

Figure 8.2 is an interpretative representation of the two organizations studied in the fieldwork. The volcano possesses many appropriate characteristics, the most striking feature being its instability and reactivity. Eruptions (major changes) occur in a seemingly unplanned way and constitute massive expenditures of energy and resources. They, therefore, tend to be spectacular but rare. When an eruption does occur the products emerge from the top and flow downwards, carrying off anything in their path. The consequences for people positioned at lower levels are drastic. This potential for danger and disaster promotes a risk averse attitude.

The volcano is divided into three hierarchical layers: strategy, functions, and people. Strategy is rolled out top-down, with minimal communication bottom-up. Little interaction occurs between the different vertical layers and career paths are funnelled towards the top of the volcano, in accordance with the hierarchical structure. This vertical division is paralleled in the horizontal plane where there is distinct divergence between functions, especially between IT and the rest. Career paths meet (if at all) at the very pinnacle of the volcano. This arrangement produces specialists rather than generalists, the 'Y career path' (a concept used by Barry Seward-Thompson, former Principal of DECollege), resulting in a skills gap. Specialisation is an effective barrier to the formulation of cross-functional teams and the transference of skills across the company. Where in-house skills are scarce, external consultancies are brought in at great expense. Heavy reliance on this tactic leads to out-sourcing of expertise in the long term. The effect is to reduce the number of core competencies to which the organization can lay claim and, if not carefully planned, surrenders business to competitors.

The 'tree' organization in Figure 8.3 contrasts sharply with the volcano, promoting long-term stability, regeneration and new growth (with the emphasis on 'pruning' not 'amputation'). A tree may be very old and its roots strong yet they support a dynamic, innovative and changing entity. The emphasis is on nourishment and a sense of balance. Energy is recycled, and when an employee leaves the tree they return to the external skills pool to become a potential source of fertilisation in the longer term. The tree is durable, flexible and responsive to its surroundings and inhabitants, providing a channel for the throughput of resources, taking from the external environment but giving back valuable resources in return. The security of the tree is ensured by successful throughput. 'Top-down' and 'bottom-up' are meaningless concepts because the tree is a network and not a distinct hierarchy. Communication flows are easier and freer. Growth (change, education and training) occur at all levels and career paths are horizontal rather than vertical. Functional hybridization means that multi-skilled teams can be formed more effectively.

The characteristics of the volcano include division, instability, hierarchy, and risk avoidance. This gives rise to complex and poor communications. The tree symbolizes integration, harmony, and conservation, promoting quality communications. Gardeners establish reputations by propagating

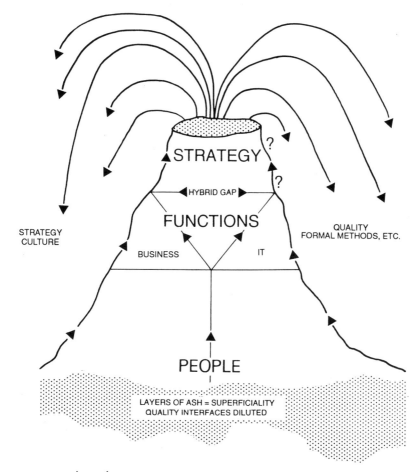

Figure 8.2   The volcano

EXTERNAL RESOURCES

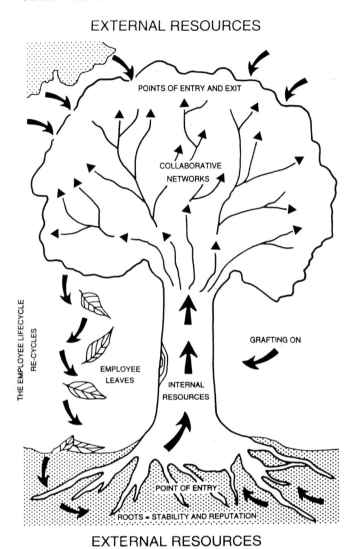

Figure 8.3 The tree

quality plants. Tree organizations establish themselves by nurturing good quality staff. Since up to 80 per cent of the future workforce is already employed (Cassels 1990: 27) it is important to be a good horticulturist. The key point is that quality now centres on the life-cycle of the employee. The volcano represents an outsider's perspective but the tree, with its human focus and attention to the needs of employees, is much more of an insider's perspective. This latter approach would seem to be more in tune with the philosophy of TQM.

How does archaeology compare?

Archaeology may regard itself as poor at handling strategic issues, especially training and career development, and so may be tempted to compare itself unfavourably with the tree analogy, but there is evidence for a more optimistic view. The key over-riding theme of the chapter so far has been culture: cultural aspects of TQM, cultural traits of organizations, and so on. The first point to make is that archaeology is heavily involved with the study of culture. That puts it in a good position to understand the sort of cultural issues that have been raised within the management context. Traditional British management culture is often described as bureaucratic, risk averse, short-termist and reactive (Rajan and Fryatt 1988; Nelson 1989). In other words, like the volcano and definitely not what is required for TQM. Many of the problems inherent in volcanoes are recognized within archaeology, in particular the effect of hierarchies upon career and skill development, and there is already evidence of 'good practice' to combat this (Locock, this volume; Cooper 1993, and this volume).

Nevertheless, archaeologists are not drawn to their discipline by good salaries, career prospects, or social status. Most are involved because they enjoy it and this motivation compares favourably with business sectors. This is particularly noticeable on site digs where scant and fluctuating resources are more immediately apparent. The one thing a site director wants to be able to rely on is the human resource. On the whole archaeologists are very committed people. In an area where so many of the labour force are voluntary or virtually voluntary this is unsurprising. It is an important point because, provided exploitation does not occur, this gives the discipline the basis of a tree-like reputation.

This is not to suggest that everyone in archaeology is happy or that everyone in commerce is miserable. What is suggested is that archaeology possesses some characteristics which give it a number of advantages in a changing and insecure business climate. The key term here is *entrepreneur*. It would be dangerous to provide a list of characteristics which constitute the entrepreneur because entrepreneurs are, by definition, individualistic. Nevertheless, it is possible to postulate that there is a closer similarity between entrepreneurialism and the tree style of management than the volcano approach. The entrepreneur, like the tree, has to be flexible, dynamic, proactive and creative. Their commitment to employees means that they put a high premium on the human resource, recognizing their skills to be a key distinguishing feature in business competition. In this environment training and development of the individual really is an investment in the future of the business. Employees are encouraged to develop their potential and to express their individuality through training, education and practical experience. Archaeology, too, is a human resource-based enterprise. It has its personalities and its teams, and to the outside world its reputation is often based on the work of a few well-known individuals and their projects. Here the author slightly contradicts Cooper's point about scant resources (Cooper 1993). Instead the archaeological project manager can be viewed as a manager of scant resources *par excellence*. Archaeology is used to justifying itself at the micro-level – specifically, at site level where archaeologists seek support for particular digs, site preservation, and so on.

It would be relatively easy to draw comparisons between the skills that are required to do this and those that are identified with the entrepreneur. Without wishing to fall into the trap mentioned earlier, some of these skills are indicated on the right-hand side of Figure 8.4. The skills of particular relevance are the ability to be creative with a limited resource base, to manipulate events to advantage, and to identify problems and turn them into opportunities. To some readers this may sound like simplistic optimism but when related back to experiences on digs, especially rescue activities, the links are more evident. If it will benefit archaeology to develop these skills, then it will have to tackle what Gibb has identified as the gap between the traditional focus of management learning and the sort of environment which develops entrepreneurial attributes (Gibb 1987; Kirby 1992). Figure 8.4 indicates the main differences. The educational focus is on typically scientific criteria and is largely objective (*etic*) in nature. The entrepreneurial focus is more subjective (*emic*). This chapter suggests that a similar situation exists in the archaeological discipline. The training and education of archaeologists tends to rest on scientific and objective traits whereas experiences in the field reflect more of the points in the right-hand column.

When applied to archaeology, the implications of this argument are more profound than is perhaps realized because they penetrate to the very core of what it is that drives the discipline and the values that underpin it. How can this gap be bridged? The response to this centres on the first item in the two columns of Figure 8.4 – i.e. focus on the past versus a focus on the future. There is an ill-defined yet important link between the tendency in archaeology to focus on the past and what now seem to be forces of change which require the discipline to focus on its future. The real ugliness for archaeology lies in the possibility that to date its prime focus has been on the past, on objectivity, on scientific criteria, yet what is required now is a more ambiguous focus, on possibilities, on uncertainties, and on values.

In business terms the idea of a successful entrepreneur conjures up personalities such as Richard Branson (Virgin Group) or Anita Roddick (Body Shop). Interestingly, it is often an entrepreneur who is cited as an example of good management practice. Deeks (1975) said that the entrepreneur's sense of social responsibility is worked out by promoting harmonious employee relationships (especially loyalty) within the organization and within the community, too (echoes of the tree in Figure 8.3). The emphasis here is on ethics and values. Ironically, when times are hard other types

EDUCATIONAL FOCUS ON	ENTREPRENEURIAL FOCUS ON
The past	The future
Critical analysis	Creativity
Knowledge	Insight
Passive understanding	Active understanding
Absolute detachment	Emotional involvement
Manipulation of symbols	Manipulation of events
Written communication and neutrality	Personal communication and influence
Concept	Problem or opportunity

Source: Gibb (1987)

Figure 8.4   The focus of learning

of management may also focus on human issues such as ethics in an attempt to gain competitive edge. Currently there is a general increase in awareness amongst the business community and ethics are appearing more explicitly on business school programmes. The trend is towards seeing ethics as integral to management practice and not as a separate issue (Ground and Hughes 1992). This is (consciously or unconsciously) an attempt to encourage success to be seen in terms of good practice and vice versa. As others have commented, there is a need to reintroduce values into the workplace (e.g. Cormack 1991; Coulson-Thomas and Brown 1990). If, as Cooper suggests, archaeology's success is partly dependent upon the social and political context, then changes in attitude towards the importance of values and ethics may appear to be good news. Yet it presupposes that those values are known and agreed. This presents a fundamental challenge.

THE UGLY

The gap between management theory and practice in relation to TQM was illustrated with reference to the conflict between the espoused philosophies of the two organizations and the experiences of staff in the workplace. The nature of the gap extends far beyond this, however. When investigated in more depth, a similar gulf was identified within the TQM literature itself. The principles of TQM are centred around matters of human resource management, especially participation and individual commitment. These are often referred to in management as 'soft' issues, yet analysis of the existing TQM literature reveals a dominant underlying philosophy which conflicts with this 'softer' profile. There are important messages here for archaeology.

Figure 8.5 illustrates that while there is a broad range of beliefs and values underpinning approaches to TQM, variability is confined to the objective and realist end of the spectrum, much as was the case with the focus of management learning environments in Figure 8.4. This has significant consequences for the management of human resources. To put it bluntly, the management discipline is far better at dealing with 'hard', quantifiable issues than with qualitative human ones. This is a legacy of scientific management; one famous proponent being Taylor (1911). The discipline of archaeology is well acquainted with scientific influence, notably with the emergence of New Archaeology. In management, the scientific paradigm holds as much sway. Where the two cross, the effect is cumulative. Witness to this is English Heritage's publication *Management of Archaeological Projects* (1991, see Andrews and Thomas, this volume) which has already been recognized as an example of classical and scientific management (Cooper 1993 and this volume). In the field of quality management the dominance of this paradigm is particularly visible. The terms quality assurance and quality control have their roots in manufacturing, engineering and production. The notion of quantifiable, controllable processes is, thus, historically entwined with that of quality. In the Tayloristic world view, quality is something that can be measured. The implicit assumption is that if it cannot be measured it cannot be 'quality assured'. The engineering model of organization is mechanistic and this gives rise to mechanistic modes of analysis and implementation. It is not the people that are the focus here but the processes.

The appropriateness of such sterile conceptions of organization and management have been challenged in recent years by people like Drucker (1988) and Handy (1988) who promote a vision of future organizations as fluid, people-centred and dynamic; characteristics shared by the tree (Figure 8.3). They argue that the need for change is vital to business success. This chapter supports that view. The current popularity of quality management methods is evidence that organizations recognize the need to change. Nevertheless, the research indicated that the dominant classical approach was strongly reflected in both organizational design and management practice, and that these had an undesirable affect on employees. The problem is that management seems to assume change can be brought about by methodologies alone. This, in itself, is a symptom of the classical management school. The objective approach presupposes that tools and techniques can of themselves provide solutions. But organizations cannot become trees by applying volcanic principles. Cooper (1993) recognized this problem when he said that it is entirely possible to follow the procedures set out in a management guide and yet still fail to achieve the desired objectives. The delusion is another legacy of scientific management.

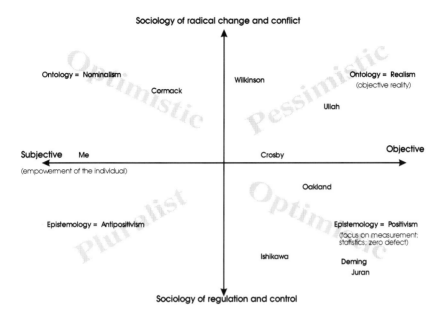

Figure 8.5   Analysis of TQM literature

Note: optimistic/pessimistic/pluralistic relates to views on effect of technology

The neglect of human resource issues, especially motivation and participation, is logical when set against the objectivist historical backdrop of management culture and teaching. Science requires that subject and object are separated and whilst this may sound like an esoteric philosophical point, it actually has influence over the way that management is put into practice. It has an influence in archaeology, too.

Reading the TQM literature suggests that some efforts have been made to 'soften up' and take better account of human resourcing issues. Even systems theory has its soft versions (e.g. Checkland and Scholes 1990). Yet these changes have been of insufficient weight to redress the balance. The resultant neglect of the soft side of TQM presents managers with a difficult task. In the absence of guidance to the contrary, human resource concerns are subsumed beneath volcanic rules, procedures and documentation. It is unsurprizing, therefore, to find a mismatch between the idea of TQM as a people-centred, participative activity and the practice of TQM as a process-oriented, impersonal management technique. The key to success (as, indeed, Crosby (1986) asserted) is people. Since the nature of people is subjective rather than objective, management styles which are biased towards the·latter are called into question. This equally applies to the discipline of archaeology. Archaeology's theoretical knowledge base more than adequately provides the means to take action. In practice archaeologists are proving themselves to be skilled in management and, in particular, to demonstrate some aspects of entrepreneurialism. Archaeology now needs to integrate these strengths.

Returning now to the 'bad news' and the gap between archaeological theory and practice, this chapter comes full circle. The gap in archaeology consists of, on the one hand, a rich and diverse theoretical and cultural knowledge base and, on the other, limited explicit incorporation of it into practice. Contrary to Cooper, this chapter argues that archaeology does not need to refer to management theory in order to bridge this gap. Archaeology is well aware of its theoretical aspects: positivism, Marxism, post-structuralism, functionalism and so on. It is not so much that archaeology is unaware of the paradigms at its disposal, but that it does not fully accept their immediate relevance to practice. This is apparent from the failure to give theory a more explicit role *vis-à-vis* graphical and statistical empirical data. The attitude towards theory is summed up by such tongue-in-cheek terms as 'armchair archaeology'. The message seems to be 'give us slides not sociology!'. Archaeology is aware of the ways in which culture may have influenced past societies, now it needs to become equally aware of the cultural factors shaping its own organization.

The relationship between the role of archaeology in society today and the mode of response which the discipline takes to the forces of change is a crucial issue. There is no one correct solution. How an archaeological 'organization' expresses itself will depend upon what it believes to be appropriate given the context within which it operates. The toughest challenge will not be in understanding the so-called 'external' environment but in understanding itself. In order to establish what is appropriate, therefore, archaeology must come to a deeper understanding of itself – what it is doing and why it is doing it (and, equally, what it is not doing and why). That means giving values a more explicit role. With reference to the tree analogy and the vision of a quality organization, it means taking less of an outsider's (etic) view and adopting more of an insider's (emic) perspective. It is also crucial to recognize that scientific (etic) modes of management are not suited to meeting the motivational needs of archaeologists (see Cooper 1993). Archaeology, then, would seem to have traits of an emic discipline. In the search for 'better' forms of management archaeology may be able to make an important contribution but only after a considerable amount of re-evaluation has been undertaken.

Probably archaeologists would not be in the subject area if they believed their work had no relevance in today's society. Each individual will hold their own views as to what constitutes relevance. This is a very important issue but it is not the problem. The problem is that each archaeological 'organization' has to convince others that archaeology deserves a meaningful place in their society. Archaeology has not had much experience of self-justification at the macro-level – i.e. as a discipline (as opposed to individual sites). Part of this self-justification involves demonstration of good management practice but archaeology should not rely upon management theory for direction here. It is clear that management today remains strongly influenced by its history. In other words, it remains firmly rooted in the scientific paradigm. The gap between management philosophy and practice discussed in this chapter supports the notion that the current dominant management paradigm is not the most appropriate route for archaeology to follow. Time and again the management discipline has failed to perform in the arena of human resource management. As the fieldwork revealed, this may be partly due to the belief that success can be achieved through the application of tools and techniques *per se*. This stems from an objectivist and etic world view, a legacy of scientific management. This chapter argues that there is a fundamental need to shift the philosophical balance from etic towards emic, and urges the archaeological discipline to consider its own position.

CONCLUSIONS

'They use statistics as a drunk uses a lamp-post – for support rather than illumination'

A comparison of archaeology and management could be like the above saying and focus on the negative aspects alone in order to fuel anxiety. If the comparison is used for illumination a rather different picture emerges. The bad news is that the management discipline cannot be relied upon to provide a positive role model. This may come as no surprise! However archaeology's cultural and theoretical knowledge base is rich and diverse. The good news is that archaeology has some management expertise of its own to offer, including entrepreneurial characteristics, which are particularly useful in an insecure and changing climate. The ugly conclusion is that in order to fully utilize these strengths, there are some fundamental issues around the role of values and their effect on practice which need to be addressed. Archaeologists as individuals and archaeology as a discipline must re-examine and make more explicit their own identity and values. They will then be in a position to make an important contribution to management and to influence its future direction.

A simple but clear statement of the required change is provided by the following Chinese proverb. Ironically, it is taken from one of the case study organizations' TQM manuals. There could be few better signposts to effective and emic management with which to end this chapter:

Tell me and I will forget
Show me and I may remember
Involve me and I will understand

REFERENCES

Brooke, C. (1992) 'Total quality management? Metaphoric plc.', in D. Winstanley and J. Woodall (eds.) *Case Studies in Personnel*, London: Institute of Personnel Management.

Burrell, G. and Morgan, G. (1979) *Sociological Paradigms and Organizational Analysis*, Aldershot: Gower.

Cassels, J. (1990) *Britain's Real Skill Shortage: and What to do about It*, London: Policy Studies Institute.

Checkland, P. and Scholes, J. (1990) *Soft Systems Methodology in Action*, Chichester: Wiley.

Collard, R. and Sivyer, G. (1990) 'Total quality', *Personnel Management* May 1990, Factsheet 29.

Cooper, M.A. (1993) 'Archaeology and management perspectives', *The Field Archaeologist* 18: 346–50.

Cormack, D. (1991) 'Excellence at work', *British Institute of Management Annual Lecture*, London: British Institute of Management.

Coulson-Thomas, C. and Brown, R. (1990) *Beyond Quality: Managing the Relationship with the Customer*, Corby: British Institute of Management.

Crosby, P.B. (1986) *Runnings Things: The Art of Making Things Happen*, New York: McGraw-Hill.

Deeks, J.S. (1975) *The Owner/Manager: Some Training Perspectives*, Furniture and Timber Industry Training Board.

Drucker, P. (1988) 'The coming of the new organization', *Harvard Business Review* January–February 1988: 45–53.

English Heritage (1991) *Management of Archaeological Projects*, London: Historic Buildings and Monuments Commission for England.

Gibb, A.A. (1987) 'Enterprise culture – its meaning and implications for education and training', *Journal of European Industrial Training* 11, 2: 3–38.

Ground, I. and Hughes, J. (1992) *Management and the Moral Point of View*, Newcastle: Applied Philosophy Trust.

Handy, C. (1988) 'Careers for the 21st century', *Long Range Planning* 21, 3: 90–7.

Hirschheim, R. and Klein, H.K. (1989) 'Four paradigms of I.S. development', *Communications of the ACM* October 1989, 32, 10: 1199–1216.

Kirby, D.A. (1992) 'Developing graduate entrepreneurs: the UK Graduate Enterprise Programme', *Entrepreneurship, Innovation and Change: An International Research Journal* 1, 2: 165–75.

Nelson, E.H. (1989) 'Marketing in 1992 and beyond', paper presented to the Royal Society of Arts, unpublished.

Rajan, A. and Fryatt, J. (1988) *Create or abdicate: the City's human resource centre for the 90s*, London: Witherby.

Taylor, F.W. (1911) *Principles of Scientific Management*, New York: Harper Row.

Ullah, P. (1991) 'The psychology of TQM', *Managing Service Quality*, 79–81.

PART III

APPLICATIONS

CHAPTER NINE

THE MONUMENTS PROTECTION PROGRAMME

Protecting what, how, and for whom?

BILL STARTIN

In England, archaeological sites which are considered to be of 'national importance' can be protected by 'scheduling'; that is, by adding the sites to the 'schedule' (i.e. list) of 'monuments' protected under the Ancient Monuments and Archaeological Areas Act 1979. Through time, the process of scheduling sites has not kept pace with the increase in knowledge about the extent of archaeological resource or with the changing perceptions of what is nationally important. Accordingly, English Heritage has embarked on a programme of work called the Monuments Protection Programme (MPP). Initially this had the limited aim of bringing this schedule up to date but its scope was soon widened in order to respond to both the limitations of the existing legislation and the complexity of the archaeological resource; the relationship between these two issues has received little formal recognition in the archaeological literature.

In a recent letter, a writer made what was perhaps a Freudian slip – he referred to the MPP as 'The *Management* Protection Programme'. In fact, as my managers will confirm, the MPP has not sought to protect them, nor necessarily to safeguard existing institutional arrangements. In practice, it has been about both asking and attempting to answer a number of questions which disturb the status quo – about opening 'cans of worms'.

Admittedly, the programme started from an established position, as the Scheduling Enhancement Programme (Inspectorate of Ancient Monuments 1984), giving a set of initials (SEP) immortalized in 'Life, the Universe and Everything' (Adams 1986: 329) as 'Somebody Else's Problem'. It was not and the name had to be changed. But the initial conception as the Scheduling Enhancement Programme was not illogical, only limited. The principal legal procedure specifically for the protection of archaeological sites was and is by 'scheduling' – adding sites to the schedule. However, a programme concerned with protecting the archaeological resource immediately faces two questions: First, can all archaeological remains be defined as 'monuments' under the terms of the Act (Section 61)? Second, are the measures introduced by scheduling appropriate under all circumstances? The answer to both these questions is 'no'.

With these thoughts in mind, the programme was broadened into the Monuments Protection Programme. This transformation was not instantaneous and there remains a strong and necessary emphasis on scheduling, but we can certainly now discuss the vision and mission of the programme in much broader terms than just scheduling, which is what this chapter seeks to do (see also English Heritage 1993: 25–31).

WHAT ARE WE TRYING TO PROTECT?

> Whereof one cannot speak, thereof one must be silent.
> (Ludwig Wittgenstein, *Tractatus Logico-Philosophicus*: 7)

The small collection of archaeological sites identified for protection under the first ancient monuments legislation in 1882 were all ancient (they were all prehistoric) and were all monumental (e.g. Stonehenge). Nowadays, the Secretary of State is content to schedule remains as unmonumental as cropmark sites and as unancient as World War II defensive installations. And change is still taking place; for scheduling purposes the term 'monument' was given and has a particular definition under the 1979 Act (Section 61) but a much broader definition of 'ancient monument' was given in the National Heritage Act 1983 (Section 33(8)): 'any structure, work, site, garden or area which in the Commission's opinion is of historic, architectural, traditional, artistic or archaeological interest'. This broader definition relates to the wider functions of English Heritage (Section 33(1)) and together these sections of the Act demanded a response more general than the SEP.

However, the descriptions under the 1979 and 1983 Acts are either too limited or too general to allow a full and focused discussion of the complexity of the archaeological resource and its management; where accepted terms are lacking, we risk having to be silent. Accordingly, an early initiative within the MPP was an attempt to define 'urban areas' and 'relict landscapes' as separate topic areas from 'single monuments' (Darvill *et al.* 1987). Also underlying this initiative was a deliberate intention to break the oversimple correlation made between nationally important remains, scheduled monuments, and management zones, however defined. This connection was obviously a fiction in the context of the major historic towns and scheduling legislation had never been developed with the aim of protecting extensive landscapes.

We are, of course, familiar with discussing and recording the complexity of the archaeological resource at micro-level. Terms like artefact, context and feature are commonplace. We are also comfortable with creating sites and monuments records (SMRs) based on recognized classes of single monument (e.g. round barrows, Roman forts, castles, and so on). But, how good have we been at recording more complex monuments, such as the large monastic sites where individual components may need to be identified in their own right and whose areal extent (e.g. precinct and associated water-control systems) is not defined by the obvious core buildings? Extensive field systems also present problems. What about the poorly defined types of archaeological remains (e.g. artefact scatters and unclassified sites discovered through aerial photography)? And what about the macro-level? Not even such well-recognized entities as round-barrow cemeteries have been systematically recorded. Without attempting to be definitive, we can identify patterning in the landscape in the form of clusters of monuments, complexes (as with many industrial sites), urban areas, relict cultural landscapes, and historic landscapes. In the terminology given here, the study of relict cultural landscapes looks at the patterning in the archaeological data (Darvill 1991) whilst the term 'historic landscapes' has developed a more general meaning (Fairclough 1991).

The above paragraph certainly exposes a good range of 'cans of worms', albeit not for the first time and even without mentioning poorly surveyed areas, the relatively neglected topic area of underwater archaeology, and the need for appropriate strategies for buried and/or drowned landscapes in general (e.g. the Fenlands or the Somerset Levels). The paragraph also invites questions about matters which are completely outside of the MPP, such as the field survey priorities of the Royal Commissions, the nature and cover of the National Monuments Record and the county SMRs (Startin 1991a), the accessibility of data from aerial photography, and the limited vocabulary, debate and strategies in the archaeological community at large. Within English Heritage, the paragraph underlines the problems we have experienced in defining the scope of the MPP (just how much can we try to tackle at one time?), in quantifying the work, in estimating the resources required, in preparing and presenting achievable targets and timetables, and in guessing the consequent increase in the work-load of our casework teams. However constrained, a project like the MPP is a vehicle of change, some of it uncomfortable.

The early work of the MPP, following the first staff appointments late in 1986, has been summarized elsewhere (English Heritage 1991, 6–7, 30, 46–9). Consideration of the above issues has now led to the work being broadly divided under five topic headings: the known and recorded resource; sites discovered through aerial photography; industrial remains; urban areas; landscapes. These last three headings are not restricted to the MPP, especially with respect to the overlap with the built environment. In addition, there are recognized 'problem areas', such as the inadequate recorded data on occupied buildings of archaeological importance or the poor understanding of artefact scatter sites, although the role of the MPP may be more in defining the problems than in finding solutions (English Heritage 1991, 51).

Given the range of issues to be tackled, work on any one issue within the MPP has taken time to bear fruits and little has yet received formal publication. The work on recognized single monument classes is fairly well known, at least to county archaeological staff, with syntheses of current knowledge in the form of monument class descriptions, the development of evaluation procedures (Darvill 1988) and the preparation of scheduling recommendations. There still appears to be a widespread naivety about the use of the scoring system as part of 'system-aided' professional judgement (an issue covered in a separate paper (Startin 1993a)), but limited dispute about which sites are identified as being of national importance.

Work on the further understanding of sites discovered through aerial photography is being taken forward by RCHME (Edis *et al.* 1989); 1993/4 should see significant progress in the form of reports on the Yorkshire Dales and the Thames Valley. The results from these areas will also be studied in landscape terms, as will the information being gathered about industrial remains. MPP work on the metal-mining industries is becoming better known with the recent circulation of consultation documents on the lead-mining and tin industries (Cranstone and Stocker forthcoming). Although the work on these topic areas may appear superficially different from that on single monuments, the same procedural sequence is adopted: a cycle of identification, recording, synthesis and classification (Startin 1991a) followed by evaluation and management action.

Work on urban areas has so far concentrated on the earlier part of this procedural sequence (Darvill 1992), particularly in asking the question, 'what is an urban area?' Accustomed as we are to studying the major historic towns with their attributes of size, complexity, longevity of occupation and depth of deposits, it is important to recognize also the smaller towns which possess these attributes to no greater degree than, say, Iron Age hillforts, normally treated as 'single monuments'. The distinguishing factor in our reaction to urban areas is, in practice, that the development pressure on this part of the resource is so great that we are forced to harder-edged decisions concerning component areas rather than the more general conservation decisions required for greenfield sites (Startin 1993a), such as the Roman town of Silchester. Accordingly, initial MPP work has concentrated on dividing urban areas both 'vertically', into types (urban area forms), and 'horizontally', into component areas and monuments. Evaluation will involve an accumulated understanding of the values of the component parts (Startin 1993a).

Work on landscapes is at an even earlier stage (Darvill 1991; Darvill *et al.* 1993) and no attempt has yet been made to define evaluation procedures; the MPP manual covering landscapes has recently been circulated

to county archaeological staff and others. At this stage we are still attempting to identify different sorts of patterning; although we are hardly the first
to make an attempt at this sort of work (Fleming 1971; Renfrew 1973), it
has not before been carried forward systematically to support preservation
policies. Apart from patterning in the data, we are also beginning to
undertake work on the distribution of recognized monument types and
the relationship of distribution and survival to geographical and topographical zones.

At the other end of the scale, consideration has also been given to the
understanding of lithic scatter sites (Schofield 1994). The salient point is
that the majority of lithic scatter sites do not of themselves allow an interpretation of the archaeological sites of which they may only be a part; our
understanding is generally insufficient to allow the identification of sites
which should be preserved *in situ*.

This account of the development and progress of the MPP is not theoretical in itself but does provide a practical expression of three underlying
principles:

1   If we are to manage the resource we must first seek to understand what
   we are trying to manage; since there is much that we do not understand, there is a continuing cycle of identification, recording, analysis
   and synthesis.
2   Understanding involves developing an adequate vocabulary (classification) in order that informed discussion can take place.
3   The management strategy for what we do not understand involves
   further study – it is not possible to move directly to specific and effective conservation action.

HOW DO WE PROTECT?

> And diff'ring judgements serve but to declare
> That truth lies somewhere, if we knew but where.
> (William Cowper, 'Hope', 1.423)

Given the complexity of the archaeological resource, it is not surprising to
find that scheduling is not the only solution. This has long been recognized for urban areas and a separate designation was included in the 1979
Act – Areas of Archaeological Importance (AAI). But this was not a conservation measure, simply a mechanism to ensure access for recording
should a site within an AAI be developed, and its intent has now largely
been replaced by the advice given in *Planning Policy Guidance: Archaeology
and Planning* (PPG 16) (Department of the Environment 1990a).

In reality, it is important to recognize that scheduling is only one option
within and one part of what can be termed the management cycle (English
Heritage 1991, 34; Startin 1993b). To assume that scheduling ensures

preservation is to confuse the intent of the legislation with its effect, which is actually to apply scheduled monument consent procedures. In short, to adopt a statement used by Neil Holbrook in a different context, it acts to identify a monument as 'a thing of the past for the foreseeable future'; the foreseeable future may be only as far as the next application for scheduled monument consent.

For archaeological remains which are sufficiently well understood, the choice of management strategy can vary from control via ownership through statutory protection to non-statutory designation, grant aid and advice. We are familiar with terms such as guardianship, scheduled monument, listed building, conservation area, historic garden, World Heritage Site, battlefield and historic landscape (Department of the Environment 1990b). Archaeological remains are also a material consideration within planning legislation (Planning Policy Guidance 16) and can be protected under more general initiatives, such as within Environmentally Sensitive Areas.

For archaeological remains which are not well understood (e.g. lithic scatter sites), further study, including research excavation, will be required before other management strategies can be clearly identified. For all remains, development may provide the opportunity for further research and this is just as much a management strategy as preservation.

Clearly, the archaeological resource is complex and there is a wide range of management options. But to what extent have these options been discussed within the archaeological community? Why is it still a surprise to some practitioners to find that scheduling is difficult to apply to artefact scatters, underwater sites, urban areas, and landscapes? Obviously, there has been too little informed debate.

For single monuments in the rural context scheduling continues as generally the most appropriate designation to identify and protect archaeological sites of national importance. To talk of the 1979 Act as 'a thinly modernized version of Victorian thinking' (Council for British Archaeology 1993, section 3.2.3) is both to deny the development of the legislation over the last century and to beg the question of what should take its place. In contrast to the position that scheduling should become all-encompassing, it can be argued that scheduling is not the most appropriate means of managing the built environment or landscapes.

Following PPG 16, the picture with respect to urban areas is reasonably clear (Startin 1991b). The relatively restricted use proposed for scheduling recognizes that the planning system provides largely the better mechanism for managing change within the built environment, providing that the archaeological and historical dimensions are properly taken into account. This is an important caveat; it explains the prominence given to the initiative on historic towns in *Managing England's Heritage* (English Heritage 1992a) where it is recognized that these towns will require databases, archaeological assessments, and explicit management strategies if protection through planning is to be successful (English Heritage 1992b; Stocker 1993). Similar, albeit less intensive work will be required for smaller towns and villages.

Policy with respect to landscapes is still developing but current thinking within English Heritage is that whilst scheduling is appropriate to the protection of individual sites or closely related groups of remains, the controls it introduces are not suited to the management of extensive areas. Given this restriction, the topic area provides an example of the process by which appropriate legislation may eventually appear, the first step being to compile a database, perhaps partly in the form of historic landscape registers (Fairclough 1991), which will allow an assessment of the implications of any measures proposed and, in any case, will provide advice to planning authorities in the meantime.

As with the first section of this chapter, this description of how we protect is not theoretical in itself but is a practical expression of an underlying principle: the management strategy chosen will reflect the nature of the resource identified and the pressures which are bearing on it. This is not, however, to deny the need to develop the concept of 'sustainable development' (Brundtland 1987) with respect to the archaeological resource (Countryside Commission *et al.* 1993); for some as yet unidentified part of the resource, preservation must be argued as the only 'sustainable' strategy (Startin 1993b).

With all the above points in mind, the overall mission of the MPP can be described as follows:

1 To review and evaluate existing information so that those archaeological remains which are of national importance can be identified.
2 To make recommendations to the Secretary of State that those remains identified as being of national importance should be legally protected through scheduling, or to identify that some alternative appropriate action should be undertaken.
3 To collate information more generally on the condition of remains of national importance so that the resource requirements for future preservation and the priorities for action can be identified.
4 To utilize the assessment of the archaeological data to frame an improved response to the problems of inadequate interpretation and knowledge.
5 To examine the existing legislative framework in order to make recommendations to Government for the better protection of the resource.

WHO IS IT FOR?

This chapter is not intended to discuss the justification for the preservation of archaeological remains; the reasons why we value such remains have been discussed elsewhere (Darvill 1993; Startin 1993a). However, one thing must be clearly understood – our preservation policies derive from the clear belief that the remains of our past belong to the future, not just the present day. Whilst this does not, indeed must not deny the rights of the present generation (Startin 1993b), we must also recognize that excavation is destructive and the accumulation of archaeological understanding is slow. Whilst seeking to act for the future may appear presumptuous, it is difficult to see that we can avoid the responsibility.

CONCLUSIONS

This chapter has not attempted a full exposition of the philosophies and vision behind the MPP (see also Startin 1993a; 1993b). It has, however, set out to provide an account of the range of work required by such a programme and to dispel any impression that it is simply a reflection of a process-based bureaucracy and that its concentration is only on the visible and easily retrievable (see also English Heritage 1993: 25–31). Whilst its outcome will undoubtedly mirror the preoccupations of its parent institution, it is to be hoped that the complexities raised by attempting the programme will provide a challenge and opportunity which will be accepted by the archaeological community at large. To manage the archaeological resource we must be clear what the resource is, what management means, and, perhaps most importantly, how the two interact.

REFERENCES

Adams, D. (1986) *The Hitchhiker's Guide to the Galaxy: A Trilogy in Four Parts*, London: Heinemann.

Brundtland, G.H. (1987) *Our Common Future*, Oxford: Oxford University Press.

Council for British Archaeology (1993) *The Past in Tomorrow's Landscape*, York: Council for British Archaeology.

Countryside Commission, English Heritage and English Nature (1993) *Conservation Issues in Strategic Plans*, Cheltenham: Countryside Commission.

Cranstone, D. and Stocker, D. (forthcoming) 'Industrial archaeology and the Monuments Protection Programme in England', in M. Palmer and P. Neaverson (eds) *Managing the Industrial Heritage*, Leicester: Leicester University Press.

Darvill, T. (1988) *Monuments Protection Programme: Monument Evaluation Manual, Parts I and II*, London: English Heritage.

Darvill, T. (1991) *Monuments Protection Programme: Monument Evaluation Manual, Part IV*, London: English Heritage.

Darvill, T. (1992) *Monuments Protection Programme: Monument Evaluation Manual, Part III*, London: English Heritage.

Darvill, T. (1993) 'Valuing Britain's archaeological resource', Professor of Archaeology and Property Management Inaugural Lecture, Bournemouth University, July 1993.

Darvill, T., Gerrard, C.and Startin, B.(1993) 'Identifying and protecting historic landscapes', *Antiquity* 67: 563–74.

Darvill, T., Startin, B. and Saunders, A. (1987) 'A question of national importance: approaches to the evaluation of ancient monuments for the Monuments Protection Programme in England', *Antiquity* 61: 393–408.

Department of the Environment (1990a) *Planning Policy Guidance: Archaeology and Planning*, PPG 16, London: HMSO.

Department of the Environment (1990b) *This Common Inheritance*, London: HMSO.

Edis, J., Macleod, D. and Bewley, R. (1989) 'An archaeologist's guide to classification of cropmarks and soilmarks', *Antiquity* 63: 112–26.

English Heritage (1991) *Exploring Our Past: Strategies for the Archaeology of England*, London: Historic Buildings and Monuments Commission for England.

English Heritage (1992a) *Managing England's Heritage: Setting our Priorities for the 1990s*, London: Historic Buildings and Monuments Commission for England.

English Heritage (1992b) *Managing the Urban Archaeological Resource*, London: Historic Buildings and Monuments Commission for England.

English Heritage (1993) *Archaeological Review 1992–93*, London: Historic Buildings and Monuments Commission for England.

Fairclough, G. (1991) 'Historic landscapes', *Conservation Bulletin* 14: 4–5.

Fleming, A. (1971) 'Territorial patterns in Bronze Age Wessex', *Papers of the Prehistoric Society* 37: 138–66.

Inspectorate of Ancient Monuments (1984) *England's Archaeological Resource: A Rapid Quantification of the National Archaeological Resource and a Comparison with the Schedule of Ancient Monuments*, London: Historic Buildings and Monuments Commission for England.

Renfrew, C. (1973) 'Monuments, mobilization, and social organization in Neolithic Wessex', in C. Renfrew (ed.) *Explanation of Culture Change*, London: Duckworth, 539–58.

Schofield, A.J. (1994) 'Looking back with regret; looking forward with optimism: making more of surface lithic scatters', in N. Ashton and A. David (eds) *Stories in Stone,* London: Lithic Studies Society, Occasional Paper No. 4, 90–8.

Startin, B. (1991a) 'The Monuments Protection Programme: archaeological records', in C.U. Larsen (ed.) *Sites and Monuments: National Archaeological Records*, Copenhagen: The National Museum of Denmark, 201–6.

Startin, B. (1991b) 'Protecting the archaeology of our historic towns', *Conservation Bulletin*, 13: 14–15.

Startin, B. (1993a) 'Assessment of field remains', in J. Hunter and I. Ralston (eds) *Archaeological Resource Management in the UK*, Stroud: Alan Sutton Publishing, 184–96.

Startin, B. (1993b) 'Preservation and the academically viable sample', *Antiquity* 67: 421–6.

Stocker, D. (1993) 'Introduction' in P. Lowther *et al.* 'The City of Durham: an archaeological survey', *Durham Archaeological Journal*, 9: 28–31.

CHAPTER TEN

SQUARE PEGS IN ROUND HOLES

Problems of managing the Palaeolithic heritage

FRANCIS WENBAN-SMITH

The aim of this paper is to try to contribute, as a Palaeolithic archaeologist, to the debate on the management of the Palaeolithic archaeological heritage. Various problems in this area are already recognized by archaeological heritage managers (Startin, this volume; English Heritage 1991: 34–5; Shaw 1988; Gamble 1992), who rely on an input from period specialists for their resolution. These problems are particularly in the areas of (a) identifying and characterizing the Palaeolithic archaeological heritage, (b) assessing the relative value of its constituent parts, and (c) developing appropriate strategies for controlling and mitigating the impact of works which affect the Palaeolithic archaeological heritage.

This chapter has four parts. In the first part, the current framework under which the archaeological heritage as a whole is managed is briefly reviewed. In the second part, the ways in which this framework serves, and fails to serve, the Palaeolithic archaeological heritage are considered. In the third part some of the problems constraining the management of the Paleaeolithic heritage are highlighted. In the fourth part a model is proposed for addressing two of the fundamental problems in the management of the Palaeolithic archaeological heritage – characterizing and assessing the basic archaeological resource. Identification of an 'important Palaeolithic heritage' does not solve the problems of effective protection and mitigation. While this chapter specifies some current weaknesses of protection and mitigation with respect to the Palaeolithic heritage, it does not attempt to prescribe improvements. Rather, it focuses on what constitutes 'important Palaeolithic heritage' as the essential basis upon which they may be pursued.

GENERAL HERITAGE MANAGEMENT

The present-day landscape of Britain is a vast archaeological resource. This landscape contains the evidence of the history of human occupation in Britain and also of the environmental and climatic context within which this occupation has taken place. Knowledge about, and the material evidence of, this past is acknowledged as an important cultural resource in the present day, serving a variety of spiritual, political, educational and economic roles. The parts of this past which are considered by society as of value are widely labelled 'heritage'. There are problems with this term, which has developed some connotations in the sense of being not only an officially propogated historical myth, but also an economically valuable commodity (see Bower, this volume). Furthermore, the concept of heritage combines both the material evidence of the past and the intellectual framework within which it is presented and understood. However, in this paper use of the term 'archaeological heritage' is taken to mean the 'material archaeological resource', i.e. actual deposits and features occurring in the landscape which are relevant to the understanding of past human behaviour. As will be made clear in the rest of this chapter, the concept of archaeological heritage should include features caused directly by human agency, deposits containing humanly worked artefacts, and also archaeologically sterile deposits which contain environmental and chronological information essential to the understanding and investigation of past human behaviour. This applies for all periods of the past, but is particularly important for the investigation of the Palaeolithic, where the range of humanly made archaeological features is minimal or non-existent.

The archaeological heritage is managed in what is considered to be the present and future public interest. Given the diversity of the public constituency, this involves recognizing and resolving the various conflicts of interest over the archaeological heritage which exist between different groups of the public, such as academics, commercial companies, development planners, and political or social interest-groups. In the UK these conflicts of interest are resolved through a framework of heritage management, based on statutes (notably the Ancient Monuments and Archaeological Areas Act 1979, as amended by the National Heritage Act 1983) and on development-control measures (Department of the Environment 1990), and administered through a combination of central government-funded organizations and local authorities.

In England, the archaeological heritage is managed at both a national level by English Heritage, and at a local authority level through the planning-control mechanisms of local planning authorities (Hunter *et al.* 1993). These bodies carry out numerous functions related to the management of the archaeological heritage. English Heritage is concerned with all aspects of the development of a national heritage, making strategic decisions to produce a heritage which is protected, preserved, researched,

and promoted for the present and future enjoyment of society as a whole
(Wainwright 1989, 1991). One aspect of this process is the maintenance
of a list or 'schedule' of nationally important monuments for which damaging activities are controlled. In addition to their responsibilities towards
remains of national importance (Department of the Environment 1990),
local authorities are concerned with ensuring that the archaeological heritage of more regional and local significance is protected from loss where
possible and, where not, that appropriate mitigation steps are taken, such
as excavation, recording and/or partial preservation.

A fundamental concern of the heritage-management process, underpinning subsequent actions, is the ascription of importance, or value, to
parts of the archaeological heritage. The value of a particular archaeological resource is currently assessed with reference to two main factors:
first, its significance within the framework of an established research
agenda and methodology for investigating the past; second, its representativeness of the archaeological heritage as a whole. This latter angle is of
importance because of the changing research techniques by which the past
is investigated and the changing political and social context within which
it is interpreted. These factors mean that the 'significant heritage' is continuously changing. Preserving a representative sample of the material
archaeological heritage of all recognized periods serves two purposes: first,
it hedges against future shifts of ideological paradigm by preserving for
future society a diverse archaeological resource from which significant heritage can be selected; second, it insures archaeological knowledge against
the development of techniques of research able to make use of data of no
apparent value in the present day. English Heritage has, over the last ten
years, set about: (a) establishing a set of academic objectives for the study
of different periods of the past, including the Palaeolithic (English Heritage
1991: 34–43), (b) producing an up-to-date record of the basic archaeological resource by investing in Sites and Monuments Record (SMR)
staff, and (c) formalizing a methodology for the characterization and
discrimination of this resource, as a basis for securing the preservation of
a nationally representative sample. This is the Monuments Protection
Programme (MPP), as described in Darvill et al. (1987), by English
Heritage (1991: 46–7) and by Startin (this volume).

Figure 10.1 shows a simplified summary of the basic heritage management process in the UK. The basis for an effective management of the
archaeological heritage is having a clear idea of what it actually is, and how
to recognize it. Then it can be inventoried and characterized, as a prelude
to assessing the value of its different parts. The value of a part of the
archaeological heritage is currently assessed by English Heritage on the
basis of eight non–statutory criteria established in 1983: survival/con-
dition; period; rarity; fragility/vulnerability; diversity; documentation;
group value; potential (Wainwright 1989). These criteria relate mainly
to representativeness, although some of them relate to significance within

1 Identification/Recognition
2 Inventory/Categorization
3 Discrimination/Assessment
4 Action:
        (i)   Protection
        (ii) Preservation
        (iii) Mitigation
        (iv) Promotion
        (v)   Research
5 Review

Figure 10.1 The simplified heritage-management process

an established research framework. It is worth noting that although these criteria pay less direct attention to research significance, English Heritage has defined key research objectives (English Heritage 1991: 34–43), which makes it likely that research significance within the terms of these objectives should also be a factor in attributing value.

Having identified a part of the archaeological heritage as being of national importance, appropriate action can be taken. This can involve the following:

1 legal protection from damage or disturbance, including scheduling;
2 maintenance arrangements to ensure that natural decay does not destroy the archaeological resource;
3 mitigation arrangements, such as archaeological fieldwork in advance of destruction;
4 dissemination and promotion, making people aware of what particular parts of the archaeological heritage tell us about the past;
5 research to investigate particular periods or questions, even when a part of the archaeological heritage is not under threat.

The archaeological resource can also be protected through the planning process so that in cases where disturbance or destruction is unavoidable, appropriate steps are taken to mitigate the loss of archaeological knowledge. Finally, it is necessary to continuously review the value-judgements made and the actions taken, and to consider whether they have been satisfactory or require modification.

THE PALAEOLITHIC HERITAGE

While the Palaeolithic archaeological heritage needs to be managed within this framework, the details of how this framework is applied need to be different. It can be argued that the established practices by which the archaeological heritage is identified, characterized, evaluated for significance, and protected (involving both legislation and also strategies for mitigation) are a series of round holes into which the square pegs of the Palaeolithic archaeological heritage cannot be hammered.

There are specific problems in the areas of:

1   recognition and inventory – identification of what constitutes the basic Palaeolithic archaeological resource, and then inventorying and characterizing it;
2   discrimination – assessing the significance of different parts of the Palaeolithic archaeological resource;
3   statutory protection – legislation which provides the foundation of archaeological heritage management by providing a legal basis for influencing development proposals and commissioning mitigating work;
4   mitigation strategies – selecting portions of a threatened archaeological resource for preservation, adopting appropriate research methodology in advance of loss.

Recognition and inventory

Figure 10.2 represents the areas in which the square peg of the Palaeolithic heritage does, and does not, fit into the round hole of the established general framework. Inside the round hole, and overlapping with the centre of the square peg, is the standard view of what constitutes the archaeological heritage, and how it is recognized and inventoried. There is a focus upon its humanly made, or humanly modified, nature. Because the bulk of the archaeological heritage post-dates the end of the last ice age, it is generally found close to the surface of the present-day landscape, leading to its relatively easy identification. These factors combine for the archaeological heritage to be conceived as an aggregation of 'Sites and Monuments' as reflected in the terminology of the heritage management sector, which maintains Sites and Monuments Records (SMRs) as the basic tool for knowing where archaeological resources survive. Recent programmes of inventory and characterization, such as the Monuments Protection Programme (MPP), have been based almost entirely on existing records of sites and monuments, rather than primary field surveys.

This framework accommodates the needs of the Palaeolithic heritage to a certain extent. Find-spots of many Palaeolithic artefacts were collated by Roe (1968) and are included in county SMRs. In addition, the Southern Rivers Project (SRP) has set about recognizing and characterizing the artefactual content of the Pleistocene deposits of the southern river valleys (Wymer 1991; Gamble 1992). However, despite the welcome appearance of the SRP, some problems remain. Highlighted in Figure 10.2, on the outside of the hole, are the parts of the Palaeolithic archaeological heritage

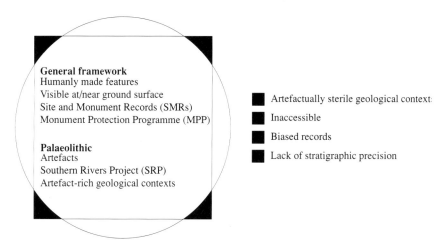

General framework
Humanly made features
Visible at/near ground surface
Site and Monument Records (SMRs)
Monument Protection Programme (MPP)

Palaeolithic
Artefacts
Southern Rivers Project (SRP)
Artefact-rich geological contexts

■ Artefactually sterile geological context

■ Inaccessible

■ Biased records

■ Lack of stratigraphic precision

Figure 10.2   Recognition and inventory

which do not fit. The main point which has to be recognized is that the Palaeolithic archaeological resource consists of natural Pleistocene deposits, some containing humanly modified artefacts and others not. The investigation and understanding of the Palaeolithic period depends, more than for other periods, on the analysis of evidence not caused by human activity. Artefactually sterile geological deposits can be investigated from a number of different angles (absolute dating of sediments, lithological and geological analysis, floral remains, faunal remains, among others) to provide the fundamental chrono-stratigraphic, climatic, and environmental framework of the Palaeolithic. The artefactual evidence of human behaviour needs to be placed within this framework if it is to be fully understood, and if we are to provide a full picture of the changing behaviour and cultural development through the Palaeolithic, which is one of the goals stated for Palaeolithic research by English Heritage (1991: 34–5).

Having recognized the broad base of what constitutes the Palaeolithic archaeological heritage, there are a number of practical problems associated with carrying out an inventory of it:

1   Inaccessibility – the Pleistocene deposits which constitute the Palaeolithic archaeological heritage are relatively inaccessible, having been buried and distorted over 500,000 years. Therefore they cannot usually be characterized by superficial observation. Auguring and the examination of sections are required to identify the sequences within Pleistocene deposits, and even these often only give a patchy idea of the full range of deposits in a Pleistocene unit.

2   Biased records – the record-based inventory process is affected by biases of discovery. The inaccessibility of Pleistocene deposits, or of artefact-

bearing contexts within Pleistocene deposits, has made the discovery of artefacts dependent upon there being both commercial quarrying and knowledgable collectors operating in the same time and place. Particular quarries in the Lower Thames area, such as Barnfield Pit and Baker's Hole, have achieved their current status as a result of these factors. The intensity of commercial quarrying which took place on the banks of the Lower Thames in the late nineteenth and early twentieth centuries was due to the combination of valuable mineral deposits with easy water-access. Equally significant deposits probably exist, or existed, elsewhere in the Lower Thames area but have not been exposed, or did not happen to be recognized by alert local collectors. A second significant bias affecting the existing records of the Palaeolithic heritage is that a significant part of that heritage is, and has always been, excluded *a priori*. As argued above the Palaeolithic archaeological heritage includes artefactually sterile deposits. Therefore a record-based procedure for inventorying the archaeological heritage (such as the SRP) produces not only a Palaeolithic heritage biased by factors of recovery, but also a Palaeolithic heritage missing a major part.

3   Lack of stratigraphic precision – the records of Palaeolithic finds often lack the stratigraphic or locational detail which would allow us to pinpoint a particular geological context within a Pleistocene sequence as being the source of an artefact or assemblage.

Discrimination

Figure 10.3 summarizes the situation with regard to identifying the significant Palaeolithic heritage. In the hole are summarized the basic criteria

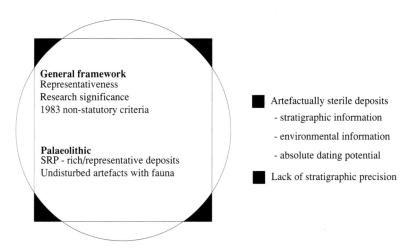

Figure 10.3   Discrimination

underlying the discrimination of the valuable archaeological heritage in general. These are representativeness and research significance, with the assessment based upon the eight non-statutory criteria established in 1983. This framework covers the Palaeolithic heritage to a certain extent. The SRP will provide a basis for identifying the variety of artefact-bearing Pleistocene deposits and hence identifying both the richest ones and also a representative sample. Also, undisturbed artefacts preserved in association with biological remains are specifically recognized by English Heritage as being of research significance.

However, on the outside of the hole are criteria for identifying significant parts of the Palaeolithic heritage which are excluded from the standard discrimination procedure:

1 the potential of artefactually sterile deposits for contributing to the chronological and environmental framework of the Pleistocene (biological remains, absolute dating potential, stratigraphical significance);
2 the potential significance of disturbed assemblages of artefacts for investigating behavioural trends over longer periods of time than the minute portions represented by assemblages of undisturbed lithic artefacts. Furthermore, there are various grades of disturbance between totally undisturbed (such as Boxgrove Unit 4b – Roberts 1986) and highly disturbed (such as the Lower Gravels at Swanscombe – Conway and Waechter 1977). This diversity in the Palaeolithic archaeological record makes it a rich academic resource which could be used to answer questions at a variety of chronological and spatial scales. The potential of both undisturbed and also disturbed assemblages for investigating the Palaeolithic should be recognized. Even if academics have not yet developed means of using the disturbed Palaeolithic resource, it should not be destroyed as the bulk of the Palaeolithic artefactual resource is disturbed, and hence we would be constraining future researchers by writing off a large proportion of the Palaeolithic heritage.

Statutory protection

Figure 10.4 summarizes the statutory base of heritage management, and how this serves the Palaeolithic heritage. In the hole is the legislation by which the archaeological heritage is protected, and also the details of how the archaeological heritage is defined in the protective legislation. The main act is the Ancient Monuments and Archaeological Areas Act (1979), as amended by the National Heritage Act (1983). This legislation clearly defines the archaeological heritage as being humanly modified monuments and sites, including caves. At the discretion of the appropriate Secretary of State (currently that for National Heritage), and under the advice of English Heritage, nationally important buildings, structures, works and the sites of such buildings, structures and works (s.61(7)) can be scheduled, permitting the control of activities which would otherwise cause damage (s.2(2), s.2(3)).

With respect to the Palaeolithic heritage, this legislation specifically includes cave-sites, which were at the forefront of the general consciousness of prehistoric research in the late nineteenth century when early legislation was enacted, but no other part of it. All other Palaeolithic sites are not covered by the definition of 'monument' so they fall outside the hole, and are excluded from formal legal protection on archaeological grounds. The excluded Palaeolithic archaeological heritage includes natural geological deposits both with and without artefacts, and regardless of their stratigraphic, dating, or biological evidence. Even undisturbed artefacts associated with biological remains, officially recognized by English Heritage as being of central significance in the study of the Palaeolithic, cannot be scheduled as an ancient monument and hence statutorily protected. While scheduling is not the only approach to preventing damage to archaeological sites it still plays a central role. Scheduling also establishes unambiguously the national importance of the site for development control purposes, and it provides that people who carry out unauthorised activities can be prosecuted as criminals.

Some Pleistocene deposits containing Palaeolithic artefacts are statutorily protected as Sites of Special Scientific Interest (SSSI). However, these designations are generated through nature conservation legislation, and administered by nature conservation agencies. They are designated by reason of their flora, fauna, geological or physiographical features (Countryside Act 1968 s. 15(1), Wildlife and Countryside Act 1981 s. 28(1)); they are not intended to protect the archaeological heritage.

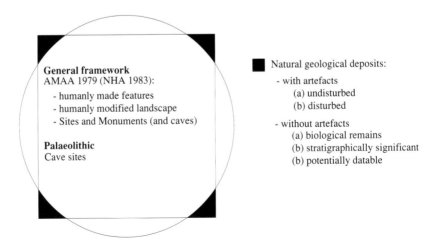

General framework
AMAA 1979 (NHA 1983):

- humanly made features
- humanly modified landscape
- Sites and Monuments (and caves)

Palaeolithic
Cave sites

Natural geological deposits:

- with artefacts
  (a) undisturbed
  (b) disturbed

- without artefacts
  (a) biological remains
  (b) stratigraphically significant
  (b) potentially datable

Figure 10.4 Statutory protection

Geological SSSIs are identified on the basis of their being important exposures through a sequence of deposits, without consideration of any Palaeolithic archaeological factors. Many sites of Palaeolithic significance (both with and without artefacts) are not recognized as SSSIs. For sites which do not achieve SSSI designation (requiring national or international significance) there is no formal safety net in the local planning process for sites of more regional significance equivalent to the protection offered by PPG 16 for standard archaeological remains.

In England, responsibility for designating and administrating SSSIs rests with the Nature Conservancy Council for England (known as English Nature). Its statutory functions relate to nature conservation, meaning the conservation of flora, fauna or geological or physiographical features (Environmental Protection Act 1990 s. 131(6)). Consequently the task of inventorying and protecting Pleistocene deposits with respect to their Palaeolithic archaeological significance is beyond English Nature's remit. In the absence of legislation to amend its statutory functions, English Nature cannot be presumed, expected or obliged to play a direct role in protecting the archaeological heritage, despite its incidental role in protecting sites in some cases.

Mitigation strategies

Figure 10.5 summarizes the framework of mitigation mechanisms in place to counteract threats to the general archaeological resource, and the ways in which these serve the Palaeolithic heritage. For a scheduled area, the Secretary of State must authorize any work which affects the site, and the fact that it has been scheduled, indicating national importance, may discourage the submission of planning applications. However, as discussed above the great majority of the Palaeolithic heritage cannot be protected by scheduling, therefore it must be protected by other mechanisms.

In the hole are the procedures by which the loss of the locally and regionally important archaeological heritage is mitigated. These are increasingly carried out under PPG 16 as a part of the planning process. This means that archaelogical input can happen at a sufficiently early stage in the development process to influence the location and extent of archaeological loss. The application of mitigating strategies under PPG 16 is based upon information stored in the SMR, and controlled by county or district archaeological staff. This mechanism can work for the Palaeolithic, provided that significant deposits are specified in the SMR and that county or district archaeological staff have access to appropriate expertise in Quaternary research. Certain find-spots of artefacts are recorded in the SMR, although not always with high precision, and the SRP should lead to the identification of certain Pleistocene deposits as requiring protection, or mitigation in advance of loss.

However, the problems with relation to the Palaeolithic heritage are,

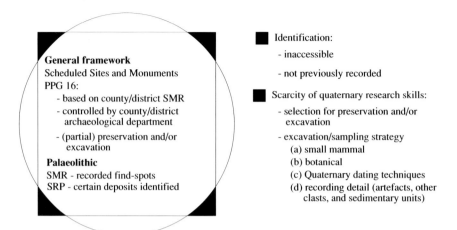

Figure 10.5 Mitigation strategies

once more, recognizing it is present in the first place, and second, knowing what to do with it. This involves (a) deciding which bits should be preserved and/or excavated, and (b) knowing how to research the bits which are excavated. This in turn involves knowing protocols for: small–mammal recovery, botanical recovery, Quaternary dating techniques (which require appropriate treatment of datable items such as molluscs, large fossil teeth, and sediments; and also appropriate background readings – see Smart and Frances 1991) and recording detail (which attributes of lithic artefacts, sedimentary units, and other clasts should be recorded). These skills are not widely present in local authority offices or in contracting units which have the main expertise in dealing with the more frequently met archaeological remains of later periods. These problems might be solved most effectively by the creation of a Quaternary research service with specialists available to provide relevant advice and to carry out fieldwork.

PROBLEMS AND PRIORITIES

The central point of this paper is that the Palaeolithic heritage must be recognized as including artefactually sterile geological deposits. These are fundamentally important for the investigation of human behaviour in, and through, the Palaeolithic period. Once this central point has been accepted, there are a number of practical problems in the management of the Palaeolithic resource which need to be faced. Two fundamental problems which need to be recognized are (a) that the basic inventory has not been carried out to establish the range and amount of the Palaeolithic heritage remaining in England, and (b) that there need to be some agreed criteria for identifying its most significant parts. These criteria need to be formulated within the context of a defined set of priorities for Palaeolithic research and the evidence necessary to achieve them. Obviously a total concensus is unlikely in view of the diversity of current thinking on how to study the Palaeolithic and on what parts of it are interesting or important (e.g. amongst many others: Roe 1981: 8; Collcutt 1986; Gamble 1987; Roebroeks *et al.* 1988; Wenban-Smith 1990; Kuhn 1991; Wynn 1991; Sinclair 1992).

However there is common ground within this diversity. Although cultural remains themselves (artefacts and humanly modified faunal remains) can be analysed and interpreted in a variety of ways, the environmental and chronological framework of this cultural evidence is universally recognized as vital to its understanding. First, the absolute age of our earliest ancestors, information on the interglacial and glacial climates in which they survived, and information on the megafauna with which they were contemporary, are topics of proven general interest. Second, environmental and chronostratigraphic information plays a central role in the application of ecological approaches to Palaeolithic research. Such approaches (e.g. Gamble 1987) often make little use of artefacts, except as signifiers of hominid presence, and are not concerned with whether lithic artefacts have been disturbed or not, except insofar as this complicates their association with a particular climatic regime and consequent floral and faunal environment. Such approaches operate at gross locational and chronological scales, identifying the presence or absence of hominids in European geographical provinces covering hundreds of thousands of square kilometres. Yet such approaches attempt to provide answers to some fundamental questions on the ability of archaic humans in the early Palaeolithic to plan ahead intelligently and organize themselves logistically. Third, Palaeolithic archaeology is a historical discipline. Observations and conclusions in all spheres of research (such as typological and technological analysis of lithic artefacts, the study of microscopic cut-marks on faunal remains, and ecological approaches) become more significant when their changes through time can be identified and interpreted. Fourth, chronological controls allow correlation of cultural evidence with the very rare skeletal evidence of Palaeolithic humans, allowing us to investigate the relationship between biological species (identified on skeletal morphology) and cultural behaviour. The basic chronological and environmental framework is provided by a combination of geological studies (Jones and Keen 1992; Gibbard 1985; Bridgland 1986), botanical studies (Turner 1975; West 1977) and faunal studies (Stuart 1982; Currant 1989).

Finally, with respect to cultural remains, it is necessary to question the primacy generally given to accumulations in undisturbed contexts. Such undisturbed accumulations of artefacts, particularly when in association with biological remains, are widely and correctly recognized as being able to give a deep insight into behaviour during a short period at a single location (cf. Roe 1980), for instance in Unit 4b at Boxgrove where the microscopic cut-marks on the fragmentary fossil remains of single horse have provided evidence of hunting and systematic butchery in the earliest period of the Palaeolithic (Roberts in preparation; Parfitt 1991). However, Palaeolithic research requires that attention also be paid to cultural evidence in disturbed contexts. Accumulations of artefacts in more disturbed contexts can give insights into patterns of behaviour over longer periods of time and wider areas, as the possible territory from which an assemblage might have been gathered can be deduced. In some ways disturbed accumulations could be more useful in investigating patterns of cultural change over long periods as they are less subject to idiosyncratic variability, as suggested by Newbury (1987).

A MODEL FOR CHARACTERIZING AND DISCRIMINATING PALAEOLITHIC DEPOSITS

Having briefly discussed some goals of Palaeolithic research and of the different sorts of evidence potentially of use in achieving them, this paper concludes with a preliminary model of how the Palaeolithic heritage could be characterized in a basic inventory, as a prelude to discriminating its most significant parts. Figure 10.6 shows seven areas of potential significance by which a Pleistocene deposit could be characterized, as a basis for assessing its value as a part of the Palaeolithic archaeological heritage. This model should be applied to individual geological contexts within a sequence of Pleistocene deposits, each of which would need to be characterized and assessed separately.

The first of these areas (nature of geological context) cannot be present, absent, or quantitatively assessed in the same way as the other areas. A Pleistocene context would always have a nature of some kind (i.e. be identifiable as a fluvial gravel, a marine beach, an estuarine mud-flat, a solifluction deposit, and so on). It would be necessary to record this

1 Nature of geological context
2 Disturbance of context
3 Absolute datability of context
4 Chrono-stratigraphic geological evidence
5 Botanical remains
6 Faunal remains
7 Artefactual remains

Figure 10.6 Preliminary model for the characterization of Pleistocene deposits as a Palaeolithic archaeological resource

information, to build up a picture of the range and relative frequency of Pleistocene deposits in England independently of their research significance and artefactual content, as these constitute the evidence of the landscape within which Palaeolithic people existed. Furthermore, to identify a representative sample of the Palaeolithic heritage, it would be necessary to select a sample which included a proportion of all types of deposit, and which also took account of the range of association of the other areas of significance with each type of deposit.

The other six areas listed in Figure 10.6 summarize the potential significance of a context for the investigation of the Palaeolithic period, with attention paid to the sorts of information of use for environmental and chronological purposes, as well as to the quantity and disturbance of cultural remains. It should be possible to score the significance of a particular context in each of these areas quantitatively, for instance on a scale of 1–5. These scores could then be amalgamated to provide a total score for each context within a deposit, and for the Pleistocene deposit as a whole. The greater significance of a deposit should lie not so much in whether one of the areas has evidence which rates a 5, but in the quantity of different areas represented at the same site, and in particular the association of behavioural and environmental evidence with dating evidence. Extra value should be placed upon the co-occurrence of significance in a high proportion of the suggested areas of possible significance. Such a co-occurrence would be of more value for Palaeolithic research than a high score in just one area, combined with an absence of significance in the other areas.

This model is intended as a preliminary 'Straw-man/Aunt Sally' to be modified in the light of further debate between specialists of the different disciplines which combine in Quaternary research, and between those who organize the framework of heritage management. However, it is hoped that the body of this person, even if highly mutated, will survive, and that a basic survey of the whole Palaeolithic archaeological resource can be undertaken leading to identification of its most important and representative parts. After this step has been taken, it will be necessary to confront the problems of providing appropriate protection and mitigation arrangements which recognize the specialist techniques and knowledge required in Quaternary research.

CONCLUSIONS

This chapter has tried to demonstrate that the environmental and geological evidence from artefactually sterile Pleistocene sites is of central importance to the study of the human presence in England during the Middle and Late Pleistocene. Such evidence, together with similar evidence recovered from sites with lithic artefacts, helps to create the basic environmental and chrono-stratigraphic framework within which to place the human cultural and skeletal evidence recovered from Pleistocene contexts, leading to the identification, and hopefully understanding, of its changes through time.

Therefore it is necessary to consider initially how to identify artefactually sterile deposits which are significant to Palaeolithic research, and subsequently how to ensure that the threats to them are controlled and mitigated in the same way as for other parts of the archaeological heritage. This chapter has attempted to initiate debate by suggesting six attributes, besides artefactual content, by which Pleistocene deposits might be characterized as the basis for discrimination of the potentially significant Palaeolithic heritage. Once a record has been created of the locations of this resource, the problem arises of how to ensure appropriate mitigating responses to threats posed by development, when the relevant expertise is itself a scarce resource. It is suggested that one way of dealing with this problem is to form a central service, or directory, of Quaternary specialists to provide advice and carry out fieldwork.

REFERENCES

Breeze, D.J. (1993) 'Ancient monuments legislation', in Hunter, J. and I.B.M. Ralston (eds) *Archaeological Resource Management in the UK: An Introduction*, Stroud: Alan Sutton Publishing, 44–55.

Bridgland, D.R. (1986) *Clast Lithological Analysis, Technical Guide 3*, Cambridge: Quaternary Research Association.

Collcutt, S.N. (ed.) (1986) *The Palaeolithic of Britain and its Nearest Neighbours: Recent Trends*, Sheffield: Department of Archaeology and Prehistory, University of Sheffield.

Conway, B.W. and Waechter, J. d' A. (1977) 'Barnfield Pit, Swanscombe', in E.R. Shephard-Thorn, and J.J. Wymer (eds) *South East England and the Thames Valley*, X INQUA Congress, excursion guide A5, Norwich: Geo Abstracts, 38–44.

Currant, A.P. (1989) 'The Quaternary origins of the modern British mammal fauna', *Biological Journal of the Linnean Society* 38: 23–30.

Darvill, T., Saunders A., and Startin, B. (1987) 'A question of national importance: approaches to the evaluation of Ancient Monuments for the Monuments Protection Programme in England', *Antiquity* 61: 393–408.

Department of the Environment (1990) *Planning Policy Guidance: Archaeology and Planning*, PPG 16, London: HMSO.

English Heritage (1991) *Exploring our Past: Strategies for the Archaeology of England*, London: Historic Buildings and Monuments Commission for England.

Gamble, C. (1987) 'Man the shoveler: alternative models for Middle Pleistocene colonisation and occupation in northern latitudes,' in O. Soffer (ed.) *The Pleistocene Old World: regional perspectives*, New York: Plenum Press, 81–98.

Gamble, C. (1992) 'Southern rivers Palaeolithic project', *Quaternary Newsletter* 66: 38–40.

Gibbard, P. L. (1985) *Pleistocene History of the Middle Thames valley*, Cambridge: Cambridge University Press.

Hunter, J., Ralston, I. and Hamlin, A. (1993) 'The structure of British archaeology', in J. Hunter and I. Ralston (eds) *Archaeological Resource Management in the UK: An Introduction*, Stroud: Alan Sutton Publishing.

Jones, R.L. and Keen, D.H. (1992) *Pleistocene Environments in the British Isles*, London: Chapman & Hall.

Kuhn, S.L. (1991) '"Unpacking" reduction: lithic raw material economy in the Mousterian of west-central Italy', *Journal of Anthropological Archaeology* 10: 76–106.

Newbury, M.G. (1987) 'A research project in the Lower Paleolithic of the Hampshire Basin', Paleolithic and Mesolithic Day Meeting, 24 October, Torquay.

Parfitt, S. (1991) 'Horse butchery at Boxgrove', paper given to Lithic Studies Society, British Museum (Franks House), 24 April.

Roberts, M.B. (1986) 'Excavation of the Lower Palaeolithic site at Amey's Eartham Pit, Boxgrove, W. Sussex', *Proceedings of the Prehistoric Society* 52: 215–45.

Roberts, M.B. (in preparation) Final report on excavations at the Lower Palaeolithic site of Boxgrove.

Roe, D.A. (1968) *A gazetteer of British Lower and Middle Palaeolithic sites*, CBA Research Report 8, London: Council for British Archaeology.

Roe, D.A. (1980) 'Introduction: precise moments in remote time', *World Archaeology* 12, 2: 107–8.

Roe, D.A. (1981) *The Lower and Middle Palaeolithic periods in Britain*, London: Routledge & Kegan Paul.

Roebroeks, W., Kolen, J. and Rensink, E. (1988) 'Planning depth, anticipation, and the organization of Middle Palaeolithic technology: the "archaic natives" meet Eve's descendants', *Helinium* 28, 1: 17–34.

Shaw, T., (1988), *Saving our Prehistoric Heritage: Landscapes under Threat*, London: The Prehistoric Society.

Sinclair, A. (1992) 'Post-Processual Palaeolithics: a 'p' too far', paper given at the annual conference of the Institute of Field Archaeologists, University of Birmingham, 6–8 April 1992.

Smart, P.L. and Frances, P.D. (1991) *Quaternary Dating Methods – a User's Guide*, QRA technical guide no. 4, Cambridge: Quaternary Research Association.

Stuart, A. J. (1982) *Pleistocene Vertaebrates in the British Isles*, London: Longman.

Turner, C. (1975) 'The correlation and duration of Middle Pleistocene interglacial periods in northwest Europe', in K.W. Butzer and G.L. Isaac (eds) *After the Australopithecines*, The Hague: Mouton, 259–308.

Wainwright, G.J. (1989) 'The management of the English landscape' in H.F. Cleere (ed.) *Archaeological Heritage Management in the Modern World*, One World Archaeology, vol. 9., London: Unwin Hyman, 164–70.

Wainwright, G.J. (1991) 'Preface', in English Heritage *Exploring our Past: Strategies for the Archaeology of England*, London: Historic Buildings and Monuments Commission for England.

Wenban-Smith, F.F. (1990) 'Researching the Early Palaeolithic: an organizational manifesto', *Lithics* 11: 16–23.

West, R.G. (1977) (2nd edn) *Pleistocene Geology and Biology with special reference to the British Isles*, London: Longman.

Wymer, J.J. (1991) 'The Southern Rivers Palaeolithic Project', *Lithics* 12: 21–3.

Wynn, T. (1991) 'Tools, grammar and the archaeology of cognition', *Cambridge Archaeological Journal* 1, 2: 191–206.

CHAPTER ELEVEN

THE IMPACT OF INFORMATION TECHNOLOGY ON THE PRACTICE OF ARCHAEOLOGICAL MANAGEMENT

DAVID WHEATLEY

The relationship between the theory and practice of management on one hand, and the tools of management on the other is usually regarded as a simple, linear one: it is assumed that operational requirements simply dictate the tools selected for management practice. Tools and technologies are consequently regarded as products of management ideas, as passive elements in the development of management practices and of management theories. This chapter argues, contrary to this view, that new tools are occasionally assimilated into existing practices whose use alters the preconceptions of managers, thus acting to change profoundly those practices and theories which caused their adoption. In these instances the relationship between tool and practice may be regarded as reversed, and management practices and theories can be seen to be partly driven by their available tools. At least part of the reason for this is that tools adopted into management to serve a particular function may prove to have unforeseen and far more valuable applications within other areas. These tools and technologies then become active elements in the formulation of management strategies, whose role in the development of management practice should not be ignored or dismissed.

Naturally this is something of a simplification, because new tools and technologies are not always instantly or easily absorbed into the practice of management, and management practice itself inevitably exhibits considerable inertia when undergoing change. The relationship between practice and technology must therefore be regarded as a reflexive one: management practice initially determines which tools and technologies are adopted (within the range of currently available technologies) but these tools then serve to actively reformulate management theory and participate in the transformation or reproduction of the practices which constitute management.

One class of tools which has and will continue to play an active, rather than passive role in the formulation of management practice is the group of tools collectively known as information technologies. These include computer databases, electronic communications and Geographic Information Systems (GIS). GIS have recently received extensive attention from archaeologists in both research and management contexts (e.g. Allen *et al.* 1990; Harris 1986; Kvamme 1989; Gaffney and Stanicic 1991) and considerable effort and expenditure has been recently directed towards the acquisition of GIS software and the development of the skills required to apply GIS technology to archaeology. There is general agreement that GIS technology has the potential to alter radically archaeological practices. For example Marble has recently commented:

> it is only rarely that a change occurs which revolutionises a field to the point where many of the things we do must be looked at from a completely different viewpoint. It is my contention that GIS is beginning to do this for Geography, and that it will also do so for those portions of the social sciences which are, or at least should be, concerned with the spatial aspects of human society.
>
> (Marble 1990a: 9)

The Chorley report on the handling of geographic information left even less doubt about the significance of GIS: 'It is the biggest step forward in the handling of spatial information since the invention of the map' (Department of the Environment 1987: 8). Although this may overstate the case a little, it would seem that the examination, in general terms at least, of the relationship between GIS and the management of archaeology might be of considerable benefit.

GEOGRAPHIC INFORMATION SYSTEMS

Just as databases are computer systems for the storage, retrieval and processing of textual and numeric information, GIS are computer systems for the storage, retrieval and processing of geographic information. Although GIS technology in its entirety is relatively new, its constituent elements have been in existence for some time. GIS software is a combination of database, computer-aided mapping, and spatial analysis software. Until the development of explicitly geographic information systems, geographic data was stored and retrieved as textual data in traditional databases. Computer-aided cartography (CAC) and computer-aided design (CAD) software has been available since the 1960s, developed to automate the repetitive stages in the production of maps or engineering drawings.

As these systems developed through the 1970s and 1980s they became increasingly able to order and manipulate spatially referenced information in a variety of ways. More recently, the need to store large amounts of data for some engineering or cartographic applications led to the linking of CAC and CAD systems to traditional database systems, essentially allowing the CAD or CAC software to draw on the storage and retrieval mechanisms of the database while itself acting as a graphical 'front end' to the database. This provided the incentive to develop data structures for the storage and retrieval of spatial information and the creation of arc–node topographic models for the representation of spatial data. These developments, together with the phenomenal rate of hardware development (resulting in vastly increased processing speeds and storage capacity), made it possible during the 1980s to create systems which stored spatial information with a genuine representation of its spatial attributes, to extract and represent this information in a map format and to analyse the spatial content of this information.

It is worth emphasizing that it is the spatial nature of the representation and display of information which sets GIS apart from traditional information systems, and has led to such widespread interest in the technology. GIS data structures not only store the attributes of data objects, but fully represent the spatial organization of the objects, and so form a model of how they are related to one another in space. Traditional database systems are not inherently capable of retrieving or manipulating the data attributes held about objects which are in spatially related locations – for example the names of streets whose postcodes reveal that they are adjacent. As Kvamme explained 'GIS are distinct from traditional database management systems because of this spatial referent; indeed it is the geographical structure that give GIS added capabilities over traditional database management systems' (Kvamme 1989: 139).

It is the contention of this chapter that GIS technology is likely to play an important role in the formulation of management practice in the UK during the next decade. In order to understand the nature of the changes which may take place, it is necessary first to consider the *operational requirement* for GIS within archaeological management, in other words the motivation for adopting the technology in the first place, and secondly (perhaps more importantly) to speculate about the active role the adoption of GIS may have in the formulation of management theory and practice.

THE OPERATIONAL REQUIREMENT FOR GIS

One of the most significant changes to occur within archaeological management in the UK over recent years has been a perceptible shift of emphasis away from legislative approaches and towards planning approaches to conflict resolution.

Legislative approaches to the management of the archaeological resource have a long history in the United Kingdom, beginning with the first monument protection legislation enacted in 1882, primarily through the efforts of John Lubbock, later Lord Avebury. This legislation included a list of protected sites referred to as the Schedule of Monuments, and allowed for the purchase of scheduled sites if they were offered for sale. Later changes to the legislation strengthened the protection afforded to monuments by requiring land owners to give notice before disturbing or destroying scheduled monuments, and providing for the issue of compulsory purchase orders. The most recent act, the 1979 Ancient Monuments and Archaeological Areas Act as amended by the 1983 National Heritage Act, still requires the Schedule of Monuments to be maintained as a list of sites of 'national importance'. This legislation prohibits the destruction of scheduled monuments 'without lawful excuse' and prohibits all works which affect a scheduled monument, unless the permission of the Secretary of State is first obtained (see Startin this volume).

It has been widely recognized for some time that the management practices dictated by the framework of this legislation are far from ideal. For example, Francis Wenban-Smith (this volume) has argued that some types of Palaeolithic remains are extremely difficult to protect under the legislation for a variety of reasons. More generally, it is clearly not possible within the framework of the legislation to afford protection to sites quickly following their discovery: for a site to be protected it must be included in the schedule, which in turn requires that it is deemed to be 'nationally important'. This can be time-consuming to establish, and in the case of a site discovered during development means that protection under the legislation is difficult if not impossible.

Partly as a reaction to these problems, the management of archaeology in the UK has gradually shifted from the legislative mechanism of 'scheduling' towards the use of a planning approach. This shift of emphasis has recently resulted in the issue of Planning Policy Guideline note 16 (PPG 16) (Department of the Environment 1990). This document effectively defines a new framework for the management of archaeology within local government planning machinery (predominantly under powers granted by the 1990 Town and Country Planning Act) and among a number of important and reasonably clear policy statements, two relevant features may be highlighted:

1 Archaeological remains *and their settings* whether scheduled or not are explicitly stated as a material consideration in the determination of planning applications. This effectively compels local government planning authorities to consider the archaeological impact of any activities which require planning permission.
2 It emphasizes the importance of consultation between planning authorities, archaeological curators and developers before planning permission

is granted, and has consequently resulted in a growth of archaeological evaluation prior to planning determination, and an associated reduction in 'rescue' excavations.

At a practical level, these changes have had several effects on archaeological curators which are relevant to this discussion. Firstly, the type of information which is the currency of archaeological management has altered. The increase in archaeological evaluations has resulted in an increase in information resulting from fieldwalking, survey, geophysical survey and the interpretation of aerial photography. All these types of information, which are essentially spatial in nature, are difficult to store and manipulate in traditional database systems.

Archaeological evaluations generally involve the integration of some or all of these types of data with existing sites and monuments records (SMRs). In the UK these county-based records have a long history, mainly stemming from the appointment of O.G.S. Crawford as the first Archaeology Officer of the Ordnance Survey and the resulting systematic survey of archaeological sites. As Lock and Harris (1991) have argued, the existence within the structure of UK archaeological management of these extensive and now almost entirely computerized records has of itself provided a significant motivation for the adoption of GIS technology. Prior to computerization in the last ten years, these records were almost always maintained in the form of card-index site records, each card containing a reference to a mark on a map – a manual system with obvious similarities to GIS. It is therefore no surprise that county archaeologists in the UK see the value of a technology which can realize the latent potential of this data, and allow rapid access and integration of this data with other spatial information. At the same time, the need to consider the settings of archaeological monuments has been a huge incentive to archaeological curators to become involved with the analysis of more than simple text-based records.

The ability of GIS technology to allow quick and intuitive manipulation of a variety of spatial information, including existing SMRs, survey data, geophysical data and remotely sensed data, makes it an ideal tool for the collation and analysis of data for archaeological evaluations. As a result of these new operational requirements, a number of large archaeological organizations have invested heavily in CAC, CAD or GIS equipment, and in the acquisition of additional regional data such as elevation, geology and hydrology.

THE EFFECTS OF GIS ON MANAGEMENT

So far this chapter has observed some of the reasons why GIS technology has started to be adopted within archaeological management – in other words it has reviewed GIS as a passive technology. It is now possible to

review the effects of the adoption of this technology beyond this operational requirement and progress to consider the active role that GIS technology may play in the formulation of management practice. This section
will claim that one of the areas in which GIS could have greatest effect is
in the formulation of methodologies for the ascription of value to the
archaeological resource, and that this in turn could alter the cognitive definition of the archaeological resource itself. In this context, the archaeological resource should be taken to exclude portable antiquities, whose
spatial context is not fixed, but changeable and whose archaeological context is frequently absent. This should not be taken to imply any belittle-
ment of the value of the portable (aspatial) archaeological resource and
indeed for a discussion of the nature of value systems as applied to aspatial
as well as spatially referenced archaeological material see the chapter by
Carman (this volume).

The process of archaeological management, as of all management, is a
process of conflict resolution and this frequently involves the mitigation of
alternative actions which are advocated by different conflicting interest
groups through the consideration of archaeological value (see Bower;
Carman; Darvill; and Firth, all this volume). The notion of archaeological
value is clearly controversial, although it is rarely debated: some archaeologists seem to regard any explicit discussion of the value of archaeological
remains as either irrelevant, uninteresting or subversive while others (e.g.
Lipe 1977; Darvill *et al.* 1987; Darvill, this volume; Carman, this volume)
accept that archaeological remains are valuable and strive to understand the
nature and sources of this value. This is a general position with which I agree,
without necessarily accepting the specific definitions and formulations of
archaeological value which have been presented by these workers.

Without becoming embroiled in tortuous justification of this position,
it is the contention here that while archaeology clearly has no abstract
inherent value (any more than anything has inherent value), it equally
clearly acquires value or has value ascribed to it by the actions of archaeologists, planners, developers and all other interest groups whose actions
may modify archaeological material. By value I do not mean to imply
specific monetary value, but I accept the position of Darvill (this volume)
that a value system is essentially a social concept of desirability, and as such
the value of archaeology (or anything else) is not static and unitary, but
variable and plural, and heavily dependent on context.

Archaeological management, therefore, generally involves the mitigation
of alternative possible courses of action with the aim of minimising the
overall loss of this ascribed archaeological value, or the justification of
the loss of archaeological value by an increase in some other type of value.
It is only by the ascription of values to archaeological material that alternative courses of action may be evaluated, and conflicts which involve the
modification of the archaeological resource can be resolved. Therefore
whether it is admitted (and consequently made explicit) or not, archae-

ological managers are involved in the ascription of value to archaeological remains. It is not the purpose of this chapter to discuss the alternative value systems applied to the archaeological resource or to analyse the mechanical processes which have been created for the determination of archaeological values within a management context (see for example Groube and Bowden 1982; Darvill *et al.* 1987; Darvill, this volume; Startin, this volume). Each of these may be affected in various ways by technological changes within management. However it is the nature of the archaeological resource itself – the object of the valuation process – which will be most affected by the adoption of GIS technology.

To justify this assertion, it is first necessary to characterize the archaeological resource, and to consider why it should be altered in any way by a new technology. The first thing to note is that the archaeological resource in this context is an artificial construction. There are obviously tangible things which constitute the material archaeological resource (earth, pottery, flint, walls, etc.), and these things are not physically altered by the application of a tool or technology to their description and representation. However the process of archaeological management is not carried out on these material things, instead the object for which management strategies are devised is a theoretical, notional resource. Although not tangible, this archaeological management object may be seen to possess certain properties which are revealed through its representation by archaeological managers.

Currently, the most obvious characteristic of the archaeological resource is that it is site-based. This is to say that archaeology is typically described as a series of spatially bounded entities (archaeological sites) to which is ascribed archaeological value. It follows logically from this that the space between archaeological sites is deemed to be of no archaeological value. This conceptualization of the archaeological resource is most clearly revealed (in the UK) by the legislative mechanism of scheduling – this is a particular instance of a bounded spatial entity which is ascribed a particular instance of archaeological value: 'national importance'. However, the nature of the representation of the archaeological resource within Sites and Monuments Records (SMRs) also reveals this conceptual model: originally these were recorded in the form of pins or marks on a map, to which an entry within a card index is linked; more recently the computerization of SMRs has fossilised this mental template into a database schema, within which archaeological records are typically linked to a single grid reference for ease of storage.

Of course this notion of the archaeological resource as a spatially discontinuous variable of archaeological value has limitations, and these limitations have occasionally been addressed within archaeological management. The definition of 'Archaeological Areas' as well as archaeological sites within the 1979 legislation addressed it to some extent by offering legislative protection to larger spatial areas than sites. However, this merely recognized larger areas of archaeological value, still set within a milieu of no 'national importance'. More significantly perhaps, the shift from a rigid legislative approach towards a more flexible planning approach (as represented by PPG 16) has allowed recognition that the *settings* of archaeological monuments are important. On the face of it, this would seem to accept that archaeological value is spatially continuous because the setting of a monument could mean almost anything; however closer consideration reveals that this is not the case. In order to have a *setting*, there must be a *site*, and the site must be distinguished qualitatively from its setting or the two terms are meaningless. Thus it can be seen that PPG 16, by creating the distinction between site and setting merely represents a change from the model of the archaeological resource as bounded areas of archaeological value within a background of no value, to a new model which recognizes two types of archaeological value: the value ascribed to sites themselves, and the value ascribed to the setting. This is a slight conceptual improvement, but does not alter the essentially discontinuous nature of archaeological value.

ARCHAEOLOGICAL VALUE AS CONTINUOUS VARIATION

It should be apparent from the preceding discussion that both the legislative framework of archaeological management (such as the 1979 Act) and the tools available for management practice (such as the SMR database) have acted as a restriction on the development of a more mature conception of archaeological value. Recently, a number of developments within archaeological thinking have made this far more apparent, and have acted to highlight the schism between the management model of the archaeological resource and that of archaeologists generally.

Firstly, the growth of non–site-based archaeology (e.g. Dunnell and Dancey 1983; Shennan 1985; Thomas 1975) has criticized the centrality of the archaeological site in regional analysis. Non–site-based archaeology recognizes the archaeological site as an artificial construction and, as an alternative to this, places the emphasis on archaeological remains revealed from fieldwalking and survey and on issues such as sampling which arise from the use of this evidence. Secondly, and possibly related to this, there has been an increasing interest in the concept of landscape (e.g. Wagstaff 1987; Crumley and Marquardt 1990). Although difficult to define, this certainly incorporates the 'spatial manifestation of the relations between humans and their environment' (Crumley and Marquardt 1990: 73), and generally represents a more holistic approach to archaeological interpretation both in terms of the spatial distribution of archaeology and the temporal persistence of natural and cultural landscape features. Landscape archaeology also encompasses both natural and anthropogenic processes which are involved in the formation and transformation of the environment, and aims to explore the relationship between the two.

Because of these developments in archaeological thinking, it will soon be impossible to justify the discontinuous management model of the archaeological resource described above. The notion of archaeological value consisting of discrete components set within a background of no archaeological value can be seen to be in conflict both with the non-site-based methodology for regional analysis and with the interrelatedness which is embodied in the idea of landscape. It is in the context of this problem that GIS technology will have the greatest effect, because with GIS the archaeologist finally has a tool which is capable of manipulating the archaeological resource as a spatial surface: of representing archaeological values as continuous variables (see Figure 11.1).

Examples of the potential of GIS to reformulate the archaeological resource are too numerous to recount here, but two recent areas of application may provide some enlightenment. Firstly, there has been considerable effort expended on the development of predictive modelling (e.g. Kvamme 1990; Warren 1990). This is a general term for methodologies which attempt to model the distribution of archaeological material in unsurveyed locations. These generally operate by generalizing the environmental and landscape characteristics of a known set of archaeological material in order to estimate the probability of an unsurveyed area of landscape containing similar archaeological remains. Archaeologists have known instinctively that some areas may be more likely to contain archaeology than others, and therefore that some areas with no known archaeology have some sort of high archaeological value because of this. GIS methodology offers the possibility of incorporating the notion of archaeological potential into the representation of the archaeological resource, and so to conceptualize the resource in this way as a surface of continuous variation.

A second area of potentially revolutionary importance is the area of visibility and proximity analyses (e.g. Ruggles *et al.* 1992; Wheatley forthcoming). As discussed above, it is intuitively the case that some places are more archaeologically sensitive than others because they are within sight or sound of or are close to archaeological remains. The landscape setting of monuments has therefore been recognized in a rather vague way by recent developments in archaeological management such as PPG 16. However, GIS technology allows the development of explicit methods (such as cumulative viewshed analysis) for comparison of places in terms of their visibility and proximity to one another.

Lastly GIS offers the opportunity to develop a common methodological framework for archaeological conservation and other conservation interests. This discussion has focused on the attribution of archaeological values to landscapes, and the potential impact of GIS on this field. However the application of GIS to the management of natural resources as various as tidal mudflats, urban clearways and endangered species has been developing within the UK at an equally rapid rate.

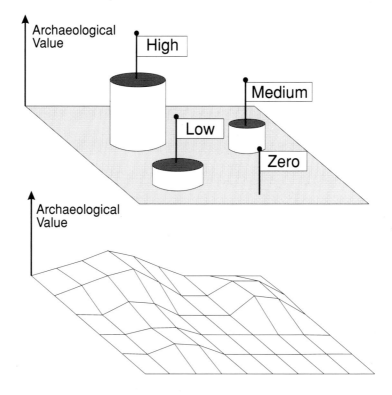

Figure 11.1 Management models of archaeological value

This technological innovation has presented archaeologists and natural scientists with a tool capable of providing a common framework for environmental assessment.

CONCLUSIONS

The adoption of new information technologies within the sphere of archaeological management can be viewed both as a response to an operational requirement for this type of technology, and as an active participant in the reformulation of management ideas. In a passive sense, some recent changes to archaeological management practice – which are themselves responses to changes within a wider archaeological sphere – can be seen to be driving archaeological managers towards the acquisition and application of particular information technologies for the storage and manipulation of georeferenced data. Once assimilated into current management practice, however, such technology can be seen to have a potential which far exceeds this operational requirement. In the case of

Geographic Information Systems specifically, it allows archaeological managers to redefine the notion of the archaeological resource, currently conceptualized as a series of discrete units of archaeological value in a landscape of no archaeological value, as a surface of continuously varying archaeological value.

ACKNOWLEDGEMENTS

The author gratefully acknowledges the support of the Royal Commission for Historic Monuments (England) and the Science and Engineering Research Council, and also the valuable advice and assistance of Dr Tim Champion and Dr Stephen Shennan.

REFERENCES

Allen, K.M.S., Green, S.W. and Zubrow, E.B.W. (1990) *Interpreting Space: GIS and Archaeology*, London: Taylor & Francis.

Crumley, C.L. and Marquardt, W.H. (1990) 'Landscape: a unifying concept in regional analysis', in K.M.S. Allen, S.W. Green and E.W. Zubrow (eds) *Interpreting space: GIS and archaeology*, London: Taylor & Francis.

Darvill T., Saunders, A. and Startin W. (1987) 'A question of national importance: approaches to the evaluation of ancient monuments for the Monuments Protection Programme in England', *Antiquity* 61: 393–408

Department of the Environment (1987) 'Handling geographic information', report to the Secretary of State for the Environment of the Committee of Enquiry into the Handling of Geographic Information chaired by Lord Chorley, London: HMSO.

Department of the Environment (1990) *Planning Policy Guidance: Archaeology and Planning*, PPG 16, London: HMSO.

Dunnell, R.C. and Dancey, W.S. (1983) 'The siteless survey: a regional scale data collection strategy', in M.B. Schiffer (ed.) *Advances in Archaeological Method and Theory* 6: 267–87, New York: Academic Press.

Gaffney, V. and Stanicic, Z. (1991) *GIS Approaches to Regional Analysis: A Case Study of the Island of Hvar*, Ljubljana: Filozofska fakulteta.

Groube, L.M. and Bowden, M.C.B. (1982) *The Archaeology of Rural Dorset*, Dorset Natural History and Archaeology Society Monograph 4, Dorchester: Friary Press.

Harris, T.M. (1986) 'Geographic information system design for archaeological site information retrieval', in S. Laplin (ed.) *Computer Applications in Archaeology 1986*, University of Birmingham.

Harris, T.M., and Lock, G.R. (1991) 'The diffusion of a new technology: a perspective on the adoption of Geographic Information Systems within UK Archaeology', in K.M.S. Allen, S.W. Green and E.B.W. Zubrow (eds) (1990) *Interpreting Space: GIS and archaeology*, London: Taylor & Francis.

Kvamme, K.L. (1989) 'Geographical information systems in regional archaeological research and data management', in M.B. Schiffer (ed.) *Studies in Archaeological Method and Theory* 1: 139–202, Tucson: University of Arizona Press.

Kvamme, K.L. (1990) 'The fundamental principles and practice of predictive archaeological modeling', in A. Voorips (ed.) *Mathematics and Information Science in Archaeology: A Flexible Framework*, Studies in Modern Archaeology 3, Bonn: Holos-Verlag, 257–95.

Lipe, W.D. (1977) 'A conservation model for American archaeology', in M.D. Schiffer and G.J. Gumerman (eds) *Conservation Archaeology: A Guide for Cultural Resource Management Studies*, New York: Academic Press.

Lock, G. and Harris, T. (1991) 'Integrating spatial information in computerised sites and monuments records: meeting archaeological requirements in the 1990s', in K. Lockyear and S.P.Q. Rahtz (eds) *Computer Applications and Quantitative Methods in Archaeology 1990*, BAR International Series 565, Oxford: BAR, 165-173.

Marble, D. (1990) 'The potential methodological impact of geographic information systems on the social sciences', in Allen, K.M.S., Green, S.W. and Zubrow, E.B.W. (1990) *Interpreting Space: GIS and Archaeology*, London: Taylor & Francis.

Ruggles, C.L.N., Medyckyj-Scott, D.J. and Gruffydd, A, (1993) 'Multiple viewshed analysis using GIS and its archaeological application: a case study in northern Mull', in J. Andresen, T. Madsen and I. Scholar (eds) *Computing the Past. Computer Applications in Archaeology '92*, Aarhus: Aarhus University Press.

Shennan, S.J. (1985) *Experiments in the Collection and Interpretation of Archaeological Survey Data: the East Hampshire Survey*, Sheffield: Sheffield University Press.

Thomas, D.H. (1975) 'Nonsite sampling in archaeology: up the creek without a site', in J.W. Mueller (ed.) *Sampling in Archaeology*, Tucson: University of Arizona Press, 61–81.

Wagstaff J.M. (1987) *Landscape and Culture: Geographical and Archaeological Perspectives*, Oxford: Basil Blackwell.

Warren, R.E. (1990) 'Predictive modelling of archaeological site location: a primer', in K.M.S. Allen, S.W. Green and E.B.W. Zubrow (1990) *Interpreting Space: GIS and Archaeology*, London: Taylor & Francis.

Wheatley, D.W. (forthcoming) 'A view to a hill – the use of line-of-sight maps to understand regional variation in earlier Neolithic Wessex', in H. Maschener (ed.) *GIS and the Advancement of Archaeological Method and Theory*, Carbondale: Southern Illinois University Press.

CHAPTER TWELVE

PREPARING ARCHAEOLOGISTS FOR MANAGEMENT

TIMOTHY DARVILL

The success of any organization depends on a continuous supply of competent, experienced, and well-trained staff who are alert to the changing environment in which they have to operate. This is as true in archaeology as in any other profession, and the changing working practices and organizational structure within the archaeological profession over the last two decades have provided major challenges for training providers.

Training in its most general sense – the process of teaching or learning a skill or discipline – has long been a feature of archaeological endeavour in Britain. Training excavations have featured in the summer calendar for decades, and there can be few archaeologists working today who have not attended either as pupil or tutor one of the many evening classes, day schools, summer schools, or similar events that happen every year. But when we talk of training the question that always comes to mind is: training who for what?

Training providers constantly ask themselves this question, and in working out an answer find that they are being both pushed and pulled by a series of competing internal and external pressures. Starting from the central position of a core discipline with established principles, practices and understandings, there is firstly a strong pull from the dynamics of the discipline itself; the constant need to explore new avenues and refocus attention on different aspects as consensual frameworks shift about. Associated with this there is the need to be reactive by adapting programmes to suit changing demands from potential employers and from students themselves. Pushing in another direction is the need to predict what will be required several years hence when students now entering the system leave college or university and seek employment in the wider world.

None of this is easy, especially when the political agenda within which public funds for education and training are provided is in constant flux, and the operational context regularly modified (Austin 1987). Writing in 1977, Roger Mercer examined the contributions that universities could make to rescue archaeology and vice versa (Mercer 1978). Some of the problems raised at that time are still with us: for example, the difficulty of providing a comprehensive undergraduate programme on archaeology in only three years. Others, for example involving universities in rescue excavations and training graduates for life in the rescue circus, have now been superseded by new issues. Two stand out for special mention as they both embody the concept of 'management', although apply it in rather different ways. First is the matter of managing the heritage itself and the expansion of archaeological resource management as the principal sphere of work in which archaeologists are employed. Second is the question of managing the way archaeologists do their work and the increasing expectation that archaeologists go about their business in a professional, structured, logical, and accountable way.

Responses to the first of these two changes have recently been considered in some detail by Andrew Saunders (1989) and Peter Fowler (1991). It is not proposed to say much more about this here except where there is an overlap with the main theme of the present chapter, namely the matter of preparing archaeologists to be managers.

In tackling this aspect of management – 'business studies for archaeologists' as it might more realistically be phrased – I would like to consider three aspects. First, the general background to the inclusion of management studies in archaeology. Second, the present arrangements, such as they are, for training programmes in archaeological management. Third, to consider how the situation might change in future.

As a prelude, however, two points must be made. First, very little detailed quantified information is available concerning the provision of training in archaeology. As a result there is a danger that the information used here may be incomplete or unrepresentative. Second, I have to declare an interest in the courses run in the Department of Conservation Sciences at Bournemouth University as I shall draw heavily on their content and on the market research carried out for their design and validation.

BACKGROUND

Traditionally, recruitment to archaeology has been heavily reliant on educational and training attainment in knowledge-based skills; indeed archaeology is a knowledge-based profession in which theoretical perspectives, conceptual frameworks, data categorization, sampling, and comparative analyses underpin everything that is done. The key skills required of an archaeologist are those of structured analysis, reasoned argument and careful presentation.

Established posts are mainly held by individuals with first degrees, and higher degrees are fairly common. Professional qualifications offered by the Institute of Field Archaeologists (IFA) also, in the main, build from foundations represented as academic qualifications by grafting on the recognition of increasing levels of experience and competence to achieve progression through the principal membership classes of Practitioner, Associate, and Member. Practical skills in field archaeology, such things as excavation, survey, or aerial photography, are highly valued too, and many of the most successful archaeologists are those who have combined academic and practical abilities.

The explicit need for business skills and management expertise is relatively new in archaeology, although, as will be examined later, elements of what might now be regarded as essential management skills have been practised by archaeologists for a long time. The enhanced profile of business skills is no doubt partly connected to wider changes within the profession as a whole (including the academic sector) over the last decade. Equally important, however, is the effect of the changing place of archaeology as a discipline in the public perception. Three main reasons for the incorporation of business skills in archaeological work over the last fifteen years or so can be identified, all of them relevant to the question of training in such matters.

First is the intrinsic attraction of using business management experience to do a job better and more efficiently whether this is an excavation programme or a piece of academic research. Anyone who has had to write up a back-log excavation from the 1970s or before will know of the problems caused by the fact that those working in the field at that time were encouraged to focus on doing the excavation itself without proper resources for the work in the wider context of a single project which involved the successive stages of planning, execution, analysis and reporting as would nowadays be expected.

The second main prompt for greater attention to business skills is the fact that archaeology involves considerable expenditure of public funds. The political philosophies of the 1980s in particular emphasized the need for accountability, efficiency, performance monitoring, targeted approaches, and the delivery of quality products and services. Business studies offered the frameworks and procedures within which these philosophies could be played out, and as a result were widely adopted.

The third main prompt, rather more particular to archaeology, was the changing environment in which archaeological organizations were operating. In the public sector, archaeological operations became more closely integrated with mainstream divisions or sections, for example planning departments, and these already had a corporate culture which archaeologists were expected to fit into. In the private sector, many units and trusts found themselves drawn into business arrangements with major public and private companies who also had their own operating environment, generally one in which competition for work and adherence to contractual obligation were important features. Again, archaeological organizations swam or sank according to their ability to adapt to these changing environments. In 1989, English Heritage reinforced the need for proper project management in the context of archaeological programmes which it funded with the publication of *The Management of Archaeology Projects* (English Heritage 1989), a set of guidance that has since been updated and greatly expanded (English Heritage 1991).

Having recognized that business skills are a relevant part of the way that archaeologists are expected to operate, the question that now faces us is to what extent existing courses include business management skills in their curriculum. Here, however, we move beyond the simple equation that archaeology courses mainly exist to provide the next generation of archaeologists. As a number of surveys and studies have shown, archaeology graduates are more likely to become civil servants, teachers, or entrepreneurs than archaeologists (Austin 1987: 234). Thus perhaps it is especially appropriate that they should be exposed to the business applications within the discipline as well as to the academic foundations.

EXISTING PROVISIONS

Training in archaeological work is provided in Britain at a number of different levels and through a variety of organizations. For the purposes of this review consideration is given to four categories: non-degree courses; undergraduate programmes; taught postgraduate programmes; and continuing professional development (CPD) programmes.

Non-degree courses

The two most widely known non-degree courses in archaeology are probably the Certificate in British Archaeology run from the Department of Continuing Education at Oxford University (in association with the Open University), and the Higher National Diploma (HND) in Practical Archaeology which for many years was run at Weymouth College but which from Autumn 1993 is offered by Yeovil College. There are others too, for example at London and Bristol, but Oxford and Yeovil illustrate the range of coverage represented in these kinds of courses.

The Oxford programme is modular in construction. Content is restricted to what is known about Britain in archaeological terms from the Neolithic period through to medieval times. There are five modules in all but each student takes only two, one in each of two years. Each module is designed to be equivalent to one Open University full credit at second level. Study is part time through evening sessions and a summer school.

By contrast, the Yeovil HND is a two-year full-time programme which has a strong practical and vocational orientation. There is a clear vision of how students will use their qualifications to develop careers in archaeology, in some cases building on the Diploma to take a degree course (the Higher National Diploma is recognized as an entry qualification by most universities). One of the eight stated objectives of the course is to give students 'the ability to work in a professional and business-oriented environment'. Another is for students to have 'substantial transferable skills' (Anon. 1993: 2). The first of these objectives translates into two professional studies units out of a total of fifteen units on the whole course. The first is mainly concerned with the structure and organization of archaeology in Britain, the second deals with such matters as legislation, local government systems, planning, and human resource management. The HND is a Business and Technical Education Council (BTEC) qualification and accordingly seeks to develop seven common skills as an essential part of the learning programme. These are:

1   managing and developing self;
2   working with and relating to others;
3   communicating;
4   managing tasks and solving problems;
5   applying numeracy;
6   applying technology, and
7   applying design and creativity.

It is easy to see how all of these skills can be brought together in a course in practical archaeology, and perhaps this represents one of the attractive features of such a programme.

Undergraduate programmes

Non-degree courses in archaeology are relatively rare, but full undergraduate programmes are fairly common. Archaeology of one sort or another is taught at undergraduate level at about a quarter of the higher educational institutions now classed as universities in the United Kingdom: twenty-four such institutions being included in the 1992 Higher Education Funding Council (HEFC) research review exercise under the subject area of archaeology. The 1994 Universities and Colleges Admissions Service (UCAS) *Official Guide* lists thirty first degree courses in archaeology in the UK, to which must be added three or four times that number of combined honours and closely related degrees (e.g. Heritage Conservation). This compares with fifty-six courses in history, and seventy-five in mathematics, both again having numerous permutations with other subjects as combined honours degrees (Universities and Colleges Admissions Service 1993).

The content and scope of these archaeology degree courses varies considerably between different universities. It has long been recognized that three years (four in Scotland) is insufficient time to provide a comprehensive programme in such a broad subject as archaeology (Mercer 1978: 56), and there has been some debate about exactly what should be covered by an undergraduate archaeology course (Austin 1987: 230–1). The result has been that, in terms of the subject matters covered, courses have tended to become more specialized in recent years. Thus some courses place more emphasis on archaeological theory, others on practical skills; some focus on the British Isles, others on Europe as a whole or some other part of the world; some are more concerned with prehistory and less with post-Roman periods, other the reverse. Covertly at least, in the language of business studies, courses are increasingly defining for themselves a 'market position' and 'unique marketing features' (UMF). The problem now is whether potential students are sufficiently discerning to realize that opting for one course as against another is no longer straightforward and carries with it a decision about the very focus of the studies that are provided and the kinds of job opportunities likely to be available at the end.

While differences in detailed course content measured in terms of the subject matters covered are diverging, the key general themes that might run through undergraduate archaeology programmes are more widely agreed. In 1990, the IFA and the Standing Conference of University Professors and Heads of Archaeology (SCUPHA) agreed a core syllabus as an aid to recognizing and defining undergraduate courses in archaeology. The six features of such a course were defined as:

1   the history, contemporary role and organization of archaeology and its public dissemination;
2   theoretical and methodological studies including, for example, experimental archaeology and ethnoarchaeology;
3   analytical approaches to science-based archaeology, including mathematical and quantitative techniques;
4   extensive fieldwork experience;
5   a range of studies across a broad chronological and geographical spectrum, and
6   systematic experience of handling primary evidence.

No survey data is available to document the extent to which different courses conform to this model. The practical element represented by item 4 is certainly widely pursued, although it is unclear how many courses stretch this item to include any consideration of research designs, specifications, or the MAP2 guidelines for archaeological project management issued by English Heritage (English Heritage 1991).

Business studies of a more general kind which are relevant to archaeology do not figure in the core syllabus. As far as I am aware, Bournemouth is the only university currently offering courses which include a significant element dealing with management issues, although other degree courses certainly include some consideration of such things. The BSc Archaeology course includes consideration of human resource management in the second year, building into a full single unit in year three (one hour per week plus seminars and directed reading) which includes lectures grouped under the following headings: project planning and design; financial management; computers and accounts; computers and project management; competitive tendering; dealing with developers; monitoring projects; project assessment.

The BSc in Heritage Conservation at Bournemouth includes rather more in the way of management studies, and has a full unit (two hours a week in lectures (one hour in third year) plus seminars and directed reading) in each of the three years of the course:

Year 1 Principles of management; marketing; using computers in management;

Year 2 Business and financial management, including accounts, cash forecasts and balance sheets;

Year 3 Project management, including specifications and design, costing, tendering, contracts, model project management systems (e.g. MAP2; British Property Federation (BPF); Environmental Assessment programmes etc.), project execution, monitoring, reviewing.

Including this material means that other things have to be excluded, and at present the penalty is paid by limiting the geographical scope of much of the other teaching to the British Isles and near Continent. For this reason alone one cannot expect all undergraduate courses to include management elements since other course delivery teams will no doubt identify different priorities.

Taught postgraduate programmes

The 1992 edition of the IFA's *Directory of Educational Opportunities in Archaeology* (Institute of Field Archaeologists 1992: 4–12) lists 77 taught postgraduate courses in universities around the country. Of these about 20 have a practical or vocational orientation and about 10 deal at least in part with archaeological resource management. A survey of these courses in 1990 by Peter Fowler revealed that seven main elements were commonly included:

1 principles and theory of conservation;
2 practice of conservation planning;
3 the nature of the resource;
4 issues and skills of communication and interpretation;
5 relevant legislation;

6   management theory and principles, and
7   field visits and project work.

This was borne out in 1991 by a survey of potential competitor courses in advance of designing what is now the MSc in Archaeology and Development at Bournemouth University. However, of those universities and colleges contacted in 1991 only York and Birmingham (Ironbridge Institute) included more than a small element of management studies. In the form in which it is now taught, the Bournemouth Archaeology and Development course includes consideration of: financial planning, project-management systems, costing, negotiating, contracts, timetables and schedules, project monitoring, cash-flow, agreements, organizational structures, human resource management, and presentation.

A variation on this range of conventional postgraduate opportunities is represented by the Postgraduate Diploma in Field Archaeology taught by the Department of Continuing Education at Oxford University in association with the Oxford Archaeological Unit. This is a one-year course (also available in modular form spread over a period of up to three years) leading to a postgraduate diploma. The main aim is to involve students in a broad range of professional archaeological activities.

Continuing Professional Development (CPD)

The idea of training as a continuing process rather than a once-and-for-all event is relatively new in terms of its application among professionals. Its widespread adoption and the recognition of continuing professional development as an important contribution to the maintenance of high standards of professional practice is perhaps in part due to the needs of keeping up with rapidly changing technologies and, in sectors such as planning and environmental studies, to changing legislation. Many professional bodies require their members to undertake prescribed levels of CPD each year. Such requirements are an indication of the quite proper recognition of the fact that membership of a professional institute is not simply about the attainment of set standards but equally about the maintenance of standards of performance.

The IFA has yet to embrace the integration of CPD with the maintenance of membership standards, although possible schemes have been discussed (Fraser 1993). It has, however, embarked on the provision of short training courses. In March 1990 a questionnaire was circulated to all IFA members soliciting their views on what training courses were most needed and what format they should take. The two most popular topics identified were project management, with 51 per cent of responses, and legislation, with 43 per cent of responses (Fraser 1991). The first is particularly telling with such a high proportion of those archaeologists who responded recognizing for themselves that this aspect of business skills is something they feel they should know more about. The IFA promptly responded by establishing a common curriculum for short courses in these subjects and inviting universities and other training institutions around the country to submit proposals for running them. In the 1992/3 academic year courses were run at Southampton, Bournemouth, Leicester and Bradford universities, in all cases with the support of the IFA and English Heritage. Similar courses are proposed for the 1993/4 academic year (Fraser 1993).

The success of the IFA's important initiative in this field can be judged from the fact that other training providers have independently begun to run similar courses, as for example with the Project Management course run by the Department of Continuing Education at Oxford University in December 1993.

LOOKING BACKWARDS AND FORWARDS

Optimists would probably argue that the current provision for management studies in archaeology is in a healthy state and that the increased provision over the last few years is a promising sign for the future. For those who wish to include business management among their archaeological skills there are certainly opportunities at many different levels from foundation-level non-degree courses through to CPD. As the application of business studies in archaeology becomes more widespread the content of the units taught on these courses will develop, and the overall level of integration of such units into degree courses as a whole will no doubt reflect changing perceptions as to the value of such skills to graduates.

Pessimists, especially those who strongly support business studies in archaeology, might say that as a proportion of all courses currently on offer, those which include business studies represent a pitifully small group. They might point out that archaeology already relies on business skills to a high degree and that not covering such topics in the basic educational programme from which most archaeologists build their careers is like leaving out a consideration of European Neolithic or the Roman conquest of Britain.

Cynics might wonder what all the fuss is about. Over the last century or so archaeology has established itself as a recognized and respected profession without the help of all this business management stuff. This point of view raises an interesting question because in a way it is right: how have archaeologists gained an understanding of management skills? The answer to this seems to lie in two main directions, both of which have implications for future developments.

First, many practising archaeologists over the last century or so have brought management skills in from other walks of life. For many, archaeology has been a second career, either by choice or fortune. Military service and the management skills inherent in a military training have made a major contribution to archaeology. The work of Pitt Rivers is an early case (see, for example, McAdam, this volume). He attended the Royal Military College at Sandhurst for six months in 1841 and was commissioned as a lieutenant into the footguards, the Grenadier Guards, in 1845. This training seems to have contributed much to his ability to use surveying instruments, make models, and draw sections and plans (Thompson 1977: 14). It appears, however, to have helped little in the planning and running of his early excavations at Cissbury in 1867 and 1868 which mainly seem to have been in the antiquarian tradition of collecting objects for his collection, although sections were dug and recorded in a systematic way (Thompson 1977: 48). He returned to soldiering in 1873, accepting command of a brigade depot at Guildford, the greatest responsibility of his military career. He was promoted to major-general in 1877. This experience of service seems to have contributed greatly to his expertise in organizing and maximizing the results from fieldwork (Thompson 1977: 54).

Of more recent date is the experience of Sir Mortimer Wheeler. Prior to military service in 1914 Wheeler had not been involved in excavations, but there can be little doubt that his experience on active service influenced his management style in later life. Under the conditions of active service, decision-making is intense as instincts are for survival rather than academic niceties; Wheeler himself records having once experienced the sudden and unforgivable urge to put a bullet through the head of one member of a raiding party who was not pulling his full weight as part of the team (Wheeler 1955: 43). In comparison, planning and executing an archaeological excavation project must have seemed a doddle.

The second source of understanding in this area comes from self-teaching of some sort. For some this means learning on the job from others (including those already mentioned who have brought in outside skills) and following their example. More recently it has involved simply buying a book on business management and picking up ideas in this way.

Looking ahead, where do these ideas lead us? Three areas of change seem relevant as endorsing the hopes of the optimist, redressing the imbalance perceived by the pessimist, and rectifying the short-fall identified by the cynic.

Revision of teaching programmes

The content and structure of most existing courses in archaeology probably owe more to gradual evolution, and the interests of those delivering them, than the critical appraisal of what such courses should concern themselves with in order to provide students with the best possible exposure to the subject and the greatest chance of using what they have spent their time learning to get a worthwhile job. Assessment of skill needs and further market research on the orientation of courses will no doubt help this, and perhaps lead to the further revision of the core curricula considered above. Unlike many professional fields, the Department of Trade and Industry do not at present carry out routine reviews of vocational needs and skills shortages for archaeology. This is perhaps something which in the first instance could be developed by the IFA, following on from the surveys of training needs already carried out.

Implementing the conclusions of such studies will require liaison with representatives from the training providers which in the absence of an organization to represent those interests has to be done on a centre-by-centre basis. The evolution of course content based on proper market research would seem the most appropriate way of developing the core curriculum and keeping it up to date and relevant. Such research might also, however, identify the need for joint-honours programmes in which archaeology is available in combination with management studies.

Other changes on the horizon will also have their effect. The European context of courses will have greater relevance in future. Chapter 3 of the *Treaty on European Union* (the Maastrict Treaty) deals with education and training. Article 126 covers the development of quality education by encouraging cooperation between member states. Article 127 deals with the implementation of a Union-wide vocational training policy to supplement and support what is being done by member states. In this the EC will aim to:

1 facilitate adaptation to industrial changes, in particular through vocational training and retraining;
2 improve initial and continuing vocational training in order to facilitate vocational integration and reintegration into the labour market;
3 facilitate access to vocational training and encourage mobility of instruction and trainees and particularly young people;
4 stimulate cooperation on training between educational or training establishments and firms; and
5 develop exchanges of information and experience on issues common to the training systems of the member states.

How this will be translated into action has yet to emerge, but the emphasis on vocational (also called 'near to market') skills is noteworthy and has recently appeared in the British government's revision of the arrangements for the funding of the Research Councils announced in a White Paper (Her Majesty's Government 1993).

Recognizing and supplementing existing knowledge and skills

Archaeologists are generally highly trained, knowledgeable and skilled people. Traditionally, those skills are recognized through academic and professional qualifications, but with the development of National Vocational Qualifications (NVQs) and Scottish Vocational Qualifications

186 Timothy Darvill

(SVQs) there are new opportunities to recognize other kinds of skill sets. Although originally conceived as providing an alternative entry route to vocationally orientated professions (Startin 1993), a more realistic initial role for such qualifications in archaeology is to provide a system for recognizing skill sets that many archaeologists have developed since leaving university. It is notable that the draft proposals for NVQs and SVQs emphasized the management aspects of archaeological work (COSQUEC 1992). Thus NVQs and SVQs look as if they will complement traditional academic qualifications rather than be an alternative to them.

NVQs and SVQs could also provide the framework for supplementing existing skills, especially in the area of business studies in archaeology: such things as management techniques and procedures; human resource management; finance and accountancy; marketing and promotion; and project management. Novel and innovative schemes for the delivery, monitoring, and assessment of learning programmes will be needed for this according to the nature of the specific subject and the level of attainment being pursued. Distance learning and action learning of various sorts will no doubt have their place, but other avenues should be considered too, for example secondment, day release courses, and project learning.

The role of Continuing Professional Development

Archaeology is not a static subject in its content (i.e. knowledge-base), its practice, or its social context. Keeping up with developments is time-consuming and while a certain amount can be done through self-directed reading and attending meetings, the opportunities for critical appraisal of developments and structured learning experiences require higher levels of commitment. The opportunities for CPD in archaeology are really only just beginning to be explored and there is a long way to go before the profession includes a strongly recognizable CPD element in its culture. Adjustments need to be made by training providers (CPD workshops are not glorified seminars or small-scale conferences in the traditional sense) as well as by the users of such facilities.

A key element to the success of CPD programmes is the identification of needs so that individuals attend programmes that are appropriate to their situation and existing knowledge. Staff development reviews provide the intra-organizational strategic context for thinking through which skills staff will need in two, five or ten years time, the balance between training existing staff or recruiting new staff to meet those needs, and the timetable and resource requirements (time and financing) for staff development. Annual staff appraisals provide a mechanism for identifying training needs, making a training plan (which might be spread over several years), and fixing targets. The problems now facing many organizations are, firstly, making time available for employees to attend training programmes, and, secondly, knowing what courses are available to achieve the goals which have been set.

CONCLUSIONS

This chapter has mainly been concerned with the preparation of archaeologists for management. Inevitably, however, it has been necessary to look more widely at aspects of the overall provision of training for archaeology. Context and balance are the important points. Business studies and management training will only ever be a small part of the wider package of knowledge and skills that an archaeologist requires. In the past, training in management skills has been rather under-represented in most courses. This imbalance is beginning to be redressed, not least because of the prevailing political climate in higher education and external pressures to promote transferable, essentially vocational, knowledge and skill sets. But there is always the danger of moving too far in the opposite direction and over-emphasizing this aspect. Business management is itself a big subject area which more than fills undergraduate and postgraduate timetables for dedicated courses. The application of business studies in the context of archaeological work must inevitably be selective and closely related to the kinds of situations that will be encountered in later life. Moreover, a good deal of management in archaeology is organizationally specific and this can only be learnt on the job (see Pryor, this volume).

Changes in course curricula can only help those coming through their archaeological training now or in the future. For those already in post CPD programmes provide the best opportunity to enhance their existing knowledge and skills. One of the problems with developing new courses of this kind, though, is the relatively small number of potential students who will be interested and suitable. In this connection support from the IFA and English Heritage for short courses is critical to their success, especially at this stage of testing and developing both the market for such courses and the culture of delivery.

ACKNOWLEDGEMENTS

The preparation of this paper has been greatly assisted by the generosity of colleagues around the country who have discussed the content and structure of courses with which they are involved. I should especially like to thank Mick Aston, Mark Brisbane, Steve Burman, Martin Carver, Chris Chippindale, Peter Fowler, David Fraser, Jane Grenville, Ian Hodder, Alan Hunt, John Hunter, Ian Ralston, Trevor Rowley and John Wood for their helpful comments and access to unpublished data and information.

REFERENCES

Anon. (1993) *HND Practical Archaeology: Course Handbook*, Yeovil: Yeovil College and Bournemouth University.
Austin, D (1987) 'The future of archaeology in British universities', *Antiquity* 61: 227–38.

COSQUEC (1992) *Draft Proposals for consultation: National and Scottish Vocational Qualifications in (a) Environmental Conservation (Archaeology) at Levels 2, 3, and 4, and (b) Archaeological Illustration Level 3*, Cheltenham: COSQUEC.

Council of the European Communities (1993) *Treaty on European Union*, Luxembourg: Office for Official Publications of the European Communities.

English Heritage (1989) *The Management of Archaeology Projects*, London: Historic Buildings and Monuments Commission for England.

English Heritage (1991) *Management of Archaeological Projects*, London: Historic Buildings and Monuments Commission for England.

Fowler, P. (1991) 'Heritage management training, UK', in Archaeological Assistance Division, National Park Service *Federal Archaeology Report*, Washington: US National Park Service.

Fraser, D. (1991) 'Professional training for archaeologists – The questionnaire', *The Field Archaeologist* 14: 244.

Fraser, D. (1993) 'The training initiative: short training courses in archaeology', *The Field Archaeologist* 19: 372.

Her Majesty's Government (1993) *White Paper on Science and Technology* (published 26 May 1993), London: HMSO.

Institute of Field Archaeologists (1992) *The Institute of Field Archaeologists Directory of Educational Opportunities in Archaeology*, Birmingham: Institute of Field Archaeologists.

Mercer, R, (1978) 'The university department of archaeology – its position vis à vis Rescue Archaeology', in T.C. Darvill, M. Parker Pearson, R. Smith and R. Thomas (eds), *New Approaches to our Past: An Archaeological Forum*, Southampton: University of Southampton Archaeological Society, 53–62.

Saunders, A, (1989) 'Heritage management and training in England', in H. Cleere, (ed.) *Archaeological Heritage Management in the Modern World*, London: Unwin Hyman, 152–63.

Startin, B, (1993) 'Developed in archaeology by archaeologists for archaeology?', *The Field Archaeologist* 19: 375–78.

Thompson, M.W. (1977) *General Pitt-Rivers: Evolution and Archaeology in the Nineteenth Century*, Bradford upon Avon: Moonraker Press.

Universities and Colleges Admissions Service (1993) *University and College Entrance: Official Guide 1994*, London: Universities and Colleges Admissions Service.

Wheeler, M. (1955) *Still Digging*, London: Michael Joseph.

Wood, J. (1993) 'Digging ourselves into holes? Education, training and professional development in heritage conservation', in H. Swain (ed.) *Rescuing the Historic Environment: Archaeology, the Green Movement and Conservation Strategies for the British Landscape*, Hertford: RESCUE, 77–82.

CHAPTER THIRTEEN

THE MANAGEMENT OF ARCHAEOLOGICAL PROJECTS

Theory and practice in the UK

GILL ANDREWS AND ROGER THOMAS

Project management has been the focus of much discussion in recent years. This chapter considers the way in which project management has been approached in a specifically archaeological context in the UK in recent years, and looks in particular at a document, *Management of Archaeological Projects* (English Heritage 1991a) which has aroused considerable interest in the archaeological profession since its publication. This document, widely known as MAP2 was, prior to this volume, the only published literature available on the subject of archaeological project management. This chapter will examine the background to, and reasons for the production of, MAP2, outline the approach to archaeological project management which is exemplified by MAP2 and consider the implications of the document for the theory and practice of archaeological management in the light of experience gained since 1991. The chapter will conclude with a brief discussion of the changing relationship between academic concerns and managerial ones in British archaeology since the early 1970s.

BACKGROUND

Current approaches to archaeological project management in the UK are the product of the particular arrangements which exist here for the organization and funding of archaeological work. A consideration of those arrangements and of their evolution over the past twenty years is therefore important for an understanding of our approaches to archaeological project management and for an appreciation of the purposes of MAP2 itself. For a fuller account of the nature and development of archaeological arrangements in the UK, readers are referred to chapters in Hunter and Ralston (1993).

Prior to about 1970, 'public' archaeology in the UK was, with some important exceptions, conducted on a relatively modest scale, with limited funding and with organizational arrangements and procedures which were largely *ad hoc*. Around 1970, however, deep professional and public concern about the widespread destruction of archaeological sites by development led to a steep increase in the level of government funds available for 'rescue' archaeology and, consequently, to the establishment of a network of permanent and professionally staffed archaeological units to undertake this work. Initially, funds were made available to meet the running costs of archaeological organizations, but in 1980 the central government body responsible for providing the bulk of funding for archaeological work in England (now English Heritage) introduced a policy of 'project funding'. Under this policy, funds were no longer provided for the support of organizations, but were only made available for specific archaeological projects of defined scope, duration and cost. The purpose of this policy was to ensure that funds were allocated to projects which represented value for money in academic terms.

The second half of the 1980s saw further developments in archaeological policy in England, notably the incorporation of archaeological considerations into the statutory processes of town and country planning. These developments culminated in the Department of the Environment's Planning Policy Guidance note 16, *Archaeology and Planning* (PPG 16) (Department of the Environment 1990). PPG 16 emphasises the role of local planning authorities (LPAs) in protecting archaeological remains from development through the planning process, including, where necessary, ensuring that investigation and publication take place. Furthermore, PPG 16 stipulates that the responsibility for any archaeological work made necessary by development falls on the developer. As a result, much archaeological work which would formerly have been funded by central or local government is now paid for by developers, the work usually being carried out by archaeological units working under contract to the developer and in accordance with the archaeological requirements of local planning authorities and the archaeological officers who advise them. Consequently, there is now a range of different kinds of organization involved in 'public' archaeology in the UK. Their roles, and the relationships between them, are relevant to archaeological project management and to the origin and purposes of MAP2.

Within the present arrangements for archaeology in the UK, one can identify three principal kinds of roles. First, there is the protection of archaeological remains and monuments under the ancient monuments or planning legislation, and the provision of statutory or quasi-statutory advice on archaeological matters (including the response to development proposals). This 'curatorial' role is the province of English Heritage and the LPAs. Second, there is the provision of funds for carrying out specific archaeological projects (English Heritage and developers). These sponsors may use consultants or other qualified professionals to advise on the scope and cost of projects and to supervise their execution. Third, there is the role of providing archaeological services (such as assessment, excavation or analysis) to developers and other funding bodies. This 'contract' role is performed mainly by archaeological units. It may be noted that the same body may perform more than one of these roles at the same time.

In essence, then, the division of roles is between those who specify what work should be done (and to what standard), those who commission and pay for that work in order to meet the specified requirements, those who advise on how the work is carried out, and those who execute that work in accordance with the specification and standards set. This division of roles underlies, and is of importance to understanding, the approach to archaeological project management which is advocated in MAP2.

It may be remarked that this structure reflects a much broader trend in Britain since 1979 to adopt 'market-based' solutions for the provision of services of all kinds. Such arrangements, which are now found very widely (for instance, in the now-privatized utility companies) involve a separation of roles between 'consumer' or 'client' (in this case, developers), 'provider' or 'contractor' (in this case, archaeological units) and 'regulator' (here, local and central government bodies) and are underlain by notions of competition between providers and freedom of choice for consumers. This supposed commercialization of an activity which was formerly centrally funded and controlled has provoked much comment (e.g. Swain 1991) and distinguishes the present situation in Britain from the 'state archaeological service' model found in some other parts of Europe.

THE DEVELOPMENT OF ARCHAEOLOGICAL PROJECT MANAGEMENT AND THE GENESIS OF MAP2

Interest in and awareness of the importance of archaeological project management has been growing since the 1970s as the scale and complexity of archaeological projects has increased and as the policy frameworks for archaeology have developed. The sharp increase in the early 1970s in the amount of archaeological information being recovered as a result of the rescue archaeology programme led to a growing backlog of unpublished excavations. The need to address this problem led to the production, in 1975 and 1982 respectively, of two influential reports which have been of fundamental importance in developing approaches to the management of archaeological projects. These reports – *Principles of Publication in Rescue Archaeology* (Department of the Environment 1975, a report by a working party of the Ancient Monuments Board for England and commonly known as the 'Frere Report' after the working party's chairman) and *The Publication of Archaeological Excavations* (Department of the Environment 1982, a report of a joint working party of the Council for British Archaeology and the Department of the Environment, referred to as the

'Cunliffe Report') gave rise to a set of archaeological management concepts and terms which have achieved a wide currency. These reports were influential in the development of MAP2.

The Frere Report addressed the problem of how to publish an ever-increasing quantity of archaeological data. The report put forward a model of archaeological projects which saw data managed at a series of levels (I to IV) which equated to successive stages in the life of a project, from excavation through to final publication. This report was important in providing a logical structure for the processing of excavated data, but the sheer volume of the data being recovered meant that the objective of prompt and economical publication remained elusive. In addressing this problem the Cunliffe Report stressed the need for the critical selection of data. Particular emphasis was put on the role of the research design (the part of a project design which sets out the academic objectives of the project) as a means of ensuring this selectivity, and the need for 'well defined thresholds for review and forward planning' was identified as a means for achieving this selectivity. This concept of regular critical review as the key to successful archaeological project management is central to the model put forward in MAP2.

Following the introduction of project funding, the early 1980s saw the establishment of archaeological projects of increasing size and complexity. However, it also witnessed continuing difficulties in achieving the completion of projects (and post-excavation analysis and publication projects in particular) on time and within budget. These developments led to an increasing interest in issues of management within the archaeological profession. This interest was manifested in particular by the production by English Heritage, from the mid-1980s onwards, of a series of documents dealing with archaeological project management.

The first of these documents, the *Design, Management and Monitoring of Post-Excavation Projects* (English Heritage 1987) was circulated to all archaeological units which were receiving grants for projects from English Heritage, the major provider of funds for archaeological work in England at that time. Adherence to the principles of the document was made a condition of grant. In 1989, a more wide-ranging document, *The Management of Archaeology Projects* (English Heritage 1989), was published. This document gave a fuller definition of the terms set out in the Frere and Cunliffe Reports, and foreshadowed MAP2 in setting out the different stages in an archaeological project and the types of documentation which should be produced at each stage.

Building on this foundation, *Management of Archaeological Projects* (MAP2) was published by English Heritage in 1991 (English Heritage 1991a). MAP2 attempts to analyse and to set out clearly the processes and the logic that are involved in executing an archaeological project. MAP2 also provides some guidance on the use of project management techniques in archaeology, and includes a series of specifications for the documentation which should be produced at each stage in the life of a project.

Since the publication of MAP2, over 3,000 copies (at the time of writing) have been distributed within and beyond the archaeological profession, in the UK and abroad. The document has aroused widespread interest and discussion. It has been adopted by most archaeological units and its principles applied to their projects (whether funded by English Heritage or from other sources). Many local authority archaeological officers, and some developers and consultants, have also begun to incorporate MAP2 into project briefs and specifications as defining a standard to which work which should be carried out (e.g. Association of County Archaeological Officers 1993).

The interest with which MAP2 has been greeted indicates a perceived need for guidance on archaeological project management and it is appropriate to explore briefly the reasons for this. The factors which led to the production of MAP2 and its predecessors can be discussed under two main headings: factors which are essentially internal to the archaeological profession and ones which relate to the wider policy context of archaeological activity in the UK.

The principal internal factor which led to a concern with project management was the sustained growth in funding for archaeology which occurred from 1970 onwards, first from government and subsequently from developers. The change in scale of archaeological operations which increased funding made possible meant that it became necessary to formalize and make explicit project management procedures which had previously been largely implicit, intuitive and undocumented. Thus archaeological project managers who wished to make best use of their resources while finishing projects to timetable and within budget, had a stimulus to begin to develop formalized project management procedures for their work. Similarly, those archaeologists (notably in English Heritage) who were responsible for allocating resources, for controlling expenditure and for ensuring that projects were properly managed to completion needed to establish common mechanisms which would enable proposals to be assessed and projects to be monitored.

The external factors which exerted pressure in the same direction fall into two main areas, both of them essentially concerned with control and accountability. The first was the growing demand for accountability in the public sector, and the second was the incorporation of archaeology into the planning process through PPG 16 and the consequent introduction of private-sector developer funding for archaeological work.

Throughout the public sector in the UK, the 1980s saw an increasingly strong requirement for accountability and the need to be able to demonstrate that value for money was being obtained. This requirement posed a significant challenge to those responsible for archaeology in this sphere. Two main issues presented themselves. First, it was necessary to demonstrate that the results of particular pieces of archaeological work were likely to be of value and that expenditure on them would be justified. Second,

194 Gill Andrews and Roger Thomas

it was essential to ensure that publicly funded archaeological projects were carried out efficiently and cost-effectively, with the desired outcome being achieved within the planned timetable and budget for the project. Thus archaeologists in government who were responsible for allocating funds had not only to satisfy themselves, but had also to be able to demonstrate to their financial supporters in central government, that both the 'academic' and the 'operational' aspects of those projects had been considered thoroughly, were being monitored carefully and were under proper control.

Issues of control and accountability also arose, although in a slightly different form, from the introduction of the policies for archaeology and planning which are contained in PPG 16. PPG 16 states that where remains are threatened by development and cannot be preserved it is for the developer to make 'satisfactory and appropriate provision' (in other words, provision to the satisfaction of the LPA) for the archaeological excavation and recording of those remains and for the publication of the results of the work. This is usually achieved by a developer engaging an archaeological unit to carry out the work under contract. The developer may be assisted in this by an archaeological consultant who can negotiate with the LPA over the archaeological requirements, assess and advise on a unit's project proposals and monitor the execution of the work.

The policies of PPG 16 make the existence of formalized project management procedures desirable from a number of different points of view. The archaeological officer advising the LPA will wish to see a fully documented statement of the developer's proposed archaeological provision in a given case, so that judgements can be made over whether what is proposed is 'satisfactory and appropriate' in the circumstances. The developer or their consultant will wish to ensure not only that a project proposal will meet the reasonable requirements of the LPA but also that the work has been properly planned and costed by the archaeological unit and that the project will be executed to the requisite standard, on time and within budget. The unit will also find it useful to have common and agreed guidelines for project management as these can assist project staff in working up and executing projects which will conform to accepted approaches and standards.

The introduction of 'developer funding' to archaeology also resulted in the growth of competitive tendering for archaeological projects. In discharging the archaeological requirements of an LPA, a developer is entitled to seek proposals and costings from more than one archaeological unit in order to ensure that value for money is being obtained. In a competitive tendering context, all parties (LPA, developer, unit, consultant) will find it helpful to have a common set of approaches, concepts and terms, so as to provide a 'level playing field' for the preparation, costing and comparison of different proposals for the same project.

MAP2 seeks to respond to the needs identified above by presenting a research–driven model of archaeological project management. First, MAP2 makes explicit the need for selectivity in the recording and analysis of archaeological information: clearly, resources must be targeted onto those things which are most important in academic terms, so the need to formulate an archaeological research design (or statement of academic objectives) before a project commences, and to maintain, update and review it subsequently, is a central principle of MAP2. Second, MAP2 acknowledges the applicability of project management techniques (drawn ultimately from industry, and concerned with the control of activity, expenditure and quality of product) to archaeology. Third, by setting out a structure for the conduct of archaeological projects and a set of specifications for particular pieces of project documentation and products MAP2 contributes to the creation of a 'level playing field' for archaeological work in an era of competitive tendering.

MAP2 – THE MODEL

Projects of any kind (archaeological or non-archaeological) have particular characteristics which differentiate them from other kinds of activity, such as cyclical or repetitive ones. Projects have a short, clear list of objectives; they have a fixed time-scale and budget; they will very often be executed by a team; they do not allow scope for practice or rehearsal; they frequently entail the need to confront and deal with uncertainties or unexpected eventualities which arise during the life of the project; and they are intended to result in the creation of a definite end product.

MAP2 considers how these general characteristics of project-based activities can be approached in a specifically archaeological context. It does this by attempting to analyse and to set out clearly – in other words, to expose to view – the processes and the logic, both intellectual and managerial, that are involved in executing an archaeological project from conception to completion. In doing so MAP2 draws on established project management techniques and applies these to the particular problems of archaeological projects.

One of the most obvious difficulties of archaeological project management is the unpredictable nature of the archaeological resource. A project may start from a position of considerable uncertainty about its subject matter; both the academic objectives and the resourcing and programming of the work will often need to be reviewed and modified as the work progresses and as uncertainty about the nature of the material is reduced. In order to provide a clear and logical structure within which this process can take place, MAP2 advocates a staged approach to the execution of archaeological projects, with a strong emphasis on the importance of project planning at the outset of a project and with provision for a review at the end of each stage.

Of the project management techniques which MAP2 considers, the most important relate to project planning. Good planning is critical to the success of any projects and involves a range of activities. These include defining clear objectives and standards, making soundly based estimates of the resources required to achieve these objectives and standards, programming activities and the use of resources so as to attain project objectives, appointing a project manager who can coordinate project activity and motivate the project team, and assembling a project team which contains the experience and skills necessary to execute the project. MAP2 works through these general principles in the context of a large-scale excavation project and its subsequent programme of post excavation analysis leading to publication.

Applying the concept of a staged approach to such a project, MAP2 defines five principal phases of activity (see Figure 13.2):

- project planning (Phase 1)
- field work (Phase 2)
- assessment of potential for analysis (Phase 3)
- analysis (Phase 4)
- dissemination (Phase 5)

Each of these phases is based on an underlying, more fundamental cycle of activities (Figure 13.1) which is repeated through the successive phases of the project. The components of this cycle are:

1 Proposal: a project is made, setting out the objectives of the project and the means of achieving them.
2 Decision: a decision is taken to proceed (or not) with the project.
3 Data-collection: the project is carried out – data (in a wide sense, including artefacts, samples and so forth) are gathered and appropriately documented.
4 Review: the results of the work are reviewed, and consideration given to the next steps to be taken.

Thus, at the end of the cycle there is the opportunity to formulate a further set of proposals and the cycle begins again. In its generalized form, taking stage 3 to cover any kind of activity, this cycle underlies a very wide range of different kinds of activities; choosing and taking a holiday or carrying out a large construction project may involve the same basic cycle of 'proposal, decision, action, review'. As far as archaeology is concerned there is nothing new in this: a process of data-collection and review followed by selection, further study and ultimately publication has always been implicit in the structure of archaeological projects. Making the process explicit for the successive phases of a project has, however, allowed a clear distinction to be drawn between the different activities which occur at each phase, which has in turn enabled the identification of the

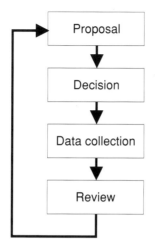

Figure 13.1   Archeological project management: the basic cycle (MAP2, Figure 2)

'well-defined thresholds for review and forward planning' which the Cunliffe Report advocated.

In MAP2, consideration of the cycle of activities just described in conjunction with the five main project phases resulted in a model for archaeological projects which can be depicted as a flow–chart (Figure 13.2).

First of all, it is worth noting that three 'review thresholds' are identified, at the end of phases 2, 3 and 4. At each of these points, the documentation resulting from data collection is reviewed. This review provides the basis for planning the next phase, allowing objectives to be redefined and the content and costing of the next phase to be firmly established. If review of the results of any phase indicate that no further work is merited, the project is brought to a close by proceeding to publication and deposition of the project archive.

The purpose of the initial planning phase is to formulate the proposal or project design which sets out both the academic objectives of the project (the research design) and the means (staffing, resources, timetable) of achieving them. Once completed, approval of the project design will need to be sought both from the funding body (English Heritage or a developer) and, in many cases, from those responsible for protecting the archaeological resource (LPA or English Heritage).

Following a decision to proceed, data collection (excavation, fieldwalking, geophysical survey and such like) will result in the production of a site archive. Again MAP2 provides a specification for the site archive (MAP2, Appendix 3).

However successful the fieldwork phase has been in terms of meeting the original objectives, the data collected is bound to require a period of

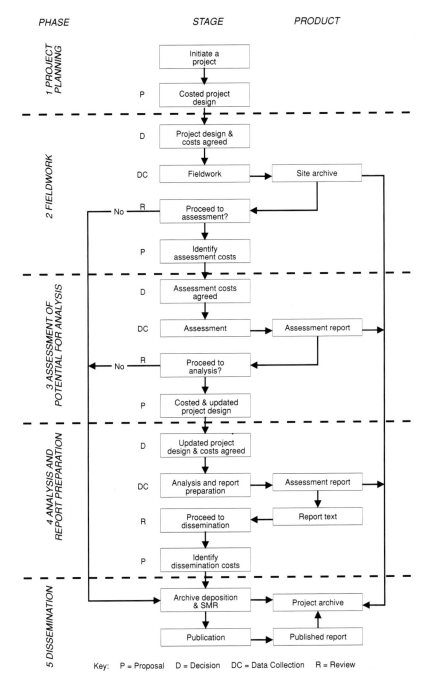

Figure 13.2   A model for the management of archaeological projects (MAP2, Figure 1)

appraisal before the commencement of post-excavation analysis leading to publication. Post-excavation analysis is particularly time-consuming and expensive and justification for such work must be carefully made. Some kind of selectivity will almost always be needed when planning post-excavation analysis, and the more we already know about a particular aspect of the past, the more carefully that selection will have to be made so as to avoid the danger of producing results that are repetitive or of limited value in some other way. Making the necessary selections and decisions about analysis and ensuring that a publication is produced which accurately reflects the academic importance of the results of fieldwork, within the resources available, are two of the most demanding aspects of managing an archaeological project. The larger the project, the more demanding these tasks, and it was in this area that difficulties were encountered with some large post-excavation projects in the 1970s and 1980s.

It was for this reason that MAP2 introduced a formal 'Assessment of Potential for Analysis' phase into the model of archaeological project management. Making the necessary decisions about selection takes time, effort and expertise and it has become clear that, in order to ensure that post-excavation resources are allocated to best effect, a formal review phase is needed between the end of fieldwork and the commencement of post-excavation analysis. This assessment phase is the pivotal point in the life of an archaeological field project. Its purpose is to establish the value for post-excavation analysis of the data collected during fieldwork and contained in the site archive, and to indicate what further study may be merited.

The results of the assessment phase are presented in an assessment report (a specification for which is given in MAP2, Appendix 4). This report will include all the information needed to make decisions about the future direction of a project, including comments on the quantity and quality of the data in the site archive, a statement of its potential value for analysis and recommendations for the storage and long-term curation of that data.

The statement of the potential value of the data is unquestionably the most challenging aspect of the assessment, and is critical if the research objectives of the project are to be accurately redefined. It is not possible to be prescriptive about exactly what work, and how much, should be done during the assessment phase because of the variety of archaeological data. The guiding principle, however, is to do the minimum amount of work necessary to enable sound judgements about the value of the material and the future scope of the project to be made. Such judgements require considerable expertise and the best staff available should be used for such work. It is also important that assessments are integrated pieces of work, in which members of the project team communicate with each other so that the potential of relationships between all the elements of the total data-set can be established.

Once completed, the assessment report is reviewed to define whether, and what, further work is justified. Where assessment demonstrates that the site archive does contain material which has the potential to contribute to the pursuit of worthwhile research objectives, the analysis phase must be planned. When identifying data for analysis, the objectives of the analysis phase must be borne in mind: that is, the production of a report for publication supported by a research archive. Analysis must be planned with publication firmly in view, and the publication synopsis is therefore an important element of project design at this stage.

Just as the project design specifies the programme for fieldwork, so the up-dated project design should outline the specific research aims of the analysis phase and the contribution which the work will make to archaeological knowledge, together with a statement of the resources needed to achieve those aims.

Data collection during analysis should be approached in two stages. Detailed work on stratigraphic records, artefacts and environmental material will result in the production of catalogues, data-files and reports which together will go to make up the research archive. It will then be necessary to finalize the content of the publication. Assessment will have removed many of the uncertainties about the results of analysis, but cannot eliminate those uncertainties entirely. It is therefore important that any material which does not meet its potential as predicted at assessment is identified at as early a stage in the analysis phase as possible, so resources are not wasted on it (by the same token, if material proves to be more worthwhile than expected, it may be possible to reallocate resources from elsewhere in the project to that material).

Once data collection is complete, a draft text and illustrations for the final report can be produced, in accordance with the publication synopsis (as amended). MAP2 provides broad guidelines for report-writing (Appendix 7) and English Heritage has produced more detailed advice on this subject (English Heritage n.d. a, b).

The final phase of the MAP2 model is the dissemination phase. This phase covers the editing, production and printing of the report, and the deposition of the project archive in good order in an appropriate museum or other repository. The dissemination phase will involve members of the project team in liaison with those who are editing and publishing the report and those who are to receive the archive.

Publication of the report and deposition of the archive mark the formal end of a project. However, it will be recalled that the basic cycle of activities on which the MAP2 model is based ends with 'review' and it is this which enables individual projects to be seen in the context of wider cycles of research. 'Review' of a completed project – whether in the form of a published academic review of the report or through reflection (by members of the project team or by others) on the results of the project – should suggest future lines of work and research. These can then be incorporated into proposals for future projects, thus beginning the cycle again.

WORKING WITH MAP2 – EXPERIENCE TO DATE

It is (at the time of writing) nearly three years since MAP2 was published and the archaeological profession in the UK is still coming to terms with its interpretation and the practical problems posed by its implementation. Few major projects have been run on MAP2 principles from inception to completion so it is not yet possible fully to estimate its effects. However, the document seems to have been generally welcomed (but see Barrett 1992; Pryor this volume) and MAP2 is now being used in a wide range of contexts. It is appropriate, therefore, to review the operation of MAP2 in the light of experience of working with it to date. Comments fall under two main headings: those relating to interpretation and those relating to implementation.

Interpretation

The reason for which the MAP2 model has been generally accepted is, we believe, because MAP2 simply attempts to formalize and to set out clearly processes which have always existed, but which were in the past largely intuitive and undocumented. MAP2 provides a basic framework and set of principles, and a number of archaeological organizations and groups have, as the preface to MAP2 suggested, begun to produce their own internal guidelines which seek to marry MAP2 principles and terminology to particular sets of working practices or areas of interest.

The area of interpretation which has given rise to the most discussion is that concerning the assessment phase. In the past, some kind of review of the results of fieldwork will always have preceded the commencement of post-excavation analysis, but the innovation which MAP2 introduces is the definition of a formal phase of assessment in which the potential of material for analysis and publication is explored and documented, as the basis for planning the analysis phase.

The nature of the assessment process has been widely discussed, and a range of differing views have been expressed. Two main issues have emerged: the amount of work which it is necessary or appropriate to undertake at the assessment stage and the relationship between the assessment report and the updated project design.

On the first point, some have argued that it is cost-effective to undertake, as part of the assessment process, recording of data which will contribute to the eventual analysis. This is to misunderstand the nature of assessment. As indicated above, assessment should involve the minimum amount of work necessary to enable reliable judgements to be made about the potential for future analysis, in order to ensure that available resources are targeted onto the most worthwhile material. This purpose is entirely defeated if recording for analysis is brought into the assessment phase. That said, arriving at a satisfactory definition of 'minimum amount of work' has proved a challenging task. Meeting this challenge has involved developing a range of new methodologies specifically for assessment (such as pilot studies and sampling approaches) and has also involved recognizing that what is appropriate at the assessment phase will depend heavily on the details of specific instances: the nature of the material, its quality and quantity and the research objectives of particular projects.

In discussing the second point, the original focus of MAP2 and the documents which preceded it is relevant. The initial impetus for their production came from the need to bring under control major post-excavation projects arising from programmes of excavation which had been carried out often without clearly documented research designs to guide data collection. Accordingly, assessment was initially seen as an attempt to establish *de novo* the character and range of potential excavated assemblages, with the 'updated' research design for analysis selecting those aspects of the potential which were to be exploited. In the case of projects which have started life with a clearly-defined research design, the position may be rather different. In such cases, the primary purpose of assessment is to 'measure' potential against the original research objectives, with the identification of new and unexpected areas of potential as a second objective. Here, the assessment process and updated research design will be much more in the nature of a review and revision of the original research design for fieldwork than is the case with 'backlog' post-excavation projects in which assessment and the resulting research design for analysis may often be the first systematic attempt to establish potential and the direction of the analysis project. Thus, there is a degree of overlap between the specifications in MAP2 for the assessment report and the updated project design which may be unnecessary for projects which have been properly documented from the start. This may be a point to consider for the future.

Implementation

The successful implementation of MAP2 requires those involved to be skilled in the application of project management techniques. These techniques include project planning and estimating, controlling time and resources, tracking progress, and communication and team-working. The formal application of these techniques to archaeological projects is relatively new, so a range of new skills has had to be learned by archaeological project managers and this has been a key issue for the implementation of MAP2. Four aspects in particular may be discussed.

First, project planning and documentation. At first sight the amount of documentation required to support MAP2 project proposals may seem rather daunting. However, initial resistance to investing the necessary time and effort at this stage is generally overcome as the advantages of doing so, not only to satisfy the project sponsor but also for enabling the project to be properly managed by the organization undertaking it, come to be appreciated.

Second, estimating. Good estimating is critical to the success of any project, but until recently there has been no significant body of experience and knowledge in this area of archaeology, and this has been a problem for archaeological project management. As lessons are learned from reviewing projects undertaken with MAP2 procedures, a body of knowledge about work-rates will be built up which will facilitate the process of accurate estimating for future projects.

Third, programming of work. In any project, establishing the correct sequence of activities and the links between them, so that a smooth flow of activity is maintained, is crucial (this is the issue which the Critical Path Analysis method is designed to address). Again, this is an area in which archaeological project managers can usefully learn from experience.

Finally, communication and team-work. Traditionally, many archaeological projects have comprised a range of separate individual contributions to a joint enterprise. Successful management of a complex archaeological project demands a fully integrated approach, in which all those engaged on the project work as, and consider themselves to be, part of a team with a common goal. There are two key aspects to this: proper briefing of all members of the project team at the outset, and effective communication within the team as the work proceeds. Such an approach is essential to the successful implementation of MAP2, and achieving integrated team-working may demand adjustments to working practices and roles.

A second major issue of implementation concerns broader questions of organization. The use of project management techniques and, indeed, the concept of project-based funding and project-oriented organizations, raises the question of what kinds of organizational structures and skills are most appropriate for project-based operations. This issue is outside the scope of this paper (but see Nixon, this volume; Locock, this volume) but is obviously closely linked to the question of managing individual projects.

Finally, a more general comment may be made concerning the nature of MAP2. The document is a set of guidelines intended to assist those engaged in carrying out projects: it is not a rigid prescription to be applied mechanically without regard to the circumstances and character of individual projects. Understanding this point will ensure that implementing MAP2 does not become unduly time-consuming, costly or restrictive. MAP2 is intended to facilitate, not to hinder, effective project management.

PROJECT MONITORING AND MAP2

MAP2 is concerned with project management, which is the responsibility of those undertaking the project. As was discussed above, however, the origins of MAP2 lie in the need for accountability on the parts of those funding projects, or specifying project requirements. The issue of 'external' monitoring of projects may therefore be commented on briefly.

Internal progress tracking and quality control is integral to good project management, but additionally the project sponsor may wish to undertake external monitoring of a project, particularly if payment is being made in stages against the completion of specified blocks of work. A MAP2 project design sets out the objectives, methods and standards, and resourcing and programming of a project. The purpose of monitoring is to ensure that the intended outcome of the project is being achieved in accordance with the project design and to identify areas where corrective action may be necessary, either because of problems in executing the work or because the potential of the material has proved less, or more, than originally expected. Experience suggests that there are considerable benefits on both sides in having projects monitored by an appropriately qualified person who is not a member of the project team and can therefore take a detached view of the progress of the project. Such monitors will often be used by, and report to, the project sponsor although the curatorial body may also wish to be involved in the external monitoring of the project.

Thus MAP2 and the internal and external monitoring which it facilitates can serve the separate needs of the project team, of the project sponsor and of the curatorial body whose requirements the project is intended to meet. At one level the needs of each are different, but at root the purpose of project management and monitoring is to ensure that resources are always targeted onto the most worthwhile areas for archaeological study. Both day-to-day project management and formal periodic monitoring will identify areas where decisions need to be made about the use of resources, and the monitoring process provides a forum for discussion and agreement between all parties on these decisions. The criteria by which these decisions are made will be discussed in the next section.

MAP2: MANAGEMENT AND RESEARCH

It may seem slightly perverse to conclude a chapter on archaeological project management with a series of comments on the research-based nature of archaeology. In fact, we think that one of the most significant aspects of MAP2 is the emphasis that it throws onto the academic criteria which drive managerial decision-making in archaeology.

It is a characteristic of the archaeological profession in the UK that it is now operating on a scale and under circumstances which demand the routine use of management techniques which are more commonly associated with commerce and industry. However, the values which drive our management decisions are fundamentally academic ones. This basic fact means that we have always to attend equally to academic issues on the one hand and managerial concerns on the other. MAP2, in setting out a model which is essentially research-driven but which is implemented through the application of established project management techniques, seeks to address this issue in particular.

MAP2 lays constant emphasis on the need to justify the academic objectives that are proposed for a project, and on the need for appropriate selectivity in data collection. By clarifying and exposing the managerial procedures of archaeological projects, MAP2 has thrown the spotlight onto the academic criteria by which we make our project management decisions. Both day-to-day managerial decisions and the major decisions following review stages have to be made on the basis, ultimately, of archaeological value – in other words against a research agenda of what we want to know about the past. With the greater emphasis on the explicit justification of our objectives, it is becoming increasingly important that we articulate our research agendas fully.

It is at this point that we would like to broaden the perspective somewhat and to consider how MAP2 may fit into broader patterns of archaeological thinking and policy development, particularly those of English Heritage and its predecessors concerned with archaeology in England. We refer above to the need, when managing archaeological work, to keep academic and managerial considerations in balance. Taking a broad view, we believe that it is possible to detect an oscillation, in terms of the dominant concerns at any one time, between managerial and academic concerns in archaeology, extending back for over twenty years.

The picture presented below is in effect a commentary on the descriptive account presented above of the development of archaeology in the UK since the 1970s. The commentary is given from a particular point of view, and certainly represents a gross simplification of events over that period. However, we believe that the account does have a basic validity.

Prior to the early 1970s, archaeology was generally on a small scale. Project management was largely intuitive and undocumented, and the distinction between academic and managerial problems probably received little explicit consideration. From about 1973 to about 1980, however, government support for archaeology was largely concerned with establishing and supporting archaeological organizations in the form of units of various sizes and types up and down the country (Thomas 1993: 138). This was essentially a problem of management – how to create stable organizations capable of responding to the need to carry out rescue excavations and surveys. This period represents our first phase, in which managerial concerns were prominent.

By about 1980, it was felt that the financial needs of these organizations were overwhelming the academic needs of archaeology, limiting the scope for new work and fresh ideas. In response, the policy of project-funding was introduced with its emphasis on the need for research designs and clearly defined academic objectives. Thus in this second phase, attention was directed towards academic issues (Thomas 1993: 138–9).

During the mid-1980s it was realized that the scale and complexity of many projects, and particularly of large urban post-excavation projects, had become such that far closer attention needed to be paid to project management in order to ensure that the academic objectives of those projects were actually achieved as intended. This concern led to a series of English Heritage papers, prompted largely by the demand for accountability, from 1987, culminating in MAP2 in 1991. This period also saw the development of the policies of PPG 16. Thus in the later 1980s and early 1990s, our third phase, there was a strong focus on the management of archaeological activity.

As already indicated, MAP2 has, by establishing a model for archaeological project management, thrown the spotlight back onto the question of the academic values which drive that model. Similarly PPG 16, by establishing firm policies for managing the archaeological resource, has brought into sharp focus questions of what should be managed, and how – in other words, questions of academic importance.

We believe, therefore, on the basis of extrapolation from this brief analysis of past developments, that we are now entering a fourth phase, in which attention will be directed to issues of archaeological importance, academic objectives and the archaeological research agenda. *Exploring our Past* (English Heritage 1991b) represents an early response to this concern, setting out a very broad academic framework for future work. *Exploring our Past* is necessarily very general in scope and more detailed studies (e.g. Fulford and Huddleston 1991 on Romano-British pottery; see also Wenban-Smith, this volume) will be important in amplifying the research agendas for particular topics. Such research agendas are essential to the proper application of the MAP2 model, and their production is a high priority for the years ahead.

CONCLUSIONS

In this chapter we have attempted to outline the factors which have resulted in the present approaches to archaeological project management in the UK as exemplified by the document known as MAP2, to explain the MAP2 model, to explore some of the implications of its application, and to discuss the importance of MAP2 for the relationship between academic and managerial concerns in archaeological project management today. MAP2 is in many ways the product of a particular approach to archaeological organization and funding in the UK, but it does perhaps offer a number of lessons of wider applicability. Of these, we believe the most important concerns the fundamental importance of academic objectives to managerial decision-making. Archaeology seeks to study the past, and sound project-management driven by academic criteria is an essential means to that end.

ACKNOWLEDGEMENTS

Figures 13.1 and 13.2 are reproduced by permission of English Heritage. Warm thanks are due to Teresa Karpinska for typing the manuscript speedily and efficiently.

REFERENCES

Association of County Archaeological Officers (1993) *Model Briefs and Specifications for Archaeological Assessments and Field Evaluations*, Bedford: Association of County Archaeological Officers.

Barrett, J. (1992) '"Right reading lists" and "Novel Biographies"', paper given at the Archaeology in Britain Conference, Birmingham, April 1992.

Department of the Environment (1975) *Principles of Publication in Rescue Archaeology*, report by a working party of the Ancient Monuments Board for England Committee for Rescue Archaeology, London: Department of the Environment, limited circulation report.

Department of the Environment (1982) *The Publication of Archaeological Excavations*, report of the Joint Working Party of the Council for British Archaeology and the Department of the Environment, London: Department of the Environment, limited circulation report.

Department of the Environment (1990) *Planning Policy Guidance: Archaeology and Planning*, PPG 16, London: HMSO.

English Heritage (1987) *The Design, Management and Monitoring of Post-Excavation Projects*, London: English Heritage, limited circulation report.

English Heritage (1989) *The Management of Archaeology Projects*, London: English Heritage, limited circulation report.

English Heritage (1991a) *Management of Archaeological Projects*, London: Historic Buildings and Monuments Commission for England.

English Heritage (1991b) *Exploring out Past – Strategies for the Archaeology of England*, London: Historic Buildings and Monuments Commission for England.

English Heritage (n.d. a) *Academic and Specialist Publications. Preparing your Text for Publication*, London: English Heritage, limited circulation report.

English Heritage (n.d. b) *Academic and Specialist Publications. Preparing your Illustrations for Publication*, London: English Heritage, limited circulation report.

Fulford, M. and Huddleston, K. (1991) *The Current State of Romano-British Pottery Studies: A Review for English Heritage*, English Heritage Occasional Paper No. 1, London: Historic Buildings and Monuments Commission for England.

Hunter, J. and Ralston, I. (eds) (1993) *Archaeological Resource Management in the UK: An Introduction*, Stroud: Alan Sutton Publishing.

Swain, H. (ed.) (1991) *Competitive Tendering in Archaeology*, Hertford: Standing Conference of Archaeological Unit Managers/RESCUE.

Thomas, R. (1993) 'English Heritage funding policies and their impact on research strategies' in J. Hunter and I. Ralston (eds) *Archaeological Resource Management in the UK: An Introduction*, Stroud: Alan Sutton Publishing.

CHAPTER FOURTEEN

PROJECT MANAGEMENT IN A CHANGING WORLD

Redesigning the pyramid

MARTIN LOCOCK

Conventional management hierarchies are characterized by long chains of command and limited freedom of action for junior staff. While the pyramid model may have been appropriate for large-scale formal excavations, the need for flexibility and devolved decision-making when undertaking assessments has become apparent.

As part of its recent restructuring to create separate Contracts and Curatorial operations, Glamorgan-Gwent Archaeological Trust (GGAT) has also rethought its management structure to meet the perceived needs. By placing the emphasis on enabling quality project execution, and creating a series of management groups contributing expertise as needed, GGAT is now able to maintain standards of work even when the unexpected occurs.

This chapter outlines the theoretical management models available, and goes on to look at how GGAT's old and new structures operate in practice. Finally, the paper emphasizes that although structures can facilitate effective performance, the results depend critically on the attitude of staff.

MANAGEMENT IN ARCHAEOLOGY

In the early 1980s, when management courses for archaeologists were a new phenomenon, they were the subject of much ridicule. It was then widely thought that archaeologists were natural good managers, and needed no training. Now that English Heritage has designed its project planning around management, and has called its method manual *Management of Archaeological Projects* (MAP2) (English Heritage 1991), it is perhaps more acceptable to suggest that management, defined in this chapter as getting people to do their work competently and effectively, may perhaps have some relevance to the practice of archaeology.

The perception that management was irrelevant to archaeology was largely the result of a misconception of the nature of management. It may be hard to find words with the right connotations in the standard text-books on management, but it is harder to claim with any conviction that all other experience of working as a team cannot be applied to archaeology. This chapter will describe the way management structures are created and used, and the way in which the structures can create or solve problems.

A PERFECT HIERARCHY

Archaeological management, when discussed at all, was assumed to follow the hierarchical model of organization, typified by military structures (Cooper 1993). This may well be a result of the lasting influence of General Pitt Rivers and Brigadier Wheeler (see McAdam, this volume). In this model the structure is characterized by vertical ranks of increasing power and by horizontal differentiation of functions. The chain of command is clear and linear, with minimal contact between separate arms except via the head of the pyramid. This structure, as well as being appropriate to military organization, is suitable for industries with specialized tasks. A classic example of this is the Ford-style assembly line, with a front-axle section, containing the wheel-nut subsection, and the top-right wheel-nut worker. It is not, however, the only management structure possible.

OTHER WAYS OF LOOKING AT MANAGEMENT

There are occasions when the power structure of a hierarchy, in which the superior always knows better, bears little relation to actual knowledge or competence. Describing organizations in which this occurs rapidly becomes complex, because in these circumstances informed decision making requires extensive downward consultation, resulting in recursive and in some cases inverted real power structures operating within a notionally hierarchical framework. Such real power structures need not follow simple or logical patterns, and since they are organic rather than imposed creations, they cannot be predicted, and so can only be defined by detailed analysis of a specific organization. No formal classification of complex structures has emerged, although some models have been presented.

Drucker (1955) describes this as specialist or professional management: i.e., the management of specialists by non-specialists. The 'problem', in business terms, is that the head of a scientific Research and Development section may have a different agenda and set of priorities from that of the main business. Drucker emphasizes that the non-specialist must leave the specialist to know better about the operation of his section, but suggests ways in which the specialist can be brought into mainstream management decisions. In archaeological terms, this is a very relevant problem, in that the excavators of particular sites have more knowledge about the site than their managers. This means that the manager cannot say 'Layer 1 should be over layer 2': all the manager can say is 'You must decide the relationship between layers 1 and 2'.

Drucker does not address the problem of conflict of interest. The fact that the specialist has a separate agenda may mean that the interests of the business as a whole are ignored or damaged. He presented no mechanism to resolve such a problem. In archaeological terms, all personnel have two roles: as employees, and as professional archaeologists. These roles may conflict: the only acceptable solution is that the profession must come before the business. It is the manager's job to resolve such conflicts as they occur.

Drucker approaches the problem as an issue in line management: an alternative is to recognize specialist knowledge and use it as part of project management, by creating management teams with input to the project as a whole. The logical result of this approach is 'matrix management'

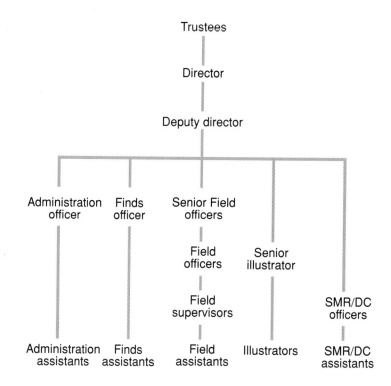

Figure 14.1 The line-management heirarchy, pre-1992

(see Nixon, this volume) in which horizontal as well as vertical control is possible. It can be argued that this structure is more closely in accord with the needs of modern archaeological projects.

GGAT STRUCTURE PRIOR TO 1992

The Glamorgan-Gwent Archaeological Trust was set up as the result of a Welsh Office initiative in 1975 to provide a service for the counties of Mid, South and West Glamorgan, and Gwent. The background to this initiative has been described by Owen-John (1986). The organization's activities developed in a typical trajectory. In the late 1970s and early 1980s work was funded directly by the government and developers, and substantial rescue excavations were carried out using government employment schemes. More recently, work has been mainly developer-funded, dominated by assessments in advance of planning determination. Despite these changes, the management structure remained fairly static, consisting of a line-management hierarchy with a director, deputy director, senior field officers, junior field officers, supervisors and site staff (Figure 14.1). Site staff included specialist planners and photographers, and recording was restricted to the supervisors. Parallel hierarchies existed for finds and administration work. This structure was in place during the successful execution of a series of major excavations.

ASSESSMENT WORK

Field evaluations and desk-top studies may appear at first glance to be simple archaeological projects. A field evaluation will expose a very small area of archaeological deposits, and not all of those exposed will be excavated. The size of the team is also small. As a result, it might be assumed that running an evaluation project is comparable to being an assistant supervisor or supervisor on a large excavation. This can lead to the ascription of a low status to this type of work, and so to poor performance. GGAT did not suffer from this problem excessively, but it did become apparent that a change in approach was needed.

The problems had arisen because of the previous structure of archaeological work. Most archaeologists start as excavators. After a few years the mysteries of planning and recording may be revealed, and finally supervisory status is reached. The work of a supervisor on a large excavation is almost wholly archaeological and the responsibilities of the post are expressed in terms of excavation. Other problems are dealt with by other people, or at least can be readily discussed with superiors. One of the reasons for the 'great divide' between directors and supervisors is that the supervisors are isolated from almost all of the management tasks required to run a project. As a result, promotion to director involves the sudden multiplication of responsibilities beyond a simple increase in personnel.

An assessment officer has to deal with a wide range of new areas, including personnel administration, contacts with clients, plant hire, deadlines and costings, sole responsibility for health and safety, and sufficient knowledge of the planning process to understand the needs of the work. These tasks can make the archaeology the smallest of problems, especially when the line manager visits rarely, and in an emergency the officer is left to decide for themself. On this basis, it is apparent that an assessment officer is better characterized as a junior manager rather than a supervisor. This change was incorporated in the new GGAT structure.

GGAT STRUCTURE FROM 1992

The publication of PPG 16 (Wales) in 1991 (Welsh Office) provided a stimulus to a reconsideration of the management structure of the Welsh trusts because it envisages a clear separation of curatorial and contracting roles. What emerged from the consultations was a structure intended to be more suited to the demands arising from developer-led archaeology, namely speed of response, quality execution, and flexibility. The new structure acknowledges that specific expertises are to be found throughout the Trust hierarchy and creates a series of management teams to allow the expertise to be brought to bear as needed by individual projects (Figure 14.2). Thus, although the two main sections (contracts and curatorial) have separate identities, and are financially independent, the structure eases communication between sections at all levels. The central services section, including administration and technical services (illustration and finds), provides services to both sections. In effect, the sections of the Trust operate an internal market, selling services to other sections. The structure is not fixed, and the post of head of technical services may be created in due course.

These changes provide the project officers with the back-up they need to carry out their new roles. Advice from the post-excavation manager, finds officer and senior illustrator can be channelled via the contracts section management team and the project manager to a project officer (Figure 14.3). Management is more flexible, so it is possible to adopt different practices depending on the individuals concerned: an inexperienced officer will be closely supervised and monitored, while more experienced staff work with minimal supervision. The structure may appear to be complex at times, because responsibility for managing a project is decided on organizational criteria rather than seniority: when the projects manager (assessments) is preparing a report on a major excavation, their manager is the projects manager (post-excavation); for an assessment project, the roles are reversed. This complexity is only superficial, however: within a single project, it is always clear who is in charge. One disadvantage of this arrangement is that the project officers are not identified as working for a particular manager, so that the next tier (principal archaeological officer)

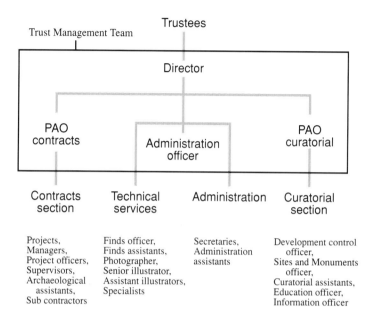

Figure 14.2   Management teams and institutional structure, 1992

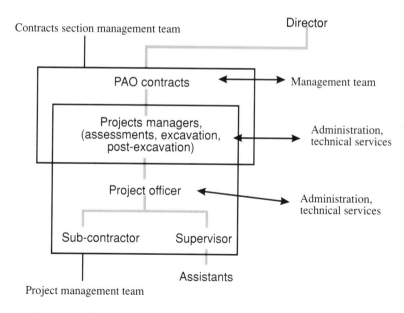

Figure 14.3   Application of the team approach

is needed for non-project personnel tasks, such as appraisal, training needs assessment and dealing with employment terms and conditions; on the other hand, it does mean that those with the greatest relevant experience are responsible for managing a project.

THE ROLE OF PROJECT OFFICERS

One of the products of the traditional excavation hierarchy is a pyramidal structure in which upward movement is restricted. The 'you cannot direct unless you have directed' paradox prevents junior staff from becoming trained and experienced in the necessary tasks. It was, until recently, normal for promotion to be achieved only by moving to a different organization. As a result, junior staff within an organization may become frustrated and do not achieve their full potential. In GGAT's new structure this problem is avoided as all staff are treated as potential or trainee project officers, and are given as much responsibility as they wish. The rapid turnover of projects, each with a definable goal (the report and prepared archive), means that the system of management can be readily adjusted as competence is proved. The individual is therefore treated on an individual basis, and the motivation of staff has ceased to be a problem.

THE ROLE OF EXCAVATORS

This chapter has concentrated on changes in the way that project officers executing assessments are managed. Alongside this has been a change in the treatment of project staff – excavators. In a structured large excavation, unless a single context planning system is used, it is usual to allocate specialist tasks to a limited group; context recording, for example, is usually restricted to supervisors. While administratively convenient this is unhelpful in professional terms as it prevents excavators from gaining experience in the skills needed for further career development. The requirements of assessment work are different. In a small team (of only two or three) it is vital that all staff should be capable of drawing, photographing, surveying and recording as well as excavating. As a result, a conscious attempt is now made at GGAT to share these skills. In addition, responsibility for logistics and administration is delegated whenever possible. This change in status is reflected both in terminology – project staff are now 'archaeological assistants' – and in salary, even though project staff are often perforce on temporary contracts.

REDESIGNING THE PYRAMID

The restructuring of the GGAT has allowed a rethink of the roles of the junior staff in projects, and it has been found that giving more responsibility, with appropriate training and supervision, has led to greater job satisfaction, improved staff morale and consequently to better performance. It is no longer a joke to talk of career development. In recognizing that the Trust's greatest resource is its skilled personnel, anything that keeps people busy and motivated is considered to be an investment in the future.

Thus effective management is seen to be the key to the achievement of quality assurance in the GGAT's work, and so a high value is placed on training, regular staff review and assessment of personal and project performance indicators. Flexibility within the structure allows rapid reward of proven skill. In quality assurance terms, no organization can afford to write off a project as a failure – this is both commercially and professionally unacceptable. Consistent staff performance is vital, and can only be achieved within an actively managed structure.

The new GGAT structure is not going to solve all management problems: in the end, it is the operation of the system, as much as its design, which will determine success or failure. However, the new structure has removed some of the recurrent problems of rigid hierarchies, and created a framework in which quality work is achieved by design, and not by accident.

ACKNOWLEDGEMENTS

The author is grateful to G. Dowdell, A.G. Marvell and other GGAT staff for their comments on the text; the views expressed are, however, those of the author alone.

REFERENCES

Cooper, M.A. (1993) 'Archaeology and management perspectives', *The Field Archaeologist* 18: 346–50.

Drucker, P.F. (1955) *The Practice of Management*, London, Heinemann.

English Heritage (1991) *Management of Archaeological Projects*, London: Historic Buildings and Monuments Commission for England.

Owen-John, H.S. (1986) *Rescue Archaeology in Wales*, Mainwaring-Hughes Award Series 3, Swansea: University College of Swansea.

Welsh Office (1991) *Planning Policy Guidance: Archaeology and Planning*, PPG 16, London: HMSO.

CHAPTER FIFTEEN

ROCKING THE BOAT

Project management means change

TARYN J.P. NIXON

In this chapter I propose to consider change in archaeology, and why archaeology is so well suited to project management. Building on this, and taking the Museum of London Archaeology Service (MoLAS) as a case study, I shall then outline how MoLAS has chosen to implement project management. Finally, I shall consider why it has or has not worked, looking at some of the benefits and disadvantages of matrix management as MoLAS has experienced it.

CHANGE IN ARCHAEOLOGY

The archaeological world is facing change from both external and internal factors. Externally there are regulatory factors such as Planning Policy Guidance: Archaeology and Planning (PPG 16) (Department of the Environment 1990) which has led to more, small projects and a different emphasis in the *modus operandi* of archaeological work; there are economic factors, including the recession, leading clients to demand increased certainty and value for money (and driving many of us to take a more 'customer'-orientated approach); there is increased competition. There are also political factors. Taking London as an example, there has been a radical change as a result of the introduction of the English Heritage Planning Advisory Service, and of the withdrawal of core funding from the Museum of London's former archaeology service.

Internally, and no doubt partly because of the external pressures, archaeologists are trying to bring about change within the profession by, for example, striving for better quality, trying to set standards against which practice can be monitored, and by designing projects with reference to regional and national as well as project specific research objectives. This attempt to improve things is partly in the interest of the resource, and partly in the interest of archaeologists themselves.

In considering how best to manage change, it is important to consider the nature of archaeology and of archaeologists. Archaeology is a discipline with unlimited potential but limited resources. There is never enough money to do a perfect job, the resource itself is finite, and there is no single 'right way' to, for example, excavate a site. So no two archaeological projects are the same, yet they all share generally similar goals. As for archaeologists, we tend to be inquisitive, analytical, dedicated, anarchical, and articulate. In addition, we require appropriate academic challenges and outlets.

These characteristics mean that it is necessary to ensure flexibility and creativity when planning and carrying out archaeological work. The treatment of different jobs of work as discrete projects – in other words the practice of project management – provides scope for creativity throughout the work: in project design; in trying to anticipate Murphy's Law; in responding to unpredictable occurrences; or in modifying a programme to accommodate another project's demands. However, the scope for creativity must be matched with accountability and control. Enter the project manager.

The project manager is distinct from the manager of classical or scientific management (see Cooper, this volume) who would generally set up systems and procedures to handle repetitive tasks in the most efficient manner possible. The success of the classical manager might be indicated by an end result where not much has happened to rock the boat, or alter the *status quo*. In contrast the project manager sets out with the intention of rocking the boat, and causing change. A project begins with a set of circumstances which will be different when the project is finished, as something will have been written, created or destroyed. Consequently project management has been defined as 'a means of bringing about beneficial change' (Barnes 1990).

As stated above, the archaeological world is changing; therefore, so given the nature of archaeology and archaeologists, it would appear that project management is an appropriate and active approach to taking control of and managing change. In other words, it can be said that change requires project management, which is itself bound to lead to further change. In sum, the adoption of a project management culture by an archaeological organization is inextricably linked with change.

THE MUSEUM OF LONDON ARCHAEOLOGY SERVICE

In considering how project management can be adopted it is apparent that archaeologists at many levels have been practising aspects of project management in varying degrees and to varying effect for many years. Certainly, archaeologists have been using Gantt and cascade charts to plan projects in stages and identify milestones; and using PERT to identify the relationships between tasks. However, this has almost always been done within the constraints of the structures of existing organizations. This chapter contends that a project-led organization can only flourish if the structure of the organization facilitates project management.

In the Museum of London until the end of 1991 the archaeological management structure was organized in hierarchical form, along the lines typified by the British civil service. There were three archaeological departments: the Department of Urban Archaeology, the Department of Greater London Archaeology and the Greater London Environmental Archaeology Service. Each had its own hierarchical substructure. It is argued increasingly that this sort of structure stifles debate (e.g. Torrington *et al.* 1989). The number of meetings proliferates but the communication of the results of those meetings is slow or breaks down completely. As debate is stifled, so is creativity, leading to reductions in the quality of work.

Matrix management, on the other hand, encourages debate (Mintzberg 1979). It places great importance on building teams (see Locock, this volume). Matrix management was originally conceived by the American aerospace industry. It was introduced in a multi-project environment, where each project was a bit different from the last, requiring creativity and innovation, but where each project followed a similar basic pattern.

As a result of the need to reorganize archaeological work in London, arising from the internal and external factors discussed above, a consultant was commissioned to merge and restructure the three Museum archaeology departments. The organizational structure of the resultant Museum of London Archaeology Service (MoLAS) is based on a matrix (see Figure 15.1). There are four departments, namely operations, specialist services, publications and finance. The departments and sections along the top of Figure 15.1 each represent functions, and are all drawn upon to meet the needs of different projects. The central features are that hierarchies are flattened and that goals are achieved through teamwork. The project manager drives each project through successive stages, drawing upon requisite skills from the different departments. Although the project manager is accountable, responsibility is decentralized. This means that the matrix has the effect of making smaller management units within the larger one.

A further result is a situation where each project team member has two leaders: their project manager and their line (or function) manager. This illustrates the presence of intentional, but theoretically healthy, tension and conflict which is a key characteristic of matrix management. This conflict often manifests itself as between those responsible for meeting the client's needs – the project manager – and those responsible for ensuring the highest professional quality – the line manager. Further aspects of this tension are considered below.

In MoLAS a project team for a typical desk-top assessment might never

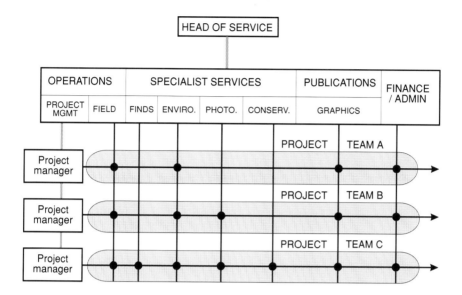

Figure 15.1 MoLAS organizational structure

actually meet as a team; most of the communications would be by internal memorandum or by telephone. In contrast, the project team for one of the large current projects, the Guildhall amphitheatre site, meets frequently as a team. The team comprises the project manager, the three site supervisors (who in turn are responsible for the twenty-five or so permanent site staff), the finds and environmental processors and specialists, the dendrochronologist, the ancient wood-working specialist and conservator, and so on according to the archaeological material being worked on at any time. Team meetings are scheduled at key points in the programme and the work is carried out in accordance with the stages identified in *Management of Archaeological Projects* (MAP2) (English Heritage 1991).

MATRIX MANAGEMENT: PROBLEMS AND BENEFITS

MoLAS was launched on 9 December 1991. So how well has the matrix management structure worked? Many employees of MoLAS might appear somewhat battle weary, testifying to the demands of introducing matrix management. Knight (1976) highlights some of the problems with matrix management: a matrix structure tends to evoke conflict, stress, poor communications or even disputes, and can be costly to administer. However, matrix management *does* have relevance to an organization like MoLAS. As management theory is quick to emphasize, the greater number of different projects an organization carries out simultaneously, the more complex its management becomes; MoLAS carried out over 400 projects during the last financial year. Writers on the subject point out that matrix management is ideally suited to multi-project organizations with similar though not identical project goals – archaeology seems to fit the bill. Also it is far easier to implement matrix management in larger organizations, and MoLAS, with a large number of functions held in-house, would seem to qualify on this account too.

Nevertheless, it would appear that MoLAS did not get it right insofar as matrix management was introduced without enough preparation. It is essential to have internal support systems established well in advance of introducing matrix management. Yet change had to be imposed on MoLAS speedily and ruthlessly, in part because of external factors like the formation of the English Heritage Planning Advisory Service and the withdrawal of the core grant. The time constraints for setting up MoLAS meant that the natural resistance to change that everybody feels had to be overcome at the same time as continuing with work and with creating and establishing all the simple but essential administrative and management support systems – even down to sorting out the new system for raising invoices.

This was undoubtedly one of the more painful lessons, which is referred to in management literature but which MoLAS was to experience for itself. The lesson is that a very strong basic management structure is needed for a decentralized organization to function well. This lesson seems ironic because strong central management seems to contradict the very idea of decentralization and delegation of responsibility. In addition, the successful introduction of project management requires not only the right structure, but also a complete project management culture in which time sheets are kept, where there is tight financial control, and where the overall picture of all the projects is kept firmly in view and becomes a driving force for the organization.

One of the most important lessons learned (and still being learned) in MoLAS is that matrix management relies not just on the clear identification of project goals, but also on a dynamic tension between project managers and line/function managers. Idealized management theory (Figure 15.2) suggests that the tension becomes constructive energy which is channeled into the project; team commitment to achieving goals results in greater efficiency, producing high quality results (Gabriel 1991). In reality, individuals have different priorities, and they get irritated and frustrated with each other. Instead of all the adrenalin being directed to finishing the project under budget, within time and to the highest quality, the tension can easily become destructive. As Figure 15.3 suggests, tension becomes conflict; conflict is expressed commonly in the form of rivalries between individuals or departments. Overt and covert criticisms of colleagues may result because within the overall project goals the team members have different priorities. The results of anxiety and aggression should not be

Figure 15.2   Idealized result of the tension between project managers and line/function managers

made light of as there can be psychological and physiological consequences and the project and the organization are likely to suffer too. This comes back to the point about a strong central management. A means of making informed decisions at a level which is more strategic than the level of projects is required to prevent tension from becoming counter-productive.

Theoretically, three main advantages arise from splitting the resources within a large organization into smaller management units:

1   the people in those units are more readily motivated towards achieving the set project goals;
2   the sum of the collective effort of a project team, developing and growing creatively, is greater than would be the sum of the individual efforts;
3   the organization achieves greater flexibility, which is an increasingly important requirement for archaeological organizations.

The degree to which a project benefits or suffers from the tension inherent in matrix management may be related to the extent to which the staff feel part of the project team. It is apparent that project teams work better on bigger, more complex projects than on small projects. The weakness of the UK economy in recent years has, however, presented an obstacle and although MoLAS recognized the potential benefits of matrix management it has had a hard time getting it to work. Over half of MoLAS 400 projects in 1992 were field evaluations and a quarter were desk-top assessments or feasibility studies. The large number of small-scale, short-term projects has made it extremely difficult to ensure the right level and speed of internal communications. Equally important, it is difficult for most people to feel part of such a project team, particularly when individuals may work on half a dozen projects within a month. No matter how valuable ultimately a field evaluation is; no matter that it does have academic value or that evaluations require extremely skilled archaeologists; pre-planning evaluation work is by and large de-motivating for field archaeologists; it does not appear to have an immediate reward and it is usually seen as offering little scope for creativity.

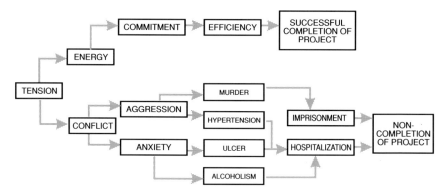

Figure 15.3 Actual result of the tension between project managers and line/function managers

CONCLUSIONS

It might be concluded that as MoLAS has not completed a sufficient variety of projects under the new organizational arrangements that it has not really tested the matrix structure. On the other hand it might be concluded that if MoLAS managed to apply the matrix as well as it has done *despite* the lack of longer-term or complex projects, and still survived, then the structure has been well and truly tested. Arguably, large complex tasks in the future, such as major post-excavation projects or urban redevelopments requiring preservation *in situ*, can only benefit from the learning experience.

Certainly MoLAS is infinitely more flexible now than its predecessor organizations were. Responsibility is decentralized with authority delegated to project managers and their teams. Procedures and systems are limited to such things as time sheets and schedules to monitor project needs in relation to what people are doing. There are still opportunities, particularly on the more complex projects, for individual and team creativity.

An important caveat is that people can feel such a strong allegiance to their projects that allegiance acts to the detriment of the organization. The next step for MoLAS must be to work on the extent to which people perceive themselves to be a part of the larger organization rather than just the project team. However, matrix management has resulted in managers and workers alike talking to each other more and pooling their creativity and expertise. Ultimately this has to be to the good of the archaeological product.

REFERENCES

Barnes, M. (1990) 'How to manage projects', in Institute of Management Consultants *Management 90 – Building the Business*, UK: Institute of Management Consultants, 367–8.

Department of the Environment (1990) *Planning Policy Guidance: Archaeology and Planning*, PPG16, London: HMSO.

English Heritage (1991) *Management of Archaeological Projects*, London: Historic Buildings and Monuments Commission for England.

Gabriel, E. (1991) 'Teamwork – fact and fiction', *International Journal of Project Management* 9, 4: 195–8

Knight, K. (1976) 'Matrix organization: a review', *The Journal of Management Studies* 111–30.

Mintzberg, H. (1979) *The Structuring of Organizations: A Synthesis of the Research*, USA: Prentice-Hall.

Torrington, D., Weightman, J. and Johns, K. (1989) *Effective Management: People and Organization*, London: Prentice-Hall.

CHAPTER SIXTEEN

MANAGEMENT OBJECTIVES

Context or chaos?

FRANCIS PRYOR

This chapter, like many of the research projects I have been actively involved in, has appeared in many different guises. It has changed and developed as ideas have matured. The way this chapter has altered as it has developed mirrors the way in which I have always done research: one digs for further questions, not answers, and the final results of the research will usually differ very markedly from one's initial research objectives. The alternative – that of working hypothesis, test, followed by validation or rejection – is altogether too simple a procedure to apply to a subject devoted to something as complex and unpredictable as the human past.

The first version of this chapter, a precis of which was circulated before the 1993 Institute of Field Archaeologists Conference, was essentially personal. It described how I learned the basics of management whilst working in the work study department of a large brewery shortly after leaving university in the late 1960s. It went on to outline how some of the lessons learned in industry were applied to archaeological fieldwork. The second version was the one I read at the conference. It was rather less worthy and far less personal. In essence it pointed out that management was about people, teamwork and motivation; management techniques were a means to an end, but it was the end that mattered. It also made the point that good archaeologists were by and large good managers and that anyone who can see a complex project through to publication cannot have a great deal to learn about management or motivation.

In this version of the evolving chapter I will return briefly to the question of motivation because it cannot be separated from the fundamental issue I have already alluded to: 'Why are we doing it?'. After developing this theme I will compare whatever it is that motivates archaeologists with what most rescue projects have to offer – which is often quite far removed from academic research. Finally I will make a few suggestions about what we might do to remedy the situation.

MOTIVATION

First I should perhaps say a word or two about my own involvement with rescue or project archaeology. Since 1971 I have carried out what is essentially a single study of the developing cultural landscape of the western Fenland around Peterborough, in the east of central England. This work has been carried out by a small and closely knit team whose composition by and large changed quite slowly. Most people stayed with us for three to five years, although some colleagues stayed with us for very much longer. It is the way of the world to have a figurehead, and that has been my lot, but the projects we undertook at Fengate, Maxey, Etton and Flag Fen, the Lower Welland survey and the Dyke survey, have all been the results of highly motivated teamwork. It was and is academic research of a hopefully highish order which was carried out in sometimes very tight rescue contexts. In pre-PPG 16 days one relied on the goodwill of the developer and sometimes this meant that work had to carried out at white heat for extended periods.

The excitement of fieldwork was one thing, but the production of a report was, and is, another. Personally I find that the unexpected patterns that develop as one extracts (or imposes!) information from data, and meaning from information, can be every bit as stimulating as the original excavation or survey. The results of our labours have been published in eight monographs and several large journal papers; one (on Etton) is in the final stages of editing; sadly what will probably be the last (on Flag Fen and the Peterborough Fenland) is in active preparation (for the various references see Pryor and French 1985; Pryor and Chippindale 1992; Pryor 1991). My MAP2 Gantt chart tells me I will hand the final completed manuscript over on 31 March 1995.

The big question that lay at the root of our teams' self-motivation was WHY? Why did people live on the Fen-edge in the way they did? Why did they parcel-up the landscape? Why did they start to group together? Why didn't they fight each other constantly? It was always WHY. It became impossible to divorce research from rescue – and that, surely, is the way things should be.

Speaking personally, the stimulus which ignites and fuels my motivation is the need to answer the 'why' questions of research into the changing nature of certain, specific prehistoric landscapes – and the people who lived there. I chose those landscapes for various reasons: they were known to be rich in archaeological remains, they were well preserved beneath alluvium and by waterlogging, and – most important of all to me – they were in an area of the country I knew and loved. In the 1970s and 1980s these landscapes, which covered a small area of the Fens, were subject to commercial, residential and agricultural development and it was consequently possible to put together and carry out successfully an integrated programme of research. Each new step forward had knock-on effects that sometimes drastically affected our understanding of the significance of earlier work (Pryor 1988). It was rather like working a complicated computer spreadsheet: one adds £2.00 to a column at the top, the machine coughs, and the bottom line moves out of profit to show a deficit of £10.19. Like my accounts, the results of new knowledge can be unpredictable. In closely integrated regional research each new discovery is therefore far more significant than the sum of its component parts. That is why site-specific, non-problem-orientated research is so uninformative, unexciting and (dare I say it?) so cost-ineffective.

CURRENT ISSUES

Despite the apparently instinctive abilities of archaeologists to manage projects, it would be foolish to deny that most of us would benefit from exposure to explicit management theory. We must be careful, nevertheless, not to disregard tried-and-tested ways of managing projects completely in our rush to embrace what are sometimes only seemingly new approaches. One of the best managers of people I know is a keen advocate of Total Quality Management (see Brooke, this volume). I suspect, however, that all the TQM in the world would be of little avail if he had been born an insensitive or arrogant person. Certain things are instinctive and cannot be taught – and imaginative, original archaeology is one of them. Various educational or training approaches can be used to improve what is already there, no matter how faint the original glimmer of inspiration might be, but in the final analysis something is required to build upon. Good archaeology can never become a mere technique.

Many modern management techniques involve review and assessment by one's peers, but peer review is a problem in that archaeology is a very small subject and everyone knows everyone else. Genuinely disinterested review will become increasingly difficult to achieve as the competetive environment hots up. Already I detect signs of friction as various competitors, between whom there is little love lost, settle old scores in the guise of consultancy. Some of these problems may be avoided if we remember that we are in archaeology to learn about the past, and that this is best done in collaboration. It would be very sad if our generation of field archaeologists was remembered for its legacy of non-publication, partial recovery, and ill-considered, narrowly site-specific research designs.

Any history of British archaeology in the twentieth century will probably show that the economic boom years of the 1980s were not accompanied (until the very end – and PPG 16 (Department of the Environment 1990)) by a commensurate rise in archaeological activity. In my own region I was only too aware that gravel pits, for example, were working flat-out to provide the much-needed aggregates for road, factory and office building, yet there were very few large-scale excavations taking place. By definition, therefore, vast quantities of archaeological data were destroyed on a scale that even the report *A Matter of Time* (Royal Commission on the Historic Monuments of England 1960), that some had considered alarmist two decades earlier, had failed to anticipate. The late 1970s and almost the entire 1980s ought, if only on a quantitative basis, to be remembered for the devastation of archaeology which occurred. Vast areas were destroyed, unseen. Even so, the period also produced the information that has inspired some major reports (for example all the recent English Heritage Archaeology Reports series) and works of synthesis and popularization (e.g. the English Heritage/Batsford series). So far the present decade – and we are approaching the mid-point – appears to be failing to produce any new or significantly original research or rescue projects, despite the lavish expenditure of developers' money. Policy statements abound and County Halls are bursting with slim ring-bound assessments and excavation reports, but in the words of former President Bush, 'Where's the Beef?'.

If the archaeological symbol of the 1980s was an over-worked field-worker fending-off a bulldozer, that of the 1990s is the numbered-paragraph report. These reports look efficient, and their production requires only a very slight ability to write English prose. In my experience, however, they are impossible to read with any actual pleasure. Indeed, I sometimes think they were written with precisely that intention. Prose aside, their actual archaeological content is probably best described as 'a summary of features encountered'. There seems to be an underlying assumption that removal of topsoil opens a book that anyone with appropriate technical expertise can read. Sadly, however, this assumption is based on a false premise: in reality archaeologists only find what they are looking for; the greatest archaeological skill is the ability to recognize the unexpected – and it is the unexpected discovery, including everything from a new category of site to a reinterpretation of the social role played by Bronze Age metalwork, that breaks the mould and takes the subject forward.

The key perhaps to an appreciation of the spiral-bound report lies in its very presentation. The medium in this instance is very much the message. The reports are terse but well-presented through use of slick desk-top publishing programmes. They are becoming de-humanized and de-cultured, and this reflects, I think, an increasing distance between archaeologists and their subject matter. It is almost as if people do not *want* to become personally involved with what they are doing; it seems to be regarded as being rather unprofessional.

THE PROMISE OF MANAGEMENT?

'But wait,' I hear a measured response, 'management will do away with time and money problems: we will assess and monitor and nothing will impede our progress'. At least that is the theory; the reality is Archaeology by Committee. Enormous committee-led projects were a phenomenon of the late 1970s and the 1980s. Their approach may be likened to that of an industrial vacuum cleaner which sucks up everything moveable with enormous power. After it has sucked its fill and passed by, it disgorges huge erudite tomes. These volumes prove beyond reasonable doubt that the topic has been dealt with comprehensively, so no further research is needed. The trouble is, however, that the most illuminating detritus will usually have slipped beneath the carpet. These things, I would suggest, are best revealed using more original, subtle, targeted, approaches.

A committee should be distinguished from a team. A team works together, as one, towards agreed goals. A committee is the sum of its parts and each person will defend their own corner. They will also usually represent other institutions or committees and will feel obliged to push their own party lines, whatever they might be. Everything the project management committee decides to do is shaped by the effort to find a path between the various personal and proxy-institutional positions. The result is an archaeology of compromise that is often hugely expensive and lacking in academic focus. But whatever its demerits, Committee Archaeology is vastly preferable to aimless archaeology.

One mistaken escape route from the byways of aimless archaeology is to procrastinate. This approach allows one to benefit from hindsight: seen thus, everything will appear to form a logical progression – part of a grand design. But there are serious problems. Practitioners of the procrastinative approach have to believe that it does not matter that the diggers and the writers-up are different people. The procrastinator says that he or she will decide what the data mean when they have all been gathered safely together. In the meantime they continue to harvest information, both relevant and redundant, like potatoes. Sadly this way of doing things fails to recognize an archaeological truth that any competent fieldworker knows from experience. We only find what we are looking for: flint people find flints, pot people find sherds, and wood people find precious little. The data we gather must depend on what we are looking for, and research objectives cannot be imposed retrospectively.

STANDARDS

If these forces can be seen to pull against the interest of research, then perhaps the biggest foe to thought is mindless standardization. By all means let us agree on sieve mesh sizes, and so forth, but let us keep a sense of proportion; such 'standards' must only be interim working arrangements, liable to instant modification when research priorities change. One only has to look at the rise and fall of the various 'seeds machines' to be reminded of the transitory nature of standardized recovery procedures. The theory that standards must be set and agreed so that all can compete fairly on a level playing field seems to fly in the face of our subject's greatest asset: the uniqueness and unpredictability of past human behaviour as manifested in the archaeological record. No two contexts are ever the same. Nothing, thankfully, in archaeology is ever standard.

Much of modern management depends upon universally agreed criteria which people and organizations can use as benchmarks for competition or decision-making. But in archaeology the benchmarks tend to move about as wildly as the subject, or at least its academic or interpretational side, progresses. I laid out a 2 per cent assessment trench pattern across the final plans of the Etton causewayed enclosure as an exercise, and revealed practically nothing; we would have been hard-pressed even to date the site with any precision. I am quite convinced that 2 per cent assessment trenches are a waste of time on alluviated sites where there is a substantial archaeological presence that pre-dates the Iron Age. But in certain circumstances, again on alluviated sites, a grid of 2 per cent sample trenches can do great damage, simply by destroying (unseen) relationships. I hate to think how Charles French and I could have made sense of certain sites in the Welland valley (which are characterized by many superimposed and intercallating lenses of alluvium and even colluvium), had we bashed them about with trial trenches.

As research into the Neolithic of Britain continues it is becoming increasingly plain that the 'pit sites', such as Hurst Fen (Clark *et al.* 1960), are not settlements at all. Similarly there are very few houses that can indubitably be considered as such; certainly the Fengate Neolithic 'house' is no such thing (Pryor 1988). So where, it is being asked, were the run-of-the-mill settlements of lowland Britain (Thomas 1991)? I suspect that the evidence for these will be extremely unexciting: a few scoops and hollows, perhaps the odd well. We found quite a good Late Neolithic candidate at Fengate in 1973, where a few desultory hollows (probably the truncated remains of undulations at the base of the ancient topsoil) were clustered around a ditched droveway (Pryor 1978). This sort of evidence would be completely missed in a 2 per cent assessment; the only way to find it would be to strip carefully a huge area of land in a region where such evidence is likely to survive. And the person who did it would have to know what they were looking for. My point is that archaeological benchmarks only make sense when defined within the contexts of an academically justified research strategy; and we have seen that meaningful research must be more than site-specific. So to answer the type of questions which I and my colleagues have attempted to address over the past twenty-five years it is necessary to paint on a broader canvas.

Site assessments generally stress the visible archaeology of cropmarks and surface scatters. These often form the focus for subsequent bids. We have learned to look for and to evaluate certain recurrent archaeological signs; what we have yet to discover is how to recognize the unexpected, the non-standard. The world of rescue archaeology is very adept at revealing the familiar and the redundant very cheaply. Perhaps a cynic might suggest that it does not matter that so much of this work remains unpublished or spiral-bound.

The Institute of Field Archaeologists have recently prepared draft Standards for Archaeological Desk-Based Assessments, Watching Briefs and Field Evaluation (Institute of Field Archaeologists 1993a, b, c). Early on, amidst the numbered paragraphs, each booklet emphasizes the need to have what are in effect research objectives enshrined within project designs. The trouble is, however, that nobody who really *knows* about a specific topic is prepared to give serious thought to the archaeological relevance or meaning of the thousands of individual research designs that are required by the implementation of PPG 16 every week. Most of the people competent to do so are either unemployed or over-worked in some university somewhere. As a result the goals expressed in project designs are often insubstantial, anodyne and absurd. In certain instances this probably does not matter too much, although it is a bit hard on developers who are forced to spend sometimes quite big money on senseless archaeological investigations; but in other cases the failure to formulate academically meaningful research goals can be disastrous. Contractors have a strong financial incentive to keep to the very barest bones of a brief. As a result, a vague or poor brief is an invitation to cut corners – and the Devil take the research. Future generations will have a very unreliable data-base to work from, even if it is impeccably stored in acid-free folders and plastic-coated paper clips.

THE IMPORTANCE OF CONTEXT

Most archaeologists today, even if they have their roots (as I do) in old-fashioned New Archaeology, must surely have abandoned the notion that archaeology will ever come up with universal 'covering laws' that are anything other than, as Kent Flannery noted from the outset, Mickey Mouse (Flannery 1973). So, for better or for worse, most of us 'do' our archaeology within the confines of context. To some, the context may be inter-continental, to others inter-state and to yet others inter-, or even intra-regional. Moreover, we generally work in time-depth, noting the processes of change over very long periods, which is another of our subject's great assets. Assuming that we all agree that archaeology without context is meaningless, then it follows that it is the changing chrono-logical, environmental and spatial relationships of artefacts, ecofacts, sites and landscapes which together constitute the essence of our inquiries.

These things, and their complex interrelationships in time and space, provide the clues that we must use to re-create our understanding of past human behaviour. Archaeological interrelationships are in fact archaeological context; it is therefore impossible to do archaeological research in the absence of context. One cannot do a 'desk-top' survey or dig a site wearing blinkers. It is also salutory to recall that county boundaries have no relevance to prehistory.

Research priorities in the various sub-interests of archaeology are often spawned within small research groups or university pubs. The topic gestates within specialist newsletters and the like, and then gradually finds its way out into the general literature, often by way of several unrelated books or papers which may refer to it obliquely. This can be a very time-consuming process. Indeed, it will only be specialists who will even be aware of the importance of the topic for several years. One result of the absence of communication between management and research is that crucially important sites are being 'rescued' by field archaeologists who are quite unaware of their sites' significance. I am painfully aware of my own limitations in this respect; my professional areas of competence are very limited. I think I can make a pretty good job of a rural Fenland site or landscape, but I draw the line at about the twenty-metre contour or at the first sign of medieval masonry. Frankly, I don't understand the current issues, both intellectual and practical, of upland or urban archaeology. They are both highly complex and demanding subjects and I would probably wreck any site I attempted to dig. I could possibly do a competent job in as much as the site grid and levels would be accurately recorded, but the meaning of the layers I encountered would be beyond me. More to the point, I would only recognize contexts and objects that were of significance to me, a prehistorian of the Fens. I might bring a minute ray of new light to the subject in question, but at what cost to the main body of the archaeology that I would be butchering? My work would lack the essential focus that is imposed by having academic research objectives: when time and money are running short one must be able to distinguish the essential from the redundant. When the chips are down, so to speak, one must know what to go for, and one must be prepared to defend those decisions.

In my own experience I have seen contract field archaeologists excavate alluviated sites, in complete ignorance of their extreme complexity. One spiral-bound site report proudly shows a photograph of a supposedly Iron Age linear ditch which has been almost entirely dug away by a machine; above it, in the massacred section can be seen a series of Neolithic features beneath an intact palaeosol. The problem is one of communication. And this, surely, is something that does urgently require management by someone. The whole basis of competetive tendering is predicated upon the confidentiality of each bid – a process that does not encourage friendly discussion. Furthermore, nobody can be expected to be an expert in all branches of archaeology everywhere in the country, and in those areas that are not of immediate personal interest it is possible to be less than completely involved with (or aware of) the current urgent research priorities. Sadly too, this usually makes for cheaper bids. So there is a positive financial stimulus to don academic blinkers. Such ignorance can be commercial bliss.

LOCAL CONTEXT AS A BASIS FOR RESEARCH IN MANAGEMENT

One way out of the failure to define meaningful research goals in rural archaeology is to recognize the importance of local context. Development sites should not be seen in isolation, but as significant elements within a sequence of evolving human landscapes. These landscapes can be compared with others elsewhere; moreoever, and just as significantly, they change as our appreciation of them changes. Nothing is static. It is far too much to expect curators to be abreast of all these developments – their work-load is simply too heavy. Instead we require explicitly formulated regional research designs which view the ancient landscape in time–depth. They would be drawn–up in close consultation with relevant academic and environmental interests, but would seek to isolate issues that could actually be resolved by individual development projects. I see the scope of these projects as being half-way between a desk-top and a field assessment: one would not do a full fieldwalking survey, but it might be useful to see whether finds did occur on the surface; similarly ten minutes with an auger would soon determine whether alluvium protected a palaeosol. The aim would be to highlight opportunities for insight into specific problems that had a realistic chance of being achieved. Inevitably there would have to be a compromise between the academic and the pragmatic, but that has always been the stuff of good archaeology. The recommendations of such surveys could be modified after individual projects had been completed and perhaps progress reports could be published (properly) from time to time. Frankly anything would be better than the rag-bag of contextless summary 'reports' that disgrace so many of our county journals.

A fresh focus upon regional research may also serve to reduce some other problematic tendencies in archaeology in the UK. Not only has professional archaeology in Britain become removed from the general public and the interested layman, but contractors and academics within archaeology are drifting apart. Our subject is fragmenting. Regional research has a role in re-integrating archaeology. At some universities (in England, for example, Sheffield, Exeter and Leicester) there is already a tradition of such work, but it now needs to be formalized and broadened. Local authority archaeologists might place greater emphasis upon integrated regional research priorities and on meaningful publication. Certain counties are already moving in this direction, for example Cambridgeshire (Bob Sydes, personal communication). County archaeological societies may have a role to play in this, which would be facilitated by the opening up of sites to local people by contractors and their sponsors. Regional archaeology does not have to be parochial or irrelevant, but it does require context and themes.

CONCLUSIONS

When I lived in North America in the 1970s, 'contract archeologists' had a dreadful reputation in academic circles; but they were nonetheless very efficient at disposing of sites. My great fear is that in Britain we have already replicated the mindless state of contract archaeology in the USA at that time. Sure, our field techniques are better and our accounting procedures are red hot. We have also embraced Management and Standards. But we seem to have stopped thinking about the larger 'why' issues of archaeology. In our rush to out-bid each other we have lost sight of context, so innovative research is becoming impossible within what was once called rescue. Our subject is a humanity, a discipline of research, and we continue to ignore that at our peril.

REFERENCES

Clark, J.G.D., Higgs, E.S. and Longworth, I.H., (1960) 'Excavations at the Neolithic site at Hurst Fen, Mildenhall, Suffolk', *Procs. Prehist. Soc*, 26: 202–45.

Department of the Environment (1990) *Planning Policy Guidance: Archaeology and Planning*, PPG16, London: HMSO.

Flannery, K.V. (1973) 'Archaeology with a capital "S"', in C. Redman (ed.) *Research and Theory in Current Archaeology,* New York: Wiley.

Institute of Field Archaeologists (1993a) *Standard and Guidance for Archaeological Desk-Based Assessments*, Birmingham: Institute of Field Archaeologists.

Institute of Field Archaeologists (1993b) *Standard and Guidance for Archaeological Watching Briefs*, Birmingham: Institute of Field Archaeologists.

Institute of Field Archaeologists (1993c) *Standard and Guidance for Archaeological Field Evaluations*, Birmingham: Institute of Field Archaeologists.

Pryor, F.M.M. (1978) *Excavation at Fengate, Peterbrough, England: The Second Report*, Royal Ontario Museum Archaeological Monograph 5.

Pryor, F.M.M. (1988) 'Earlier Neolithic organized landscapes and ceremonial in Lowland Britain', in I. A. Kinnes and J. Barrett (eds) *The Archaeology of Context in the Neolithic and Bronze Age: Recent Trends*, 63–72, Sheffield: Department of Prehistory and Archaeology, Sheffield University.

Pryor, F.M.M. (1991) *Flag Fen – Prehistoric Fenland Centre* London: B. T. Batsford.

Pryor, F.M.M. and Chippindale, C. (eds) (1992) 'Special section: Flag Fen', *Antiquity* 66: 439–531.

Pryor, F.M.M. and French, C.A.I. (1985) 'Archaeology and environment in the Lower Welland Valley', *East Anglian Archaeology* no. 27, 2 vols.

Royal Commission on the Historic Monuments of England (1960) *A Matter of Time*, London: RCHME.

Thomas, J. (1991) *Rethinking the Neolithic*, New Studies in Archaeology, Cambridge: Cambridge University Press.

CONCLUSION

Opening a debate

JOHN CARMAN, MALCOLM A. COOPER,
ANTONY FIRTH, DAVID WHEATLEY

We have said in our Introduction that this book represents an attempt to open a debate within archaeology. Having concentrated on the things on which we generally agree at the opening of the book, we want to close by outlining some areas of disagreement which we feel deserve further investigation. To some extent, these areas are already the subject of research; other areas may be similarly responsive to argument about the meanings and implications of what was previously thought to be widely known and recognized.

VALUES

The Introduction suggested that one area of dispute may be over the existence of a value for archaeological remains which can be quantified. This is the idea that lies behind the MPP, the assessment of potential for analysis in MAP2, American and Australian measures of 'significance', and similar approaches. It is an idea that informs Wheatley's paper arguing that archaeological landscapes can be represented as surfaces of continuous variation (in value terms) rather than clusters of discrete sites. It is also present in Wenban-Smith's concern for the Palaeolithic heritage and may underlie Darvill's usage of the term 'value gradient'. By contrast, Carman and Bower understand value to be something much more fluid – a 'spiritual' phenomenon for Bower; and something that lies on differing scales of intangible value for Carman. It is true that some economists – students of value *par excellance* – have turned their attention to questions of intangible value (Brown 1990; Goldstein 1990) but so far these ideas have not had much impact on archaeology. Those archaeologists who begin with the belief that archaeological value is ultimately tangible and quantifiable, whatever the mechanism chosen, have no need of such ideas. On the other hand, those who recognize the intangibility of archaeological value may be disinclined to adopt these approaches since these economists are attempting to find some appropriate measure for such value – and indeed seeking to reduce them to monetary terms (Brown 1990; Goldstein 1990).

The difference between these two approaches to archaeological value runs deeper, however, and maybe reflects other divisions within the archaeological community. If – as is often argued (e.g. Smith 1994; Cooper, this volume) – the field of AHM/ARM/CRM generally represents a view of archaeology derived from the predominately American processual school of archaeological theory, which takes a strongly realist and empiricist approach to its material, then the idea that valuation is a relatively straightforward process of measurement on an appropriate scale is a part of that paradigm (Yates 1988; Brooke, this volume). Those more influenced by post-processual archaeology and its importation of post-modernism and post-structuralism into archaeological thinking are perhaps more inclined to see the category of 'archaeological remain' as a constructed concept which although reflecting a material reality (objects you can pick up and handle) is arbitrarily ascribed to an arbitrarily created class of material ('archaeology' rather than 'nature'). In this case, the differences go deep into an understanding of the nature of the 'archaeological record' (Patrik 1985) and its implications for archaeological technique and interpretation. The possibility of a 'postprocessual CRM' which challenges many of the current understandings and techniques for managing the material of archaeology may be for some an exciting prospect; for others it may represent a *non sequitur*.

APPROACHES TO UNDERSTANDING

One of the ways in which this division between 'processual' and 'post-processual' CRMs may work itself out is in the growing concern with the history of archaeology. This forms an important part of Carman's work (Carman 1993a, 1993b, 1994) and is central to Cooper's chapter (this volume) and to McAdam's chapter (this volume). This concern derives in part from a desire to understand the specific context within which archaeology as we know it developed over time. It is becoming increasingly clear (Trigger 1989; Darvill 1993; Evans 1993; Carman, this volume) that the story of archaeology is not a simple one of increasing effectiveness but a more complex one of shifting ideology and purpose. Archaeology has a history – and that history is an interesting and important one. Archaeology need not have emerged or developed as it did; other things were possible. Even such an apparently straightforward event as the passage of the first British legal measure to protect ancient monuments (Chippindale 1983; Saunders 1983; Murray 1990), it turns out, has political and social consequences well beyond the discipline of archaeology (Carman 1993b). In the detailed study of the history of the discipline, then, lies the capacity to understand the origins, development and accumulated meanings of the basic concepts we apply in our work.

Against this long-term historical and contextual approach to understanding stands another which relies much more heavily on the analysis of the contemporary situation. Firth, for example, concentrates on the current state of what he calls archaeology underwater. This does contain an element of historical analysis, particularly so far as the development of UK legislation in this field is concerned, but this is a history of the short-term, concerning itself only with developments over the past twenty-five years. Similarly, other contributors to the volume (Brooke, Andrews and Thomas, Pryor) are concerned only with the past twenty or even ten years. The remainder are content to stay in the immediate present, or to look towards the future.

Another aspect of Firth's work is the extent to which he relies on international comparison. His is the only chapter in this collection to do so and to make explicit reference to it. By definition, a contextually based historical approach (such as McAdam's) cannot rely on international comparison. Going even further than this, however, Carman (1993b) explicitly denies the validity of such an approach – the existence of the works of Cleere (1984, 1989) and O'Keefe and Prott (1984) notwithstanding. Blockley and Brooke choose not to stress the point, but many of the approaches to management they advocate derive from the US experience and thus they contribute (albeit silently) to the belief that archaeology and the solutions to its perceived problems have similar relevance the world over. This is an idea that has been criticized by Dennis Byrne (1991), who accuses CRM of levying a 'western hegemony' on other people's archaeologies.

The underlying dispute in these differing approaches to understanding the current situation in archaeology lies in the assumption (or lack of assumption) of the usefulness of comparisons between archaeological traditions. If UK archaeology is historically contingent upon the UK experience, then it might be argued that to compare any aspect of UK archaeology with any other contemporary archaeology is misleading. On the other hand, UK archaeology does not exist (nor ever has) in a vacuum and ideas have always passed between archaeologists working on different materials, in different territories and out of differing traditions. Moreover, many aspects of management in the UK are derived from characteristics common to many western societies, which might be expected to manifest themselves equally (though not identically) in the management of archaeology in a number of countries. The extreme contextualist view – taken here by Carman, and derived from and informing his work looking at the relationship between archaeology and law in England – is that we cannot know *a priori* that preservation laws, the archaeological record or their histories are directly comparable between one country and another. Instead, he would argue that we need to examine each territory independently in order to reach an understanding that can then be compared meaningfully with the understanding of another reached by the same means. The alternative approach to understanding, adopted here by Firth, is to construct a model by reference to the situation in a number of territories and apply this to the one under specific study. The relative utility of these contrasting approaches can only be judged in the future on the basis of future research in the UK and elsewhere, and we hope that this book will help to encourage such research.

INCREASING EFFECTIVENESS

The mention of the 'utility' of research opens up a further area of potential debate. Many of the chapters in this volume seek not to express an understanding of how the world works but to change it for the better. Francis Wenban-Smith, for example, is concerned with the effectiveness of management approaches (including law) in affording adequate treatment to the material in which he is interested. He chooses not to engage in an an analysis of why the weaknesses which he has identified have arisen – for example the reasons why the law classes the material with which he is concerned as 'geology', part of the natural rather than the archaeological universe – concentrating on a pragmatic adaptation of existing approaches rather than their fundamental transformation. Similarly, Cooper and his managerial colleagues are keen to introduce into archaeology an explicit discussion of management theory rather than to understand how archaeologists do their managing, and the manner (if any) in which this differs from other types of management. This kind of research – an extension of the 'ethnography of archaeology' (Edgeworth 1990) – would constitute a valuable contribution to the field, especially by a grounding in a specifically archaeological understanding of archaeological practice.

Of course, specifically and solely archaeological understandings are impossible to reach. Despite repeated calls for the creation of an archaeology 'that is archaeology that is archaeology' (Clarke 1968) or 'a viable and distinctive archaeology' (Hodder 1986: 1), in practice archaeology relies on theories generated outside the field to develop (Yoffee and Sherratt 1993). While Clarke drew on systems theory and human geography, Hodder draws on the historical approach of Collingwood to construct his 'contextual' approach. This book is no different: Carman draws on various ideas from anthropology, sociology and political science, Firth from law and political science, Cooper from management theory and so on. None here is a 'pure' archaeologist. But the point is to what extent the ideas presented here can be *made* archaeological – that is, integrated into archaeological practice and theory – rather than remaining something separate and distinct and merely 'tacked on' to the discipline. Andrews and

Thomas, Nixon and Locock all present case studies of the introduction of specific management theories into archaeological work, but it is left to Pryor to question the validity of the process of standardization this represents.

VISIONS OF ARCHAEOLOGY

The assumption that one already knows what is happening, as opposed to seeking to identify it, is possibly a reflection of the division of those in this book into those who talk of a 'discipline' of archaeology (especially Carman and Pryor) and those who talk of a 'profession' (especially Cooper). This is a matter not for research but for argument, and it raises the question of the 'values' of archaeology mentioned in the Introduction to this book. Archaeology as a profession is, among other things, a service provided to others – something that can be bought by them as a commodity. Bower is satisfied with this, and the introduction of management concepts (by Cooper, Blockley, Brooke, Andrews and Thomas, Nixon and Locock, all this volume) are designed to facilitate it. Indeed, the idea of archaeology as a service for sale to developers and local authority planning officers under-pins much of the current structure of field archaeology in the UK. Carman, Startin, Wenban-Smith and Pryor focus on archaeology as a research disci-pline, something carried out (and legitimately so) in its own right, where the purpose is to inform about the past. Firth incorporates both terms in his institutional analysis of archaeology. Here, archaeology the institution is not reducible to a profession or a discipline – neither at the service of others nor an independent agent, but simultaneously the creation of and assisting at the creation of contemporary society (cf. Giddens 1984).

The views and opinions presented in this book are specifically those that concern the management either of archaeological remains or of archae-ological practice. But they also go deeper. They reflect the philosophical, theoretical and possibly even the political beliefs of those who present them. Our debates, then, are not just about how best to do archaeology. They are about what archaeology is, what it is for, and how it should look in the future – and by extension, how our world in all its aspects should look in the future. These are the issues that concern all those who attend TAG and IFA conferences year after year. They are the issues that concern all those who practice, read or think about archaeology. The question of 'managing archaeology' – whatever that term may mean to different people – is thus central to the discipline and to the profession and to the institution that is contemporary archaeology.

REFERENCES

Brown, G.M. (1990) 'Valuation of genetic resources', in G.H. Orians, G.M. Brown, W.E. Kunin and J.E. Swierzbinski (eds) *The Preservation and Valuation of Genetic Resources*, Seattle and London: University of Washington Press, 203–45.

Byrne, D. (1991) 'Western hegemony in archaeological heritage management', *History and Anthropology* 5: 269–76.

Carman, J. (1993a) 'Lubbock's Folly: a tale of monumental passion', paper given at the Annual Conference of the Theoretical Archaeology Group, Durham, December 1993.

Carman, J. (1993b) 'Valuing ancient things: archaeology and law in England', unpublished PhD dissertation, University of Cambridge.

Carman, J. (1994) 'The P is silent – as in archaeology'', *Archaeological Review from Cambridge* 12, 1: 39–53.

Chippindale, C. (1983) 'The making of the first Ancient Monuments Act, 1882, and its administration under General Pitt-Rivers', *Journal of the British Archaeological Association* 136: 1–55.

Clarke, D.L. (1968) *Analytical Archaeology*, London: Methuen.

Cleere, H.F. (ed.) (1984) *Approaches to the Archaeological Heritage*, Cambridge: Cambridge University Press.

Cleere, H.F. (ed.) (1989) *Archaeological Heritage Management in the Modern World*, London: Unwin Hyman.

Darvill, T. (1993) 'Valuing Britain's archaeological resource', Professor of Archaeology and Property Management Inaugural Lecture, Bournemouth University, July 1993.

Edgeworth, M. (1990) 'Analogy as practical reason: the perception of objects in excavation practice', *Archaeological Review from Cambridge* 9, 2: 243–51.

Evans, C. (1993) 'Model excavations: presentation, textuality and graphic literacy', paper given at the Annual Conference of the Theoretical Archaeology Group, Durham, December 1993.

Giddens, A. (1984) *The Constitution of Society: Outline of the Theory of Structuration*, Cambridge: Polity Press.

Goldstein, J.H. (1990) 'The prospects for using market incentives for conservation of biological diversity', in G.H. Orians, G.M. Brown, W.E. Kunin and J.E. Swierzbinski (eds) *The Preservation and Valuation of Genetic Resources*, Seattle and London: University of Washington Press, 246–81.

Hodder, I. (1986) *Reading the Past: Current Approaches to Interpretation in Archaeology*, Cambridge: Cambridge University Press.

Murray, T. (1990) 'The history, philosophy and sociology of archaeology: the case of the Ancient Monuments Protection Act (1882)', in V. Pinsky and A. Wylie (eds) *Critical Traditions in Contemporary Archaeology*, Cambridge: Cambridge University Press.

O'Keefe, P.J. and Prott, L.V. *Law and the Cultural Heritage*, Vol. 1, *Discovery and Excavation*, Abingdon: Professional Books.

Patrik, L. (1985) 'Is there an archaeologial record?', in M.B. Schiffer (ed.) *Advances in Archaeological Method and Theory* 8, New York: Academic Press, 27–62.

Saunders, A.D. (1983) 'A century of ancient monuments legislation, 1882–1983', *The Antiquaries Journal* 63: 11–29.

Smith, L. (1994) 'Towards a theoretical framework for archaeological heritage management', *Archaeological Review from Cambridge* 12, 1: 55–75

Trigger, B. (1989) *A History of Archaeological Thought*, Cambridge: Cambridge University Press.

Yates, T. (1988) 'Michael Schiffer and processualism with a capitalist S', *Archaeological Review from Cambridge* 8:1, 235–8.

Yoffee, N. and Sherratt, A. (eds) (1993) *Archaeological Theory: Who Sets the Agenda?* Cambridge: Cambridge University Press.

GLOSSARY OF TERMS

Ancient Monument   According to the Ancient Monuments and Archaeological Areas Act 1979, Ancient Monuments are either monuments (q.v.) which are scheduled (q.v.) or other monuments which are of public interest by reason of historic, architectural, traditional, artistic or archaeological interest. Ancient monuments can be placed under guardianship or acquired compulsorily (or by agreement or gift) by the relevant Secretary of State. The National Heritage Act 1983 includes an expanded definition of ancient monument that applies to the duties and functions of English Heritage (q.v.).

Archaeological Heritage Management (AHM), Archaeological Resource Management (ARM), Cultural Resource Management (CRM)   Three terms used interchangeably to designate the categorization, evaluation and decision-making on future use and/or conservation of archaeological material. While AHM is preferred internationally, ARM is used particularly in Britain and CRM in the United States and Australia where it also covers the management of the contemporary material culture of the indigenous populations.

Archaeology in Britain Conference (ABC)   The annual conference of the Institute of Field Archaeologists. The first conference was held at Birmingham University in April 1987, its venue remaining in Birmingham until 1993 when it was successfully transferred to Bradford University.

Areas of Competence (AOC)   In 1986 the Institute of Field Archaeologists (q.v.) determined that an application to become a Member of the Institute (MIFA) would be assessed against an applicant's capacity to carry sole responsibility for a substantial archaeological project embracing one, or more, areas of competence. Eight areas were initially defined: excavation, survey, underwater archaeology, aerial archaeology, environmental archaeology, finds study, structural analysis, and cultural resource management. A further area, research and development, was added in 1990.

Assessment Also termed an archaeological assessment. Assessment commonly refers to a desk-based evaluation of information regarding the presence, location and importance of archaeological remains in a particular area or site (q.v.). This may involve searches of Sites and Monuments Records (q.v.), record offices, museum archives and other collections of relevant information including historic maps. An assessment may also, however, involve non-destructive methods of site reconnaissance such as earthwork survey and geophysical survey, although these techniques, along with trial excavation, are more commonly seen as forming part of an evaluation (q.v.) programme. Assessment is referred to in PPG 16 (q.v.) sections 19-20 and is regarded as a preliminary stage in identifying whether an archaeological constraint exists to a development proposal.

Cascade charts A graphical diagram identifying the stages of a project. As a general term it would include PERT charts, Gantt charts, and Critical Path Analysis charts (q.v.). With specific reference to English archaeology it is defined in MAP2 (q.v.) as showing: all the tasks to be undertaken in the correct sequence; the interrelatedness and interdependence of tasks; time-critical elements; the length of time allocated to each task; the personnel (or grade) allocated to each task; and agreed monitoring points.

Citizen's Charter A central government initiative, which commenced in 1992, to increase the accountability of government offices and agencies to the general public. The initiative rests on the publication of 'charters' which set out the level of service that the public should expect, and against which standards of service can be monitored.

Compulsory Competitive Tendering (CCT) In the late 1980s far-reaching changes began to take place in local government in Britain as a result of central government policy. This included the passing of the Local Government Act 1988 which obliged local authorities (q.v.) and other specified bodies to contract-out manual services through compulsory competitive tendering (CCT). In 1991 the government published plans to widen CCT to other local authority functions. The approach adopted by central government is based on the philosophy that local authorities should develop their role as enabling bodies rather than as providers of services directly, taking on the role of the client which specifies and monitors the works to be undertaken by contracting organizations. This philosophy has had a widespread affect on the nature of local government in Britain and consequently upon archaeological services, many of which are based in local authorities.

Critical path analysis A technique of analysis used for planning and monitoring projects (q.v. PERT).

Development control Most forms of development and material changes of land use are subject to the approval of the local planning authority (q.v.); Development Control is the process through which local planning authorities decide whether, or under what conditions, approval can be granted to development proposals by private individuals and organizations.

English Heritage This is the popular name of the Historic Buildings and Monuments Commission for England (HBMCE), which is a quasi-autonomous non-governmental organization (quango) established by the National Heritage Act 1983, sponsored by the Department of National Heritage. Its general duties are, as far as is practicable, to:

> Secure the preservation of ancient monuments and historic buildings situated in England;
> Promote the preservation and enhancement of the character and appearance of conservation areas situated in England;
> Promote the public's enjoyment of, and advance their knowledge of, ancient monuments and historic buildings situated in England and their preservation.

Many of the functions of English Heritage had previously been undertaken within the civil service and can be traced back to the creation of the position of Inspector of Ancient Monuments within the Office of Public Buildings and Works in 1882. Responsibilities with regard to ancient monuments (q.v.) were subsumed by the Department of the Environment in 1969 and to a great extent removed from the civil service by the creation of English Heritage.

Environmental Assessment (EA) Environmental Assessment is a process through which the sponsor of a proposed development considers the effects of the development on the environment. The application and scope of EA was established through a European Community Directive (85/337/EEC) and implemented in the UK through Town and Country Planning legislation and a series of orders relating to specific industries. The 'archaeological heritage' is included in the scope of EA as a material asset which the developer must supply information about if it is likely to be significantly affected by the proposed project.

Evaluation Also termed archaeological evaluation or field evaluation. Evaluation is a programme of archaeological work, frequently comprising ground survey and small-scale trial trenching, specifically designed to help assess the character, extent and importance of archaeological remains. Section 21 of PPG 16 (q.v.) indicates that where important archaeological remains are suspected to exist, it is reasonable for a local planning authority (q.v.) to request the prospective developer to arrange for an archaeological field evaluation to be carried out before any decision on the planning application is taken. Evaluation can also be used by the planning authority to assess the weight which ought to be attached to the preservation of archaeological remains and, by prospective developers, to identify methods of minimising or avoiding damage to these remains through the use of, for example, appropriate foundation design (q.v. Mitigation).

Gantt chart A bar chart commonly used as a graphical tool for project planning and management. Individual project tasks are identified and arranged along the y-axis and time along the x-axis. They are named after their originator Henry Gantt, an American industrial engineer (1861-1919).

Geographic Information System (GIS)   A database and analysis system whose primary functions are the capture, storage and manipulation of geographic data. Geographic data contains a combination of location, attribute and topological data. See Wheatley, this volume, for further discussion.

Harris matrix   A graphical representation of the relationship between stratigraphic units based on principles of archaeological stratigraphy.

Information Technology (IT)   Any of a variety of technologies for the manipulation and communication of information held on computers including database management systems, geographic information systems, multimedia, hypertext, communications and networking, among others. See, for example, Reilly, P. and Rahtz, S.P.Q. (1991) *Communication in Archaeology: A Global View of the Impact of IT*, London: Unwin Hyman, for archaeological applications.

Institute of Field Archaeologists (IFA)   The Institute of Field Archaeologists (IFA) came into being on 21 December 1982 as the culmination of some ten years of discussion in Britain of the need for a professional archaeological institute. It was created to further the aims of archaeology in a variety of ways but principally through a Code of Conduct, the object of which is to promote the standards of conduct and self-discipline required of an archaeologist in the interests of the archaeological resource, the public, and the pursuit of archaeological research.

Local authorities   In England and Wales there is a two-tier system of local government consisting of districts set within counties. District and county councils have a wide range of responsibilities, including the implementation of planning law (q.v.), for which they serve as local planning authorities (q.v.). Many local authorities, especially county councils, are host to archaeological services within their cultural or planning departments. Local authorities have been subject to significant changes in the past fifteen years including, most recently, a local government reorganization initiative originally intended to replace the two-tier system with a single tier of 'unitary' authorities. Scotland also has a two-tier system comprising regional and district councils, although not all of these have planning functions.

Local authority (archaeological) units   In England during the 1970s and 1980s local authorities, with the support of central government, were encouraged to manage the archaeological resource in their area. This commonly took the form of the creation and maintenance of a Sites and Monuments Record (q.v.) and the provision of field teams to undertake survey and rescue archaeology. These archaeological responsibilities were frequently met by archaeological units based in local authorities (q.v.). A number of these units developed from the study of particular historic urban areas.

Local planning authority   In most circumstances in England, planning law is implemented by local authorities in their role as local planning authorities (LPAs). Where there are two tiers, county councils provide strategic advice through preparation of structure plans and determine planning applications of a strategic nature such as, for example, mineral extraction, whilst district councils determine the majority planning applications of a non-strategic nature. County Councils in England tend to hold the County Sites and Monuments Record and give curatorial archaeological advice. There has, however, been an increasing trend towards district councils employing archaeologists to give in-house archaeological advice, backed by a 'local' sites and monument record. In specifically defined areas such as national parks, separate authorities – distinct from county and district councils – have planning responsibilities and in such cases usually have both SMRs and in-house archaeological advice.

Management of Archaeological Projects 2 (MAP2)   This report released by English Heritage in 1991 outlines a model of the principles of archaeological project management based around the analysis of a large-scale archaeological excavation and subsequent programme of post-excavation analysis. It defines five main stages for a project: planning, fieldwork, assessment of potential for analysis, analysis and report preparation, and dissemination, and outlines the recommended procedures to be undertaken at each stage. The document has been highly influential in English archaeology, not least in that MAP2 guidance is to be followed in projects for which grant-aid is being sought from English Heritage. MAP2 was a developed and modified version of an earlier document (The Management of Archaeology Projects) which was released by English Heritage in 1989 (see also Andrews and Thomas, this volume).

Manpower Services Commission Schemes (MSC Schemes)   The MSC assisted a great number of unemployment-relief schemes in the early and mid-1980s. Such schemes were often run by local authorities as part of 'community programmes', directing labour to a wide variety of public uses. Many archaeological projects were set up under these programmes, such that MSC Schemes represented a major source of funding, and of new archaeologists, to the profession through the mid-1980s. Changes to the structure of unemployment-relief in 1988 effectively ended the widespread use of such schemes for archaeological purposes.

Marketing   A variety of definitions of the term marketing exist in business and management literature. Following a definition given by Philip Kotler in 1991 (*Marketing Management*, London: Prentice-Hall, p. 4), marketing can be seen as a social and managerial process by which individuals and groups obtain what they need and want through creating, offering and exchanging products of value with others (see also Blockley, this volume; Bower, this volume).

Matrix management   Traditional management theories placed great stress on the design of bureaucratic and hierarchically structured organizations, divided into specific departments or areas of expertise, in which the definition of roles, authority and chains of command were explicitly defined. While this structure favoured repetitive functions in stable environments, it can be argued that a traditional approach is less suitable for one-off activities or projects in a rapidly changing environment where it was important to bring together different expertise into a project team. Matrix management refers to the design and implementation of specific types of team structures – both temporary and permanent – comprising people drawn from across the organization. As such the teams cut across the usual bureaucratic organizational structures; authority is usually vested in members of the team on the basis of expert knowledge as they frequently have no line management relationship (see also Nixon, this volume and Locock, this volume).

Mitigation   Archaeological remains can be adversely affected by a variety of human and natural agents and processes. Mitigation refers to measures adopted to avoid, to reduce or to remedy such effects. Mitigation is particularly relevant to the development process. The approach laid out in planning guidance such as PPG 16 (q.v.) is designed to allow local planning authorities (q.v.) to identify adverse effects of development on archaeological remains prior to such development taking place. This is in order to ensure that appropriate mitigation measures are proposed as an integral part of the development process. Such proposals may, for example, include the use of particular foundation designs and the use of open space allocation to allow *in situ* preservation of significant remains, or rescue archaeology (q.v.) of remains in advance of development.

Monument   In common usage, a large artificial structure, often with some symbolic value, such as a war memorial. In the Ancient Monuments and Archaeological Areas Act 1979 a monument is defined as any building structure or work above or below the surface of the land, any cave or excavation, any site comprising the remains of buildings and so on, or the remains of any vehicle, vessel, aircraft or other movable structure. Monuments may be protected by scheduling (q.v.) or by acquisition or guardianship as an 'ancient monument' (q.v.).

Monuments Protection Programme (MPP)   An English Heritage initiative of systematic assessment – in the broadest sense – of all known monuments (q.v.) to redress national imbalances in the range and number of monuments protected by scheduling (q.v.) and other forms of management (see Startin, this volume).

Planning law   Planning law is the branch of public law concerned with the regulation of land use. In the UK it is principally directed towards 'development', including the construction of new buildings and amenities, redevelopment of existing facilities and changes in land use. Planning law is implemented by local authorities (q.v.), with recourse to central government for policy guidance and appeals procedures. The two main features of planning law in the UK are Strategic Plans (q.v.) and Development Control (q.v.). The presence of archaeological remains is a 'material consideration' in determining whether development should be allowed, so both Strategic Plans and Development Control have become significant approaches to the management of archaeological remains, as expressed in PPG 16 (q.v.).

Planning Policy Guidance (PPG)   Local planning authorities and others are guided on their decisions and recommendations by government policy. Central government guidance on planning issues is given by way of circulars and more recently by Planning Policy Guidance Notes (PPGs). The aim of PPGs is to provide concise and practical guidance on planning policies in a clear and accessible form.

Planning Policy Guidance Note 16 (PPG 16)   Planning Policy Guidance note 16, 'Archaeology and Planning' published in November 1990 sets out the government's policy on archaeological remains on land. It recognizes sites of archaeological interest as a material consideration in the planning process and gives comprehensive guidance on the various stages by which archaeological remains can be managed as part of the planning process.

Inter alia it indicates that: there is a presumption in favour of the physical preservation of nationally important archaeological sites whether scheduled (q.v.) or unscheduled and their setting; that an appropriate policy framework for the protection of archaeological sites (q.v.) should be included within local authority development plans; that it is reasonable for a local planning authority (q.v.) to request further information in the form of an archaeological evaluation (q.v.) where it believes that significant archaeological remains may be present on a site for proposed development; and, it puts the emphasis on the developer to assess the impact of proposals on archaeological remains, to demonstrate that any adverse effect of development can be acceptably mitigated, and to adequately resource any mitigation (q.v.) strategy determined as necessary.

Post-excavation   A general term applied to those tasks to be undertaken following the fieldwork stage of an archaeological project. In the general model of project management given in *Management of Archaeological Projects* (q.v.), post-excavation would include the 'assessment of potential for analysis', 'analysis and report preparation', and 'dissemination' stages of a project.

Programme Evaluation and Review Technique (PERT)   The Programme Evaluation and Review Technique (PERT) is a project planning and management technique. It is similar to Critical Path Analysis (CPA) (q.v.), the two techniques commonly being confused. Both CPA and PERT involve the analysis of projects and identification of specific project tasks. These are then arranged in the form of a network, linked by arrows denoting as accurately as possible the logical relationship and interdependence of activities. While CPA involves the provision of one estimate of time duration for each task, PERT provides three time estimates for every activity: the most optimistic duration, the most likely duration, and the most pessimistic duration. This introduction of probabilities into time-estimates can be used to perform various forms of risk analysis (frequently using computer methods).

Project Management   While there are a variety of definitions of projects, they are human activities likely to be characterized by clear objectives, fixed timescales, a team of people, no practice or rehearsal and leading to specified change of some description. Project management is a collection of loosely connected techniques, which are used to plan, implement, run and bring projects to a successful conclusion.

Rescue archaeology   Rescue archaeology is a term used to describe the excavation of archaeological remains in advance of development or other activities which threaten their survival. In Britain the term is closely associated with the large increase in the loss of archaeological sites as a result of increased development in the 1960s and 1970s. Increased concern with the unrecorded loss of archaeological remains, particularly in towns, led to the formation of a pressure group called RESCUE (Trust for British Archaeology) which vigorously campaigned for protection of archaeological remains and for increased funding to undertake rescue excavation.

Royal Commissions   Three Royal Commissions (Royal Commission on the Historical Monuments of England (RCHME), Royal Commission on Ancient and Historical Monuments in Wales (RCAHMW), Royal Commission on the Ancient and Historical Monuments of Scotland (RCAHMS)) were established in the early years of the twentieth century to establish definitive records of the archaeological resource in England, Wales and Scotland respectively. The functions of the Royal Commissions have developed considerably since their inception. The most recent Royal Warrant of each Commission, given in 1992, requires that they provide for the survey and recording of ancient and historical monuments and constructions by compiling, maintaining and curating a basic national record of the archaeological and historical environment, plus a number of further functions relating to this task.

Scheduling   The legal provision whereby it is an offence to interfere with certain selected monuments (q.v.) as legally defined. Not all monuments are scheduled: only those that are considered by the relevant Secretary of State to be of 'national importance' and for which scheduling is the most appropriate mechanism (q.v. MPP). The term derives from the practice of placing such monuments on a list (or schedule). Once so placed, they are given legal protection and it is a criminal offence to disturb or damage them without consent (see also Startin, this volume).

Site   A term used to define places of archaeological interest. Typically, they are assumed to be places where human activity took place in the past, but the term also refers to places where archaeologists are working in the present (which may not necessarily be the place of activity in the past).

Sites and Monuments Record (SMR)   SMRs are locally based records of the known archaeological remains within the area of a local authority (q.v.). SMRs are usually maintained by the local authority and are used for planning purposes, for recording discoveries and for providing information.

Sites of Special Scientific Interest (SSSIs)   SSSIs are areas of land which are of special interest by virtue of their flora, fauna, geological or geophysical features. The areas are notified by the nature conservation agencies (English Nature, Countryside Council for Wales, Scottish Natural Heritage) to the local planning authority, to owners and occupiers, and to the relevant Secretary of State. Generally, activities which are specified in the notification cannot be carried out without written consent or unless planning permission has been granted (see Wildlife and Countryside Act 1981, as amended).

Strategic Plans   Strategic Planning involves the preparation of tiered plans from regional to local levels which set out the policies which will be followed by the relevant local authority (q.v.) in encouraging and accepting development proposals. Once approved, the policies set out in Strategic Plans are binding on the authority and must be followed in the course of Development Control (q.v.). Generally speaking, central government provides Regional Planning Guidance, County Councils prepare Structure Plans, and District Councils prepare Local Plans. Structure and Local Plans may be combined as Unitary Plans in areas where the local authorities have been merged. The Strategic Plans, which have statutory support, may be complemented by non-statutory Subject Plans and Management Plans which provide further information about how the local authority intends to implement its strategic policies in relation to specific topics or areas.

Theoretical Archaeology Group (TAG)   The first public TAG conference was held at Sheffield University in December 1979. It was developed from two seminars held for students and staff at Sheffield and Southampton Universities, designed to act as a forum in which to discuss the nature and development of archaeological theory. The conference has been held annually in December since 1979, its venue moving between different universities in Britain.

Total Quality Management (TQM)   TQM is a method for introducing quality into the workplace which emphasizes each employee's responsibility for the quality of the product (see also Brooke, this volume).

Treasure Trove   An ancient legal doctrine whereby items of gold and silver (only) which can be held to have been hidden with the intention of recovery but of which the ownership is now unknown pass to the Crown (and thus today into the British Museum). The finder of such items is, by custom, rewarded with the commercial value of the find. Treasure Trove was the first law to have been appropriated for the purpose of protecting ancient remains in Britain. The scope of the law does not extend beyond items of gold or silver – not even to items found in association with such objects – and so is considered a problem to British archaeology (see Carman, this volume).

INDEX

academic interests 204–5: *see also* research, universities
accountability 193–4
ancient monument 242: *see also* monument
Ancient Monuments and Archaeological Areas Act 1979 137, 138, 142, 147, 166: implications of for Palaeolithic archaeology 153–4; limitations of 169–70; *see also* Monuments Protection Programme (MPP)
archaeological heritage: see archaeological resource
Archaeological Heritage Management 8–11, 19, 242: and accountability 193–4; archaeology and the law 19–30, 61–3; archaeological value, discussion of 168–70; business skills in archaeological management, discussion of the need for 177–8; changing trends in 165–6; comparison of archaeological and business management practices 127–8, 133; context, its effects on 57–8; critique of 10–11; effects of socio–political context on the practice of 237–8; English Heritage, its role 147–9, 153–4; functions of 58–9; future management of the Palaeolithic 156–8; Geographic Information Systems (GIS), its potential and effects on 164–5, 167–8, 171–2; the heritage industry 37–9; history of in the United Kingdom 205–6; implications of marketing theory for 101–17; importance, the role of the concept of in the management of the archaeological resource 48–9;

institutional effects of management on archaeology, discussion of 52–9, 65–6; introduction of competitive tendering to project work 194, 195; legal definition of monument 153–4; local authorities, the role of 147, 148, 190, 194; management theory, the role of 132–3, 226, 229; marketing heritage 34–5, 38, 39; marketing plan for archaeologists 103–5; marketing strategy of archaeology 102, 103, 109–10, 117; necessity for flexibility in site assessment criteria 229–30; need for promotion 113–14; planning approach to 166, 169; Planning Policy Guidance Note 16 (PPG 16) 142, 155, 166–7, 169, 171, 190, 193, 194, 206, 216, 226, 230; process of 148–9, 168, 169; project management in archaeology 75–6, 189–206, 208–15, 224–33; publication of excavations 191, 192, 200; relationship with processualism and the New Archaeology 236; the public's need of heritage 36–8; the public's role 33–4; relationship with the market 34–5; and research design 192, 195, 200, 204–5; research priorities in archaeology 231–2; role of scheduling 154, 155; Sites and Monuments Record (SMR) 139, 148, 150, 155–6; Southern Rivers Project 150–3; role of valuation 40–9, 148–9; *see also* archaeological legislation, archaeological resource, English Heritage, *Management of Archaeological Projects* (MAP2),